Customs of the Han-Chinese and the ethnic people of China

Marriage, birth & burial

Written by
Siewkuan Chee

CONTENTS

MARRIAGE CUSTOMS

About the Author

The author Siewkuan Chee is a Han-Chinese, born in the state of Selangor in Malaysia. She is the second of four siblings with an older brother and a younger sister and brother.

As a child she received two years of Chinese Primary education before switching to English education. Despite only two years of primary education she could read Chinese newspapers and books, partly due to reading Chinese novels as a teenager.

She went to Worcester University, and graduated with an Honours degree in Combined Studies: Urban Studies, British History and World History in 1991. While working on her dissertation in her final year in University, she developed an interest in writing.

Besides speaking English, Mandarin and some Malay she also speaks a few Chinese dialects such as Hakka, Fuchien and her own Cantonese dialect.

Contributors

Editor: Jayne Turnley

Production, publishing manager and cover:
John Williamson, Peter Magnus Design

MARRIAGE CUSTOMS

INTRODUCTION

According to a Chinese myth, Fu-Xi and Nu-Wa were the first couple of the universe. As stated in the Shi Ji, an ancient historical text, Fu-Xi was the first of the five mythical emperors. Reported by one source, Nu-Wa was the only female chief of high antiquity and she married Fu-Xi.

In China, at the times of high antiquity, it was the men who were married off to their wives instead of the other way round as in later times. Chinese history states, during the semi-mythical Xia dynasty (2200-1800 B.C.) and the Zhou dynasty (1122-771 B.C.), that China was a land of matriarchal society where the head of a family was a woman. In those days, only the men were married out of their families, never the women. In his book, Zhong Guo Min Jian Jin Ji, Ren Cheng said if there were any wedding ceremonies in high antiquity, it must be the women welcoming their grooms to their homes. The marriage of 'Yu The Great' known as 'Da Yu Huang' in Chinese (the subducer of the waters who controlled floods) was one example during the Xia dynasty. Before his marriage he was given his mother's surname Yi but after his marriage he adopted his wife's surname Tu-Shan-Shi. This illustrates how the women dominated family life. It was said, children of high antiquity only knew their mothers but not their fathers.

Since ancient times, the Chinese with the help of ancient texts, the Yi Jing' and the texts of the Chun Qiu period, believed in the existence of Heaven and Earth. Then it brought forth the myriad things; with the myriad things came men and women and their offspring, becoming a population that filled the earth. The Heavens and men are assimilated to the concept Yang, Earth and women to the concept Yin. Yin represents darkness and Yang represents light therefore Yin could not do without Yang and vice versa.

Another text mentioned: First, there was heaven and earth, then came the myriad things; then came men and women; then only then were husbands and wives; then only then were fathers and sons; then only then were ruler and subjects and then only then was the hierarchy.

Confucianism was brought back in favour during the Han dynasty which saw the rise of the patriarchal society. Great emphasis was placed in the concept of the continuation of the lineage of the family. According to the philosopher, Meng Zi (Mencius), there are three un-Xiao (disobediences). The greatest un-Xiao, (filial piety) which was not leaving a male heir to carry on the lineage of the family. Given this importance of the continuation of the lineage, men and women must therefore marry to produce children, especially men, so that the lighting of candles and joss sticks to worship ancestors in their ancestral halls, would not come to an end.

ANCIENT MARRIAGE CUSTOMS

'Hoon' was the ancient term for marriage of members of the ruling class during the Zhou period. However common people, (according to Van Gulik's book Sexual Life in Ancient China), were given the term 'pen' for their marriage arrangements meaning 'encounters'. Van Gulik also stated that in Spring, families of the common people left their Winter shelters and moved to the fields. Spring festivals were organised by the rural communities where young men and women performed dances together and sang catchy songs which had something to do with fertility cults. It was in these festivals that every young man courted his girl and then had sexual intercourse with her. These courting and mating activities continued all Summer and Autumn, presumably supervised by the village elders. Both the girl and boy had the same freedom to accept or refuse each other or accept and then change their minds. When this happened, both genders could start the courting and mating game again until they found someone to marry. However, (as from Nagel's Encyclopaedia Guide – China), marriages during these Spring festivals were arranged by games where the girls sang and danced on one side of a river with boys on the other. After exchanging signs during the dance, the two groups then joined up and formed engaged couples. These marriages were celebrated at the following Spring festival.

DIFFERENT KINDS OF WIVES

The marriage system in China has seen many changes throughout the course of history. In ancient times during the matriarchal society, women had more than one husband. Yet by the time of the Zhou dynasty the system took a vice versa turn. This period saw the existence of polygamy where a man could have more than one wife. There was a famous example of the two daughters of emperor Yao known as Huang and Ying who both married Emperor Shun.

'Qi' was the term given to a principal wife. According to a text, it was so called because 'qi' also means 'equal', the principal wife was on an equal level with the husband. Therefore, as the principal wife was equal to the husband, her position was higher than the 'ying'. Women who followed the bride to her husband's house as secondary wives were termed as 'ying'. The system of 'ying' was said to be the earliest kind of polygamy. These women were the 'zhi ti' probably the sisters or other female relatives of the principal wife or other women of the same 'guo' (fief) China was divided into separate administrative units known as 'guo' governed by members of the imperial family and prominent statesmen who were rewarded for their abilities. Sometimes a bride did not like the idea of bringing along the secondary wives for her husband. There was a song in the Book of Odes about the girls whom the bride wanted to leave behind.

The song comprised of the voices of these girls and it goes like this:

'The Great River divides and joins again.
Our bride went to the groom's house,
But she would not take us.
She would not take us,
But later she had to repent!
The Great River has its islets.
Our bride went to the groom's house,
But she would not be with us.
She would not be with us,
But later she had to make room for us!
The Great River has its tributaries.
Our bride went to the groom's house,
But she would not let us go with her.
She would not let us go with her,
But in the end she had to accept us! '
(see Sexual Life in Ancient China)

The Great River represented the husband and the tributaries were the female companions he was entitled to. 'Qie' was another term given to women who were either bought by a man or eloped with him. These 'qie' were the concubines and their positions were lower than that of the secondary wives. These women were called 'qie' because as stated in Li-Chi (Book of Rites), to elope was a sin and women who eloped were given the position of 'qie'. Another text mentioned that 'qie' were disgraceful women and they were added to a man's household to look after his welfare.

In the Zhou period, an emperor had one 'hou' (queen) , three 'fu-ren' (consorts) , nine 'pin', wives of the second rank, twenty seven 'shih-fu', wives of the third rank and eighty one 'yu-chi' (concubines) . Emperors, royal princes and dukes married many wives to expand the population of the fiefs and all had the same idea in mind to keep the blood pure, to produce sons to carry on their thrones, titles and lineages. High ranking officials and court officials generally had one principal wife and two concubines. This was to ensure that the many wives would produce sons to continue the lineage of the family. However, to expand the population of the fiefs was probably an excuse for marrying more than one wife. The real reason was probably to satisfy men's sexual desire. As late as the period of the Republic, 1912 onwards, China's population was already heading for explosion, surely there was no need for a man to have several wives to expand the population of the country. Chinese men married more than one wife purely for one reason, that was to gratify their carnal appetites. As one writer puts it 'Concubinage, however, continues to be practised and there are no signs of any decrease of it even in the best educated classes'. (see Things Chinese) Although concubinage together with the other marriage practices such as child brides were abolished when the communists took over China in 1949, among Chinese society, outside China, some Chinese men still have more than one wife. These days they are known as common-law wives and mistresses. Sadly, this happens even among the educated classes especially those with wealth, power and prestige.

SURNAME TABOOS

Marriage outside the clan was said to be originated from primitive society, intended to prevent clan members from marrying each other. All clan members were believed to belong to the same blood tie. It is known from numerous records, many minorities of China; the Pumi, Miao, Elunchun, Dulong, Li, Jino, Bulang, She and the Ewenke were all still practising this kind of marriage until very recently. Certain arrangements were strictly followed by some people. For example, men of family

A could take the women of family B as wives, but the women of family A could not marry the men of family B instead they had to marry the men in family C. This strict rule enabled every clan to marry outside their clans and so prevented inbreeding. Among the Yi people in Weishan, Yunnan, anyone who belonged to the same ancestor were forbidden to marry each other. This strict rule was strictly obeyed because if anyone violated this rule it was believed all clan members would have bad luck and the persons concerned would be punished severely.

Marriage within the clan was said to be another remnant of primitive society where members were only permitted to marry within the clan and within the family. Marriage was not permitted with one's parents, siblings or children. However, marriage was allowed with one's paternal male and female cousins and even different generations. For example, marrying a second cousin. This marriage system was designed to keep the blood pure within the family and the clan. Besides this, if the elder brother had passed away the younger brother would take his widow as his wife. This system was designed to stop women of the clan from marrying out so that their labour remained in the family because they were treated as property of the family. Records state that the Nu, Lisu and Bulang people had practised this practice until very recently.

In traditional China, it was a taboo for two people of the same family name to marry. This family name taboo is still observed today. At the times of high antiquity such taboos did not exist, people could marry one another with the same family name. During the reign of the Yellow Emperor who reigned during the third millennium BC, the Xia and Shang periods, say ancient legend, the family name was not an issue, people were free to marry anybody with the same surname, for example, the two daughters of emperor Yao, married emperor Shun, a man with the same family name. At that time, there were no restrictions, could be because people placed more importance on the land and the territories they lived in, rather than on blood ties.

One text tells us during the Xia, Shang and Zhou periods, in high antiquity, women had 'xing' (surname) and men had 'shi' (the area or land where people lived). At one time, China was a matriarchal society where women were heads of families. Women were given 'xing' but not men. Women were not married out of their families. Instead they brought in husbands from outside their families. The fact that society was matriarchal at that time meant that the lineage of a family was depended on a daughter not on a son.

Generally, the marriages of the Xia and Shang periods were either marrying a person with the same family name or someone with a different surname as blood ties were not considered as important, but territory was. This was recorded in the Zuo Zhuan (historical text), it said, 'shi' was the 'earth' people lived, a person without 'earth' would have no 'shi'. It was not until the Western Zhou period, that people placed great importance on blood ties. This period saw the decline of the matriarchal society and the dawn of the patriarchal society. The granting of family names to men coupled with the male's right of inheritance to land and property laid the foundation of the male position in society. At first 'xing' represented 'blood ties' and 'shi' represented 'the area where people lived' but later the two became one.

Since the decline of the matriarchal society in the Zhou period it was a taboo to marry someone with the same family name. To the Chinese, it was considered as incestuous and anyone who broke this rule exposed the man and woman concerned and their offspring to tragic disasters. The most common belief was that people with the same family name were related through blood. It was believed, a consequence of this practice was the deformity of future generations. The marriage between two

11

people with the same family name was regarded as 'against custom'. This incest rule not only applied to the Han-Chinese but also to many minorities in China and such a practice was punished severely. Many texts mentioned that the Han-Chinese, Wa, She, Achang, Ewenke, Yi, Xibo, Ta Khan Er, Bulang, Mongolians, Jino, Manchurians, Jingpo and Bai people observed this practice. It was said, throughout the period of this practice, those who broke the rule were harshly disciplined.

Among the Jino people, those who lived in the same bamboo long house were not allowed to marry each other. Although not everybody living in the long house had the same surname, for example, among the maternal cousins but marriage was forbidden as long as they remained living in the same house because they were seen as belonging to the same family. However, if maternal cousins were living in separate long houses then they could marry.

For both the Bai and She people, those who shared the same surname and the same ancestor were not allowed to marry. However, those who belonged to the same surname but not the same ancestor also known as 'same surname but different joss sticks' urn' marriage was permitted.

The Wa people believed that if two people with the same surname married it would anger the heaven and would bring disasters killing human and animals, ruining the crops and people would be hit by lightning. Those who broke this incest rule were driven out of their village and the couple were separated forever. Sometimes their fellow villagers even forced them to eat with dogs to demonstrate that their behaviour were no different from dogs and pigs.

Some minorities such as the Tujia people, in the past, had the practice of marrying one another with the same surname but later gave this up. There were some other groups of people who for other reasons also practised this practice. One example

12

was the Miao people in Guangxi as some of the mountain communities all had the same surname. This happened when women did not want to leave their place of birth. Also, the Miao people only married within their own race and this undoubtedly created serious marriage problems. Under this circumstance, a rite was performed to rid any evil that might befall a community. The chief would announce a date for the whole community to decide whether to carry out this practice. During the rite, a cow with patches of different colours was killed and everybody was given a piece of beef to eat. The fact that the cow had patches of different colours symbolised to the Miao people, a kind of chaos all mixed together and so after eating its flesh people did not have to worry about the taboo anymore and could marry anybody with the same surname. Those who attended the rite and had eaten the piece of beef had no fear of criticism from their communities. However, this rite was not a matter to be taken lightly, it was a solemn occasion. It was said, this kind of rite brought certain disasters to villages therefore it was rarely held.

In Yunnan, the Ke Mu people also had a similar practice that they would only marry people with different family names. Sons were given their father's family name and daughters were given their mother's family name and because of this the daughters of a brother had a different surname from the sons of a sister. Therefore, they were not considered as close relatives so could marry each other. However, the son of one's brother could not marry the daughter of one's sister because they were classed as close relatives.

If anyone went against this rule and married someone who was considered as a close relative, the two of them would be seen as 'zhu gou' meaning 'pig and dog' and would be punished during a rite. During this rite, the two of them would be forced to eat pig's feed, and not only that, they would be compelled to squat on the ground and actually eat like pigs! At the same time, a man would hold an axe over their heads to represent the god of thunder punishing them. Another meaning of this act was to ask for the forgiveness of the god of thunder and ask him not to punish them anymore. After this a woman would carry a bucket of water and splash the water over all those involved. This was also to ask for forgiveness from the dragon gods of the oceans so that he would not bite them in the future.

Not only was it taboo to marry someone with the same surname, but it was also a taboo to marry someone with certain surnames. The reason for this was that people with certain surnames, actually belonged to the same ancestors. According to one text, 'Inn' was the original surname of 'Qin'. Later the descendants adopted the names of the fiefs 'guo' where they lived and they were called She Shi, Dan Shi, Yuen Yen Shi, Che Shi, Zhong Li Shi, Tu Zhou Shi, Wang Shi, Jiang Liang Shi, Jiang Shi, Shou Yu Shi, Bai Min Shi, Fei Lian Shi, Qin Shi and Zhao Shi. Those who belonged to these fourteen surnames were not allowed to marry one another because they all shared the same ancestors with the surname 'Inn'. These people were not supposed to marry one another until after a hundred centuries. However, if today someone says that people with the surnames of Wang, Jiang and She should not marry one another, many people would say that was silly. Having said that, in Taiwan today, people with certain surnames will not consider marriage with one another. Examples of these are Soo, Lian, Zhou, Wu, Tao, She and Ke because it is said they belonged to the same ancestors. If people broke this rule they would have to face the consequences of having deformed children. Among the Elunchun people in the North-East of China, in Manchuria, this taboo is still observed.

There are five reasons why people with certain surnames do not marry one another. The first is these people shared the same ancestors; second, ancestors had sworn brotherhood together known as 'chet pai xiong di'; the third, their ancestors were once betrothed but did not go ahead with the wedding; fourth, their ancestors consolidated their families into one large strong family and the fifth reason is, communities were incorporated into one large community. The first reason is generally a common factor as to why this taboo is still observed among the Elunchun today.

MARRIAGE BETWEEN COUSINS

At one time marriage between cousins was practised by people in many areas of China, for example, a man marrying his maternal aunt's daughter. Many people in China, including the Han-Chinese, liked the idea of bringing in a daughter-in-law who was already known to the family instead of a total stranger. Later when new marriage legislation was introduced, this practice was abolished because it stated that people with close blood ties were not allowed to marry.

In the past, the Tujia, Buyi, Lisu, Yao and the Zhuang minorities all had a history of this practice. It was common for a man to marry his maternal aunt's daughter. If he so wished, a man was given the first right to marry his maternal aunt's daughter. Among the Buyi people, if a girl refused to marry her maternal uncle's son, her family had to pay some money to her maternal uncle as a kind of compensation. Even if a cousin was physically handicapped, too young or too old, the girl had to go through with the marriage. If the girl objected to the marriage arrangement she would be forced to marry. Only if the son of her maternal uncle had no desire to marry her was she allowed to marry someone else. Among the Yao people, if a maternal uncle had no son then he had the right to collect his niece's bride price when she married. In the past, the Miao people also had a history of paying a sum of money, livestock and goods as a compensation to a maternal uncle if a Miao girl married

15

someone else instead of her cousin. This compensation included three hundred silver monies, three hundred cattle, three hundred horses, three hundred pigs and three hundred eggs. No one was able to pay such a huge compensation therefore most Miao girls had to marry their maternal cousins even though they did not love them. Those who did not want to marry had to stay in their parents' homes as old maids. In later periods, this practice was seen as cruel and was abolished after a tragedy when a young girl of twelve was beaten to death by her father-in law who was also her maternal uncle.

This shows that marriage between cousins had something to do with the laws of people. Anyone who disobeyed this law would be criticised or even punished. Similarly, the Jingpo, Dong and Yi people, had a strict rule that children of two sisters should not marry one another. This rule was very strict and everybody had to comply by it. According to the Yi people, the son and the daughter of two sisters were like brother and sister and so they were against such a marriage arrangement. Those who disobeyed this rule were punished by death. Although the Yi people were against the marriage of a son and daughter of two sisters, ironically, the son of one's brother could marry the daughter of one's sister.

MARRIAGE DETERMINED BY CLASS

'Wooden door match with wooden door, bamboo door match with bamboo door' is a Chinese saying. 'Wooden door' means a wealthy family and 'bamboo door' means a poor family. In the old days, it was important that the rich marry the rich and the poor marry the poor. Marrying down or marrying up would attract criticism from society. In feudal society, stepping out of line was not permitted, especially for the family with a higher status in society people were careful not to choose a family with a low status. As for the family with a lower status, due to prejudices and pressures of society usually did not want to consider marrying up. Firstly, they were afraid that if the match was not successful, they would be the laughingstock of the community. Secondly, after the wedding their daughter might be looked down upon and suffer abuse.

In old Han-Chinese society, prejudices against certain kinds of occupations did exist, for example, guards who worked for the local government, barbers, chiropodists, and entertainers including actors and actresses were all considered low class occupations. Most people did not want to marry anybody who was engaged in this sort of work.

Among the Uighurs, it was a taboo for the son of a barber to marry the daughter of a silversmith. It was thought of as marrying into the wrong 'door'. There were two reasons as to why people opposed to the matching of these two kinds of trades in marriage. Firstly, people were prejudiced against certain trades. Secondly, there was a big difference in the financial rewards of these two trades. This difference in financial rewards was big enough for society to put them into different social class.

Among the Han-Chinese, it was a definite taboo for the ruling class to marry the servant class and it even became a law. According to some texts the Tibetans were just as strict about this rule and marriage was forbidden between serfs' owners and serfs. Those who broke the rule were criticised by society and even punished by the law.

The Jingpo people were like the Han-Chinese, the ruling class only married the ruling class. Marriage was forbidden between the ruling class and the ordinary people. In the past, the Kazaks were under Mongolian rule. Their sultans, the heads of communities, were Mongolian aristocrats. These Mongolian aristocrats claimed that they were the descendants of Genghis Khan and they called themselves 'tor li' meaning 'white bones'. As for the rest of the Kazak masses they were known as 'ha la' meaning 'black bones'. There were strict rules of high and low status which forbade marriage between the 'white bones' and the 'black bones'.

In the old society, the Loba people were separated into two groups, 'muk tek' the higher class and the 'nae ba' who were people despised by society. The 'muk tek' regarded themselves as pure blooded high class 'gao gu tou' meaning 'high bones'. They were people with status and were respected in society. They were free people and even if they became poor later their offspring remained as 'gao gu tou'. The 'nae ba' were regarded as 'ti gu tou' meaning 'low bones'. Even if their offspring gained wealth and kept slaves later, their status remained the same. They were not allowed to attain the status of 'muk tek' but could only acquire the status of 'wu pu', which was a little higher than 'nae ba'. Marriage was taboo between the 'muk tek' and the 'nae ba'. If a 'muk tek' broke the rule and married a 'nae ba' he or she would have to give up the status of 'muk tek' and became a 'muk zhuang' which also belonged to the 'ti gu tou' category and the 'nae ba' would be executed.

The Yi people in Sichuan are divided into two groups, some are known as Black Yi, some are known as White Yi. During the Ming and Manchu periods, the Black Yi were known as 'hei Lolo' ('hei means 'black') the White Yi were known as 'bai Lolo' ('bai' means 'white'). Black Yi were separated into three classes, known as 'inn gu tou' meaning 'hard bones', 'yuan gu tou' translating as 'soft bones' and 'huang gu tou' which means 'yellow bones'. The 'hard bones' were said to be the purest of the race and had never been enslaved by other people. The ancestors of the 'soft bones' had intermarried with slaves and this made their blood less pure. The 'yellow bones' were the least pure among the three groups, it was said they had intermarried with other races. These three groups were forbidden to inter-marry each other. The White Yi also had their sort of caste system but not as strict as the Black Yi. If the daughter of a Black Yi had sexual intercourse with a different group, according to the law, the young man would be burned alive, and the young woman would be forced to hang herself. These marriage practices were designed to ensure the purity of the race. As the saying of the Black Yi goes; 'huang niew shie huang niew, shui niew shie shui niew', meaning 'yellow cow is yellow cow, buffalo is buffalo' and 'ren yow zhong, shui yow zuan', meaning 'human is from genes, water is from spring'.

MATCHMAKER

Lax morals were regarded as a threat to the stability of family life and the continuity of the lineage by the Confucianists of the Zhou period, stressing on the principle of the separation of the sexes. As society placed great importance on a girl's virginity if she was to be accepted as a principal wife therefore, girls were under close guard indoors out of the sight of men.

As early as the Zhou period, 'mei guan' were appointed to supervise the marriages of young men and women. 'Mei guan' means 'matchmaker official. According to the Zhou Li in the Book of Rituals, (Rites and ceremonials of the Zhou period), the 'mei guan' had to make sure that a young man was married by the age of thirty and a young woman by the age of twenty.

During the Zhou period each member of the ruling class in his lifetime was only supposed to marry a principal wife once. If she died or if he divorced her, he could not marry the second time, not with the same ceremonial rites as with a principal wife. Marriage is of course arranged by a go-between as the Book of Odes, (Shih Ching in Chinese, one of the five Confucian classics), stressed the importance of a matchmaker.

It says:

'How do we proceed in hewing an axe-handle?
Without another axe it cannot be done.
How do we proceed in taking a wife?

Without a go-between it cannot be done.
How do we proceed in planting hemp?
The acres must be dressed length wise arid cross-wise.
How do we proceed in taking a wife?
Announcement must first be made to our parents.'
(see Things Chinese)

A 'mei guan' was the eyes and ears of the people with marriageable sons and daughters. At first, the task of a go-between was a male occupation but in later periods, men were replaced by females calling themselves 'mei ren' or 'mei poh' the former means 'matchmaker person' and the latter means 'matchmaker old lady'. The fact that most matchmakers were old ladies explains why they were called 'mei poh'. Although these 'mei poh' were expected to find the right match sometimes due to greed, for example, after receiving a lump sum of money from a groom's family, she would give false information to the bride's family. Since Chinese civilization began countless stories have been told about many brides, who found out when their head cloths or veils were removed, that they had actually married husbands with physical disabilities or just plain ugly.

During the Han dynasty, Han Confucianists were shocked by the marriage customs of the common people written in the Book of Odes. Rules were then laid down that all the courting and mating during the Spring festivals be under the supervision of a 'mei guan'. Names and ages of boys and girls were registered, and the matchmaker official was to make sure that the former was married at the age of thirty and the latter when they were twenty. In the Spring of each year, all the marriageable young men and women in his area were assembled or ordered to choose their mates. These unions were consummated without any ceremony of marriage. Punishment was inevitable for those who did not choose a partner. (see Sexual Life in Ancient China)

Like the Zhou period, marriage during the Sung period was also arranged by a go-between. If both families were satisfied with all the information, a meeting between the future pair was arranged in a banquet where they saw each other face to face the first time. This meeting was called 'xiang chin' in Mandarin. The two exchanged a toast and if the man liked the woman, he stuck a golden hair needle in his 'guan' (hat) but if he did not like her, he gave her two bolts of colourful satin fabrics. If this meeting proved satisfactory there was an exchange of presents and an auspicious date for the marriage was arranged.

In the Ming period, the 'xiang chin' of the future pair was scrapped. When the groom removed the veil of the bride in the ancestral hall it was the first time the couple saw each other face to face.

In the North West of China, in Gansu, the Dong Xiang people still live by their traditions. Matchmakers still have their roles to play here. Tea blocks (tea leaves are pressed to a block like a brick) and tea leaves are the traditional gifts a matchmaker brings to the girl's family. This is known as 'ding cha' meaning 'engaged tea'.

According to Ta Khan Er custom, a matchmaker must wear a hat with a red strip of material on the right side and carry a bottle of wine or spirit. As soon as people saw the hat with the red strip, they would know that the person on his way to do his duty was a matchmaker. Usually, the matchmaker was not successful in bringing the match together during the first time because the girl's family needs to think things over. When the matchmaker visits the girl's family for the second time, he will know whether they are pleased with the match or not.

If they are pleased with it, they will then go on to the next stage which is to test the young man concerned. When the young man arrived at the girl's house at the front door he would be viewed from the top to the bottom by an elderly person. This elderly person would act like one of those imperial examiners in the palace and ask him many difficult questions. If his answers were satisfactory, he would then be invited into the house as a guest of honour. At this stage, the young man would know that the marriage had an eighty to ninety percent chance of going ahead. However, the young man still had to go to the girl's house a second time. It was during this time that the girl's parents would discuss the wedding date and the bride price.

Today, the 'xiang chin' custom of the Sung period is still being practised by some Chinese. These days the meeting is not as formal as in the old days and it is known as 'xiang can't' in Mandarin or 'shiong tai' in Cantonese. If the man likes the woman then he will ask her to go out, usually with the woman bringing along a sister or a friend as a chaperone. If the man does not like the woman then he will have to give her a red pouch with some money. Red pouches with money are associated with good luck but in this case, it is to do with saving face for the woman and her family because it is a loss of face that a man has seen her but did not like her.

SINGING COURTSHIP

In contrast with the Han-Chinese, many of the ethnic minorities of China were rather free in choosing their spouses. Some did not even need a matchmaker. There were special places designed for young men and women to court each other but there were taboos to be avoided. Singing and dancing courtship was and still is prevalent among the Wa, Yao, Miao, Zhuang, Bai, Tujia, She, Jing, Lahu, Hani, Achang and Jingpo minorities.

In the Dayaoshan in Guangxi when the Yao girls are reaching courting age, parents will let them live alone in a house with a balcony right above the roadside. At night, young men will climb up to the balcony to talk to the girl. This is called 'pa lou' meaning 'climb building' and there are rules to be obeyed. Married men are not allowed to join in this 'pa lou' activity; once a girl has chosen her lover then she must stop the rest of the young men from climbing her balcony and those concerned must behave themselves otherwise they will be condemned.

Young people of the Wa minority are permitted to court each other at about fourteen or fifteen. Usually, the boy will visit the girl in a neighbour's guest room or in a widow's house. There the two will sing love songs to each other and exchange keepsakes but if the girl later changes her mind about the boy, she will return his keepsake and ask for hers to be returned. If, however they take a fancy to each other, they will sleep together and hope that they will have a good dream that night. If their dreams are of an auspicious omen such as working among the banana trees, planting bamboo or herding cattle then they will go ahead with the relationship. If they dream of bad omens like cutting down banana trees, falling trees, falling stars or sun they will go their separate ways.

Parents of the Benglong young people never interfered in their courtship. Young men could talk to young women freely, but their movements were only limited to inside the house. Meeting outside the house was not allowed. There is a front door in the camp for men to go in and out of the village and a small back gate for women to use. However, when a man is courting a woman, he must use the small back gate.

In the past, in the Qinghai region, the courtship of the Tibetans was rather interesting. Most often, young men and women did not need their parents' approval nor the matchmaker's tongue to help them get married. When they were up in the mountains herding their livestock there were plenty of chances to meet the opposite sex. When a young man or woman had found somebody they liked, they would start courting each other freely. Only when 'lien ai cheng sho', meaning 'courtship has ripen', would they tell their parents about getting married. Tibetan parents of this area usually agreed to their children's wishes and were happy to fix an auspicious date for the wedding. When the day arrived, parents of both sides met in the place in the mountain where they had agreed to meet. At the mountain, a banquet was laid out with food and wine. At this time, negotiation for the bride price began and when both sides were happy with the price, both parents then started to clap and invite the young couple to sing. Afterwards the parents then led the young couple to the interior of the mountain where out of sight from everyone, the two had sexual intercourse. Their parents, with horses ready waited patiently for their children to come out of the mountain. When they returned to the village, monks performed the wedding ceremony for them. This was only the start of the proper wedding ceremony. From the groom's family, rolls of fabrics and livestock were given to the bride as payment. The bride's dowry included new clothes and accessories. On her wedding day, the new bride had to ride to the tent to worship the deity. Inside the tent a portrait of the Buddha was installed.

In the old days, the Lisu, Nu, Hani, Jingpo, Yi and Zhuang people did not have public houses for their young people to meet each other. Nowadays, public houses are built by the villagers themselves to give their young people a place to meet at night. At night, girls and boys gather in the public house where the girls spin, weave, embroider and knit while the boys sing to the girls with their pipa (Chinese musical instrument) or other musical instruments. Only the single people are permitted to go to the public houses. The married, however, are excluded. Among the Yi people, there are a few rules to be obeyed. Those who belonged to the same ancestor, even after eight generations are still not allowed to meet in the same public house. If young men and women of marriageable age do not frequent the public house to look for future partners, they will have to face criticism from elders and be regarded as useless.

The Miao and Yao people have their own rules which must be obeyed by the young people engaging in singing courtship. As a rule, Miao people do not allow any singing courtship at home, singing is only allowed in the open fields. Young men play the lusheng flute but there is a taboo to be observed. Flutes must not be played when they are walking towards the village. The Yao people do not permit young men and women of the same village to sing to each other. Singing is not permitted in the presence of an elderly person. A young man and woman are not allowed to sing on their own or in any quiet remote place.

In the South-West of Guizhou, there is a group of Yao people with free singing courtships. Here, a young man and woman are permitted to sing to each other at home, but only under the watchful eyes of fellow young people. During the singing, they are expected to behave themselves, especially the men.

During the Spring Festival (Chinese New Year), other holidays and at county fairs, young people of the Buyi people of Guizhou are given a chance to meet and choose their lovers. Regulations are strict and there are stipulations that there must be a distance of three to four 'chi', (3 chi = 1 metre), between the men and women singing and chatting side by side or back to back. Singing is the central activity and many songs in various themes are sang. This may go on for several days without repetition. When singing, the young men and women must stand on different sides and look for the ones they like. If a man finds a woman he likes, he will ask someone to introduce her to him then go over to her side with gifts. If, for any reason, the woman is not interested she will sing a song of refusal. If she likes him, she will smile at him and together they will leave the crowd.

Among the Miao people of Guizhou and the Yao people living in the mountain ridges in Northern Guangdong, there is an annual festival for young people to select their spouses. In Guizhou, it is known as 'tel yuet' meaning 'dance the moon'. Once a year, under the Spring moon, young men and women take part in their traditional dance. When a man and a woman like each other they will kiss publicly and not feel uncomfortable about it. Their parents concern will not stop them either, providing they want each other, the matter is settled. The practice is they have sexual intercourse first, before celebrating the marriage. This practice is similar to the one used by the Yao people in Guangdong, where during the three consecutive days of the lunar New Year, young people who were single, those who had a girlfriend or boyfriend and even divorced people could all join in and court each other, singing love songs in the fields. Sexual intercourse was permitted. This practice of free sexuality before marriage is rather widespread among some ethnic minorities in the later primitive society and even among some ethnic people in class society. The Naxi people in Yongning, Yunnan, serve as the best example. The practice has to do with an uneven historical development where changes in marriage customs always drag behind economic development. Perhaps it can be argued that this practice of free sexuality is a legacy of the marriage arrangement of the common people of high antiquity.

ENGAGEMENT

In the early days of this century, the Jing people in Guangxi practised a unique engagement practice called 'matching clogs'. Before a young man and woman were engaged the parents of both sides had to take a wooden clog from their homes and the matchmaker would put the two clogs together to see whether they would match, one of each; one left and one right. If the two clogs matched, then it was considered that the partnership was matched by heaven. If the two clogs did not match, then the two families would not go ahead with the engagement. Later this practice began to lose its market because less and less people believed in it. Later, influenced by Han-Chinese customs, the Jing people adopted the practice of exchanging the Eight Characters. However, nowadays the exchange of the Eight Characters is not popular anymore.

When a Bulang woman accepts her lover's gifts of pickled cabbage, tobacco, and pork, she is now, according to the tradition, formally engaged to him. During the night they can have sexual intercourse.

Most Keerkezi people live in Xinjiang in the North-West of China. Although Islam is their religion monogamy is the norm here. Their engagement is rather interesting. Gifts are tied to a horse's head between the ears plus a small bunch of cotton. As soon as people saw this, they will know that someone is getting engaged. Usually, the man is received warmly at the girl's house by her parents. On this day they will discuss the date of the wedding and the bride price. In some areas, the man is sprinkled with white flour. This means that the girl's family has agreed with this marriage and he has the blessing of the family.

Among the Ewenke people, if the parents of a girl are happy with a marriage proposal, they will show their approval by tying a strip of red cloth on the wine bottle brought by the matchmaker from the man's parents. The matchmaker must drink four bowls of wine and will be carried back drunk to show that the proposal is successful.

During the engagement, a Dong Xiang man usually gives jewellery, cash, clothes, sugar, and tea leaves to a girl's family. In some areas, 'man tou' are also given. These are a kind of steamed dumpling, like the Han-Chinese 'pao zi', but without any fillings. Unlike the ordinary 'man tou' eaten by the Northern Chinese, these are gigantic because each one is made with two to four catties of flour. Usually only the flour of new grains is used. Each 'man tou' is smeared with turmeric on the top and a cross is cut so that as it is cooks, it opens. It is said this has something to do with blessing.

If a Lahu man wants to be engaged to his girl, he has to ask a matchmaker to take rice, wine, meat, chicken, tea and salt to the girl's house and cook a meal there for the girl's parents and relatives. After drinking and eating this meal the couple is supposed to be formally engaged. If the man is found to be a poor farmer, the girl could break off the engagement without being condemned by the community.

When a Gu-zhoong girl and young man are in love with each other, the fellow will ask an elder of the camp to act as a go-between for him. This elder will bring three squirrels and three bamboo sticks with wine inside with him to the girl's house as a gift. During the engagement, the young man must give about four to six squirrels and a kind of palm wine from two to four bamboo sticks to the girl's family. These are used by the girl's family to entertain their guests. Usually, fried squirrels, boiled white vegetables and palm wine are served to the guests. During the meal, the girl's parents will only announce the engagement if everything is peaceful. However, if the girl's parents want to change their minds about the engagement, they will not eat the fried squirrels nor drink the wine. During the drinking and eating, if the sound of animals is heard, such as a bird making a noise, a dog barking or a cockerel crowing it is considered as unlucky and the match will be called off.

The Ozbek engagement is rather unique because it is only attended by women. Men are not allowed to attend, not even the groom to be. On the designated day, the mother of the man will be accompanied by several female relatives bringing gifts of fabrics, tea, sugar, and homemade cakes to the girl's house. At the girl's house, they will be received by the girl's mother who is also accompanied by several female relatives. According to the custom, the mother of the man will say to the mother of the girl, 'Your daughter is like the moon and my son is like the sun. I think they were both husband and wife. What is your opinion? If the girl's mother approves of the proposal, both mothers will negotiate a date to hold the engagement ceremony.

'Drink soup', the name given to the unusual engagement practice of the Yi people was only observed by a bride to be. According to the practice of the Yi people, most girls of seventeen and eighteen are at a marriageable age and could be proposed to by men. If, however, a girl is still not married by the age of nineteen or twenty, nor engaged, her parents and relatives will be anxiously looking around for a man to marry her off. 'Drink soup' is a small banquet with soup as the special main dish. If the parents of a girl are happy with the proposal of a man, his family will then send a few relatives to the girl's house bringing with them food such as wine, meat, bean sprouts, tofu, and prawns. These relatives will then cook and set up a small banquet with two to three tables, inviting the girl's family and her relatives. Every table is placed with a few different dishes, but the 'soup' is the main dish. Before everyone starts to tuck in, the girl's family and her relatives will start first to taste the soup and if they say that the soup is tasty that means the marriage will go ahead. If, however, the soup is not tasty, then the marriage is called off.

To the Yi people, bean sprouts, tofu, pork and prawns are not just food but have symbolical meanings, the bean sprouts mean that the roots of both families are joined together, tofu represents pureness without blemish, pork and other ingredients represent a beautiful life and prawns mean that the couple will be blessed with many sons and daughters after their marriage.

The Kazaks have a rather humorous engagement custom. After the two sides have negotiated a date, the parent of the man and close relatives will bring along a horse and other gifts to the girl's house. To show hospitality, the girl's parents and relatives will butcher sheep for the banquet. According to the custom, the man's family must behave well throughout the ritual and do the bidding of the girl's family. After they have feasted the host will feed them yoghourt, sheep tail and liver and put yoghourt on their faces. Humiliating it seems but the guests must not flee, rather they should co-operate and show their appreciation.

In Inner Mongolia, in Yi ke zhao, the Mongolians there are still marrying in the traditional way. From engagement to the actual wedding the new couple must go through a long process which usually takes a year or two. After several trips back and forth between the two families talking about the bride price and giving the betrothal gift to the bride's family the couple will then be engaged. During this time, the groom's family will continue to pay out the bride price until it is paid in full.

Nowadays, among the Han-Chinese in Malaysia and many parts of Southeast Asia, engagement is still popular. Once the courting is successful, a young man and woman will proceed to the engagement stage. Singing is rather popular among some young people during an engagement party and I personally have been present in one of these engagement parties. Usually, people like to hire a big place such as a hall for the engagement party if there is not enough room in the house for a big party. When my cousin was engaged many years ago, she hired a restaurant for the occasion and even hired a microphone. Tables and chairs were laid in rows along both sides of the wall with white tablecloth, like a wedding reception. Apart from the parents of the young man and woman concerned, usually only young men and women are invited. On the tables, light refreshments such as soft drinks, sliced oranges, bananas, groundnuts, melon seeds, aga aga (seaweed jelly) and all kinds of cakes are placed. Usually, the guests are told to tuck in before the announcement. When the guests are halfway through the refreshments someone, usually an elder or the matchmaker, will give a speech to talk about how the couple met. After all that, the couple will be asked to stand up in front of everybody and to put on the engagement rings. Unlike the West, many Chinese still follow their own custom, both the young man and woman wear a gold ring, the man on the left hand the woman on the right. Some even have the names of their fiancés engraved on them. After all the formal part comes the informal where young men and women are called out to sing in front of the microphone, of course, only those who really want to show off their vocal cords. This kind of engagement party is known as 'cha wui' in Cantonese meaning 'tea party'.

SIX RITES

Marriage customs of the Han-Chinese were according to the Six Rites known as 'liu li' in Chinese, laid down in the Li-chi, in the Book of Rites. These six rites were the legacy of the Zhou king Zhou Wen Wang who observed these rites in his own wedding. These six rites were:

1. The man's family offered a gift through the go-between to the girl's family. Acceptance indicated that the girl's family was serious in going through with the betrothal.

2. The exchange of the Eight Characters (which is the year, month, date and hour of birth).

3. The ritual vetting of the Eight Characters in front of the ancestors of both families.

4. The payment of the bride price usually in cash and in kind to the girl's family through the go-between who had conducted the negotiations. Acceptance of the cash and goods sealed the marriage agreement.

5. Fixing the wedding date.

6. Welcoming the bride to the groom's family home, paying ceremonial deference to his family and ancestors.

Those who observed the Six Rites were nearly all members of the ruling class. As for the common people they were less rigid when following these rites. Having said that the common people also had their own marriage customs.

BETROTHAL GIFT

After Nu Wa had decided to marry Fu-Xi he presented her with a couple of deers' skins as a betrothal gift. If this story was true, then this must be the first betrothal gift a man gave to a woman.

In ancient times, live wild geese were given as betrothal gift, written in the Li Yi, an ancient text. One reason of using wild geese as betrothal gift is because it was believed that a wild goose stayed with its mate all its life and if the mate died the other would never find another mate again. Another reason was that wild geese were seen as noble birds, they could adapt to the warm weather in the South and to the cold weather in the North which had something to do with 'yin' and 'yang' because 'yin' represents 'cold' and 'yang' represents 'warm'. Since man was said to be assimilated to 'yang' and woman to 'yin' therefore the union of a man and woman was the union of 'yin' and 'yang'.

Before the Zhou period, betrothal gifts were divided into different classes. In the Li chi, it was recorded: emperors used wine, dukes and princes used jade, ministers used goats, the wealthy used wild geese, the not so poor people used chickens and the poor peasants used cloth. Despite the laying down of these rules, the fact that marriage was regarded as one of the three important events in a person's life, most people even some poor peasants used wild geese as betrothal gifts. It is said, the use of wild geese as betrothal gift was a legacy of the hunting era the Shang period.

In the Tang period, during a wedding ceremony at the bride's house, the bride would sit on a horse's saddle and the groom would throw the wild goose to a member of her family in the middle of the living room. After that, a red silk cloth was used to drape over the body of the wild goose and threads in five colours were used to tie its beak to stop it from making noise. After the ceremony, the groom's family would pay a sum of money to buy back this wild goose and let it go free. Wild geese were special birds not easy for ordinary people to obtain or afford, therefore in this period most people could only use imitations made of wood or use a pair of ordinary domestic geese as a substitute. Wealthy families usually gave two pairs of domestic geese. The feathers of the geese were dyed with red colour perhaps to resemble the wild goose or perhaps because red was the colour of good luck. Chickens were also used as betrothal gifts. It did not matter whether chickens or geese were given but they must be live and not dead because marriage was a lucky event and still is, therefore there must not be any connection with death. If a pair of dead wild geese were given as a betrothal gift it was like saying to the bride that she was to become a widow after she married her groom. Also, they must be given in pairs because even numbers meant 'double bliss' or 'double happiness'.

In Yunnan, in Lu chun and Jin ping, the Gu Zhong people of the Lahu tribe used to practise the traditional custom of using a flying squirrel as a betrothal gift. Before a young man could marry his sweetheart, he must first present her parents with a flying squirrel shot by his own hand, presumably using a bow and arrow, as a betrothal gift. To catch a flying squirrel, a young man had to go into the forest, and it was not easy to catch one, in fact it was very difficult. There was a saying in the area 'Tiger, bear and wolves are not difficult to catch but a small flying squirrel is very difficult to catch'. Therefore, a young man was seen as very courageous and clever if he caught a flying squirrel. For this reason alone, parents with a daughter picked a courageous young man for their daughter. Later, the flying squirrels are replaced by ordinary squirrels as betrothal gifts.

Many ethnic minorities still retain their own unique marriage customs, one of these are the Ka Wa people. Young Ka Wa boys and girls have complete freedom in choosing their own future spouses. As long as a young couple genuinely love each other, most parents will agree to their marriage. Their betrothal gifts are unusual. When a young man comes to his girlfriend's house to ask her parents for her hand in marriage, he needs to bring with him two essential presents; some banana leaves and a bag of salt. The former is said to represent respect and the latter represents love. If the girl's parents are happy with the proposal, they will hang the banana leaves over their front door as an act of accepting the proposal, and the couple are now engaged.

Among the Yao people in Jin siu in Guangxi, when a man is in love with a woman, he will ask a go-between to take some tobacco leaves and tea leaves to the woman's family as betrothal gifts. Some people used wine and chickens and some give money. Accepting these gifts means that the girl's family has the serious intention of going through with the marriage.

When a Lu Kai couple, (Gaoshan tribe in Taiwan), has decided to get married, the man must bring wine and areca nuts to his girlfriend's house as betrothal gifts and ask for her hand in marriage. Once accepted he will be given many gifts in return to show that they are formally engaged. After this, the young man has to go to his girlfriend's house daily to help with agricultural work or domestic chores.

Marriage is a long-winded process for the Hani people. As soon as a Hani man has found the woman of his life he needs the help of two elderly persons as a go-between to the woman's house, bringing a bottle of good wine or spirit, a bag of sugar, tobacco leaves and some cooked glutinous rice with a boiled egg inside wrapped in banana leaves as betrothal gifts. If the woman's parents are interested, they will accept the gifts and will ask the go-between to return a similar pack of gifts to the man. However, if the woman's parents do not agree to this match then they will not accept the gifts.

According to the traditions of the Ke er ke zi, Loba and the Dulong people, they must pay many betrothal gifts. Poor men who could not afford to pay betrothal gifts often had to resort to exchanging women, for example, their sisters. If a man has no sister to use as an exchange, then he would marry anybody with the help of his neighbours.

If a Lahu man wants to propose marriage to a woman, he must bring gifts for her family three times. On his first visit, he has to bring a bag of tea leaves, a bag of tobacco and a bottle of wine. On his second visit, he must bring twenty bowls of wine, two bundles of tobacco leaves and two locally made teapots. On his third visit, he has to bring some local made fabrics, one foot of green fabrics and forty jin of rice. (one jin = ½ kilogram)

EXCHANGING THE EIGHT CHARACTERS

The Eight Characters was the record of a person's name, time and date of birth and it was exchanged by the families of a young man and woman after the betrothal stage.

According to the author Ren Cheng, the rite of exchanging the Eight Characters was perhaps originated from the matchmaker official's records' keeping where names and dates of birth of young men and women were recorded, (see Zhong Guo Min Jian Jin Ji). Originally these records were used to compare the ages of young men and women, but later fortune tellers invented some mystery over it, hence, creating many superstitions about it. However, according to another source, the exchanging of the Eight Characters was invented by Li Jai of the Tang period.

There used to be an official marriageable age and it changed from dynasty to dynasty. Before and during Western Zhou, the official marriageable age for a young man was thirty and twenty for a young woman. This was the rule laid down in the Li Chi. Another ancient text mentioned that when a man had reached the age of thirty his body was strong enough, so it was the right age to become a father and a woman of twenty was just right for motherhood.

This age regulation was sometimes due to political instability in society, wars and economic developments. For instance, in the early period of the Chun Qiu period, the Duke of Qi, known as Qi Xuan Gong (685 -643 B. C.), wanted to expand the population of his kingdom to conquer the whole of China, so reduced the age of marriageable girls from twenty to fifteen. Later Gou Zan, the King of Yue, needed a large population to help him fight to get back his kingdom and issued an edict: Any man who has reached the age of twenty and any girl of seventeen still unmarried will be the fault of the parents. Later, during the Southern and Northern dynasties, the official marriageable age was reduced to fifteen for a boy and thirteen for a girl This must be the lowest official marriageable age in the history of China. In the early days of the Tang dynasty, the official age for marriage went up again to twenty for a man and fifteen for a girl. Later, during the mid and later Tang period the age was reduced to fifteen for a boy and thirteen for a girl. This survived till the Ming period and it went up again, sixteen for a boy and fourteen for a girl. There was no change in the Manchu period.

Apart from official marriageable age regulation, in the ordinary society, ordinary people also had their own regulations. Usually, country folks married at a younger age than city dwellers. In the rural areas, young men were married by the age of twenty and young women by eighteen. As for those in the cities, men were usually married at thirty and women at twenty five.

36

Eighteen was thought to be an unlucky age to get married for the She people, be it a man or a woman as it was believed, anyone getting married at eighteen would suffer 'eighteen disasters' during the marriage. Usually, a girl from a poor family would be married off by the time she was fourteen or fifteen whereas it was nineteen or twenty for a rich girl.

This practice was just the opposite to the Ta Khan Er people because they much preferred even numbers, a girl was to be married at eighteen and a man at twenty. Odd numbers were taboo to them.

Certain age differences were not approved by the Han-Chinese. If a man married a woman more than ten years younger than himself, he would attract criticism. Perhaps it was thought that the generation gap between the couple meant that they would not get along.

At one time, people who wanted to get married had to follow the hierarchy system! A younger brother must not be married before his elder brother, nor a younger sister before her elder sister because this was seen as upsetting the hierarchical system. At one time, the Han-Chinese were very strict about this rule but not anymore. However, one ethnic group, the Ozbek people are still following this strict rule. As long as an elder brother is still not married, the younger brothers are not allowed to get married first. Among the Jingpo people, if a second daughter wanted to marry before her elder sister then her husband to be had to pay some kind of compensation to her elder sister, usually a cow. The second daughter herself also had to give gold chains to her elder sister sometimes worth as much as two to three cows. It was to say that she was sorry because she had to marry before her elder sister. Among the Han-Chinese Cantonese speakers, there used to be a way to get round this problem which was to hang a pair of elder brother's or sister's trousers over the bedroom door frame for the new couple to walk under it.

Prior to 1949, it was popular among the Han-Chinese of some areas to let a ten year old son marry a girl of seventeen or eighteen. The reason was to use the daughter-in-law as a labour for the family rather as a wife for the son. However, there were other reasons too. In Honan, in the North, some wealthy families preferred to choose adult women for their young sons often in their teens. Having a much older daughter-in-law was an advantage because the adult wife was able to look after the little husband reducing the workload of the mother-in-law.

In the North-East, in the old days, the Manchurians there were said to be the ones who used to marry young. Most boys were married at the age of thirteen or fourteen. Those who married after the age of twenty were people who could not afford to marry when they were young. It was rather common that boys married older girls, for example, a boy of thirteen or fourteen married a girl of seventeen or eighteen. The reason was the same as in Honan, it was hoped that an older girl would carry out her role as a mother and wife better than a younger girl.

In the old days, there was an age taboo that the man must not be older than the woman by three, six and nine years, otherwise it might bring bad luck. There was another age taboo that the future couple must not be the same age. It was especially bad if both were born on the same month and year. There was a saying in Honan 'Same year not the same month, same month uterus deform'. This means that if a couple who were born in the same year and month married, their chances of having healthy children were in doubt. Even the Cantonese has this saying, 'Toong nin qin gor nai' meaning 'Same year is as bad as mud'.

Generally, the woman must be younger than a man like one saying which says, 'If the woman is one year older than the man, she is not a wife'. However, in the west of Honan, the people there liked the woman to be two years older than the man. According to the local saying 'If the woman is one year older than the man, gold will fly but if the woman is two years older than the man, gold will grow'. This means that if the woman was one year older than the man, his family would be poor later but if the woman was two years his senior, then his family would be prosperous afterwards.

In ancient times, the Han-Chinese practised the practice of not letting the eldest daughter marry, she was to stay single all her life. According to a Han text, during the rule of Qi Xiang Gong, Duke of Qi, (697 - 686 B. C.), in one of the Warring States, issued an order that the eldest daughter of every family in his state was not to be married and that marriage would bring bad luck to the family.

As a result of this order, it became a practice. However, that was not the real reason. The real reason was because Qi Xiang Gong had an incestuous relationship with his own sister, he invented this superstitious belief to keep her at home, with the full co-operation of his sister of course.

VETTING OF THE EIGHT CHARACTERS

Marriage divination was said to be the original form of ritual vetting of the Eight Characters. Marriage divination was said to have been invented by the first mythical couple Nu-Wa and Fu-Xi who existed since the beginning of time. Fu-Xi was said to propose to Nu-Wa. To find out whether they were meant for each other, Nu-Wa decided on a form of divination. Together the two of them went up to the top of a hill carrying two rounded stones or boulders with them. When they had reached the top of the hill Nu-Wa suggested that one of them stood on the east side and one on the west, then they threw the stones down together and if the stones reached the bottom of the hill at the same time then she would marry him. Fu-Xi agreed to her plan and the stones rolled off the hill and reached the bottom at the same time. Nu-Wa agreed that it was a sign approved by heaven and earth and that they were meant to be husband and wife.

During the Zhou period, before the invention of the vetting of the Eight Characters, a kind of divination was carried out before the ancestors' altar. This was done by shaking a long wooden or bamboo container. Inside this container, long thin wooden strips with characters written on them. During the process, the person would try to shake one wooden strip out of the container. The strip that fell out of the container was supposed to be the one with the right answer for the person. If the strip mentioned good things then the marriage would go ahead, if not, there would be no wedding. This kind of divination is still being practised by many Han-Chinese who come from ancestors' worship background and is a common sight in Taoist and Buddhist temples.

Ritual vetting of the Eight Characters did not exist before the Tang period. According to records, the Tang official, Li Jai invented the whole thing, a deception to discourage the marriage between a Tang princess and the prince of a northern country whose inhabitants were considered as barbarians to the Han-Chinese. The King of this northern kingdom tried to link his kingdom to Tang China and tried to force the Tang emperor to offer the hand of his daughter to his son, due to certain political ambition. Li Jai gathered the information of the prince's year, month and time of birth and his horoscope and produced a book of horoscopes making sure that the horoscope between the prince and the Tang princess were not compatible. This book was then buried near where the ambassador of the King was residing. One night, the ambassador saw a kind of light which seemed to be coming out from the ground nearby and thought that there might be some treasure buried underneath it. He did not know that it was a hoax.

After digging three feet deep a book was found. The book was found to contain horoscopes of the twelve animals giving details that a person belonging to a certain animal should not be marrying a person belonging to an animal that was not compatible, otherwise the marriage would be a disaster. At close examination, he found that the two horoscopes of his prince and the Tang princess were not compatible, in fact, it was very unlucky for the royal family and would even bring on the demise of the kingdom. As this was serious business, the ambassador went home empty handed. Li Jai's genius deception helped save the Tang princess from marrying a barbarian. Unfortunately for the rest of the Chinese, this hoax of Li Jai permeated the rest of society and took root as a rite.

In the old days, the vetting of the Eight Characters was of great importance. The Eight Characters were written on a piece of red paper. Red coloured paper was used because it was and still is the symbol of happiness in China. When this was done it was laid before the ancestors. Three joss sticks were lit before the ancestors. If the three joss sticks were burning evenly then the match was considered good but if they were not burning evenly 'yow zhang tuan', meaning, 'some long some short'. To the Chinese this was bad luck which probably meant that one spouse was going to die before the other.

Some people placed the Eight Characters in front of the stove god. In Zhejiang, Hangzhou, when the matchmaker brought the Eight Characters of the girl to the man's house, if it was accepted by the family, it would be placed in front of the stove god. After that, a fortune teller was hired to see whether the two sets of Eight Characters were in harmony with each other. If not, it would be sent back to the girl's family as soon as possible.

In some areas, a bowl of clear water was placed next to the ancestors' tablets and if within three days there was no dead insects in it, then it was a sign of good luck but if there were dead insects, then the marriage was called off. It seems that within the three days of receiving the Eight Characters, this was the time to listen to the wishes of the ancestors.

During the exchange of the Eight Characters, apart from the age taboo, there was also the horoscope taboo that people had to look at, known as the Chinese horoscope to Westerners. The Chinese horoscope consisted of twelve animals and is still very much in use today. Each year is represented by one animal. These animals are the rat, ox, tiger, rabbit, dragon, snake, horse, goat, monkey, rooster, dog and the pig. History is not clear when the horoscope was in use or where it originated from. According to one source, the horoscope was originated from the Xia dynasty where the Han-Chinese used it to remember the years. This way of calculating the years was also used by some minorities. Another source, (a Tang text), said in high antiquity, a minority living in the North and West of China, in a kingdom called Xia Jia Si Guo, used one different animal to represent each year. Today the Xia Jia Si people are known as Ke er ke zi and Ji er ji si people.

This horoscope was already used to record births before the Eastern Han dynasty. It was not sure why these animals were chosen to represent the years or why they were arranged as they were but once this method was adopted to record the years of the birth of people there emerged a popular belief that if a person was born in the year of, say, the tiger, he or she possessed the ferocious nature of a tiger.

By the Tang and Sung dynasties, this kind of concept had already influenced the ruling class and people perceived themselves as the animal who represented the year of their birth. There was a reference to this kind of fanatical belief. A man named Liu Zong Yuan who lived during the Tang dynasty, mentioned a man who was born in the year of the rat, made no attempt to catch the rats in his house because he perceived

42

himself as a rat and so he would not do anything to harm himself. It was said, emperor Sung Hui Zong was born in the year of the dog and his high official, equivalent to a prime minister, advised him to ban the dog trade in the capital because the 'dog' was the 'life' of the emperor. (The dogs were probably raised for consumption rather than as pets as the Chinese did eat dogs and still do, believing that eating dogs keep them warm in Winter).

Even today, there are many Chinese people who still have this kind of mentality believing that if they are born in the year of that animal, they are like that animal possessing the same nature of that animal.

In old society, this kind of belief was used in many areas especially in a marriage where it was necessary to find out whether the two animals of the future couple were compatible or against each other. During the exchange of the Eight Characters there were quite a few taboos about the horoscope. The fact that people were afraid of tigers meant a woman born in the year of the tiger was seen as fierce and capable of harming people. As tigers usually come out at night to eat people, a woman born at night was especially feared by people. Those who were born at night were separated into two groups, the ones born in the early part of the night were called 'shang shan fu' meaning 'going up the mountain tiger' and the ones born in the latter part of the night were called 'xia shan fu' meaning 'coming down the mountain tiger'. The 'going up mountain tiger' was thought to be less fierce because it already had its feed before going up the mountain so perhaps it might not harm anybody but the 'coming down mountain tiger' was going down the mountain to look for its prey, therefore it was seen as more ferocious and dangerous than the former. Some people might still consider a 'shang shan fu' for a daughter-in-law but a 'xia shan fu' was a definitely no.

In the past, the Han-Chinese in some areas in the North, thought that a girl born in the year of the goat was bad luck and after her marriage she would soon be a widow. This was mentioned in a text. People of those days thought that goats' eyes showed too much white bits and so a girl born in the year of the goat was a definitely no for a daughter-in-law because she would cause 'the husband to die young'. It was said, the Manchu Dowager Empress Ci xi was born in the year of the goat and that was why her husband the emperor Wen Zong died at the young age of thirty one. However, to get round this problem a girl born in the year of the tiger or goat would minus or add a year to her age. Those born in the first half of the year a girl born as a tiger would become an ox, a goat would become horse, those born in the latter half of the year born as a tiger would become a rabbit and a goat would become a monkey.

There was even a horoscope chart where people could choose the right future partner, for example, a rat would be best for a dragon, monkey or an ox but it was a taboo to choose a horse, rabbit or goat. There was also a proverb which goes like this:

The fight between a dragon and a tiger,
One of them will be hurt,
The fight between a dragon and a tiger,
One of them will not live long,
Two goats together will not live long,
Two tigers will not be in the same mountain,
A pig and a monkey will not reach the end,
A white horse is afraid of a green cow,
A rooster and a dog will not be a family,
A rooster and a dog is a bad match,
A green dragon is a menace to a white tiger,
A tiger and a rat do not marry.

There were similarities in the horoscope chart of Taiwan with the one in mainland China but there were also differences. If however a couple were unable to marry in one area because their horoscopes were incompatible, it might be all right for them to marry in another place. By looking at this comparison, it shows that this horoscope business was not to be trusted at all because a couple were not allowed to marry in one place but were able to marry in another. It shows that this horoscope business was really a load of rubbish.

These days, of course, a couple who are getting married will not be bother about matching their horoscopes like the old days, but many Chinese still bring up the subject and talk about it. When my cousin was getting married many years ago I remember someone made a comment, 'Oh, the future bride is a snake and the groom is a tiger'. According to the horoscope chart the tiger and the snake were a bad match.

BRIDE PRICE

If the vetting of the Eight Characters was successful, then the next step was the payment of the bride price. In ancient times, women were regarded as goods and they could be exchanged for livestock, articles and money. This exchange was the beginning of buying and selling marriage or mercenary marriage where women were sold like cattle and goods.

In ancient times, the acceptance of a pair of wild geese meant that the girl's family had the intention of going through with the marriage. Later this simple custom developed into a kind of buying and selling marriage where a specific sum of money was set for buying a wife. The bride price is actually a legacy of the mercenary marriage system.

According to a Han record, an emperor paid ten thousand 'jin' of gold, (one 'jin' is 1/2 a kilogramme), to an empress as a bride price. During the Sung dynasty, the bride price for an empress was two hundred 'jin' of gold plus twelve horses. For a consort, it was fifty 'jin' of gold and four horses. (One can see that using gold as part of a bride price has a long history that went back a few millenniums). Since then, even peasants used gold as part of a bride price.

Apart from gold, many other gifts were included in the bride price such as 'rou yi' made of gold, green jade and white jade, ('rou yi' are two characters, the symbol of fulfilling one's wishes), wine, because it symbolised the beauty of the marriage and also it was thought to be a sacrificial offering to the ancestors, carps symbolising that the new couple would be like fish and water happy with each other, clothing of four seasons in silk, cotton and fur, jewellery such as necklaces, bracelets, earrings and hairpins, a pig and a goat (poor people could only afford part of a pig and goat), wedding biscuits known as 'loong fung si bing' meaning 'dragon phoenix happy biscuits' or 'li bing', meaning 'ceremonial biscuits'. Some Manchurians and Mongolians preferred not to use these Han-Chinese wedding biscuits, they used 'man tou' instead, (these 'man tou' were made from flour and yeast with the 'double bliss' characters on them), 'si guo' meaning 'happy fruit' such as gui yuan, a small round brownish black fruit, lichees, uncooked groundnuts, chestnuts, jujubes, persimmons, apples, pomegranates and a pair of lotus stems which symbolised the love of a husband and wife that even if it broke, the fibre would still link them together, (the rest of the fruit all related to having a baby early, peace and having lots of children), tea leaves, and chicken and duck's eggs, about a hundred each, dyed in a red colour. All these gifts were packed in beautiful elaborate gift boxes.

In traditional China, the bride price was called 'li chin' meaning 'ceremonial gold'. This li chin, (money), had to be wrapped in a piece of red paper, usually known as 'hoong pao' meaning 'red pouch'. The money had to be in even numbers because everything must be in pairs including all the presents. This odd number taboo is still being observed today. Odd number implied loneliness or singleness. It was a taboo especially in a happy occasion just in case the 'singleness' became a reality, say, one of the spouses died later. In traditional China, the bride price included a ring, jewellery, coins, pieces of silk, ceremonial biscuits, wedding candles with dragons and phoenixes carved on them and some other things.

In the former province of Xi-Kang in Sichuan the Yi people there, also called Lolo, are separated into two groups; one group is called Black Yi and the other is called White Yi. These two groups never intermarried, a White Yi must marry a White Yi and it was the same for the Black Yi, though not sure whether it is still the case today. Their marriage system, at one time, belonged to the period of buying and selling marriage. Bride price was an enormous burden for a Lolo man. Any Lolo man who wanted to get married had to pay an enormous sum of 'ceremonial gold'. Some people even lost their fortunes just to get married. Some men remained single all their lives because they just could not afford to pay a bride price. Even the lowest bride price was said to be about two to three hundred ounces of silver. If anyone wanted to marry a girl from a wealthy family then he had to prepare to dish out at least two to three thousand ounces of silver. As well as receiving a lump sum of bride price from the groom's family, the bride's family also received presents in the form of cash from relatives and friends. Family income rose whenever a daughter was getting married, the sum of money received was as much as two to three working years' pay of a man. It was only natural that Lolo people preferred to have daughters than sons.

Mercenary marriage, it is said, to some extent, still exists among some people in China, for example with the Kazaks in Xinjiang.

If a man could not afford a certain sum of bride price, he will not be able to get a wife. Providing both sides have settled the bride price, a ceremony will be held, showing that the man has the serious intention of marrying the girl. During this period, the man is allowed to visit the girl and even eat and sleep with her as though they are man and wife, but she must not be pregnant. Until the rest of the bride price is paid in full, she remains with her family even if she is pregnant, she will be forced to have an abortion. Only after the man's family has paid the bride price in full, is he allowed to welcome the bride to his house.

Among the Yu gu people, livestock and clothing were the usual things that made up the bride price. In the North-East, the Ewenke people used deer, grey squirrel skins and wine as bride price. According to the custom of the Lisu people in Sichuan, twenty to thirty jin of pork, twenty or more jin of wine, four bundles of tobacco leaves and more than twenty feet of fabrics were given as bride price.

In Yunnan a Gu zhoong man, (a Lahu group), is expected to pay twelve squirrels, twelve catties of pork and twelve bowls of wine ·or spirits. As there are twelve animals in the Chinese horoscope therefore everything must be in twelve. Many Muslims live in Xinjiang the west of China and the Hui Chinese is one of these groups of people. (Their ancestors were from Central Asia, later intermarried with the Han-Chinese and settled in Xinjiang. Most of them now only speak Chinese and only a few understand a little Arabic). Marriages here are arranged by parents. Bride price is asked according to what the groom could afford. The Hui Chinese do not ask for high bride price therefore their marriage system is considered as a reasonable system.

There is a little island off the coast of Fujian called Ma-ju island. In the old days, there was an unusual practice in this place different from other areas in China. The demand for a bride price was very high compared with other areas. When a girl was one year old her price for marriage was two thousand dollars so when she reached the age of twenty she was worth forty thousand dollars. If, however she was not married by the age of twenty then each year after that two thousand dollars were minus from her bride price. This means that when she was twenty one her price would fall to only thirty eight thousand dollars. If she was still not married by the age of forty then she would not be worth even a dollar! However, most girls were married off by the time they were seventeen or eighteen years old, so most families were able to extract sums of money.

Cattle are given as bride price among the Miao people in Guizhou because they are regarded as valuable property. As bride price they must be given in pairs. In Guangdong, the Li people also give a few cattle as bride price. For the wealthy, often more than ten are given.

Once the marriage date was set, two or three months before the wedding the family of the Jing groom would send the agreed bride price, usually of pork, wine and rice about eighty catties each, and the date of the wedding to the bride's family. This was known as 'gwor zhong li' meaning 'celebrate middle ceremony'.

Old Chinese traditions and customs die hard among the Chinese. Today, this practice of paying a bride price is still observed by most if not all Chinese outside China. According to Lyn Pan, in her book, China's Sorrow, there is a revival of bride price in China today. In one case, the bride to be even asked for a coffin to be included in her bride price! The coffin was of course not for her but for her mother's future use. From this it shows that today in China the bride price is used by some people as a bargaining power to extract money and luxury goods such as television. (See China's Sorrow).

In Malaysia, bride price in the form of a large sum of money is given to the bride's family as soon as both sides are happy with the match. Besides the large sum of money, wine, a pair of live chickens, dried seafood such as sea-cucumber, (sea-slugs), ormers, dried Chinese mushrooms, wedding biscuits and a whole roast pig are also included as bride price.

FIXING THE WEDDING DATE

Fixing the wedding date was the next stage after the bride price. In the old days, in Nanjing, it was a practice to go to an astrologist to look for an auspicious date. Usually, the groom's family were responsible for taking the couple's Eight Characters to an astrologist. The astrologist had to make sure that he picked a date that was free from any 'zhoong fan' or bad luck. On a piece of red paper, he would write down the exact time for the bride to step into the sedan chair, the time to drink from the wedding goblets in the bridal chamber and the sort of people to avoid during the wedding day. Nowadays, the wedding date is decided by parents of both families.

In Malaysia, the Chinese with ancestors' worship background still look for an auspicious date from an almanac. There were superstitions surrounding this fixing of the wedding date. Some Han-Chinese in some areas of China never picked the 'gua nian' meaning 'the year without Spring' for marriage, because 'gua' sounds like 'gua fu' meaning 'widow'. For example, Chinese New Year falls on the 10th of February, the 'li chun' meaning 'beginning of Spring' falls on the 31st of January, in the following year the Chinese New Year falls on the 30th of January and the 'li chun' falls on the 3rd of February. This means that between the 10th of February till the 30th of January in the following year, the lunar year, there is no Spring.

Many people regarded the 'gua nian' as unlucky and believed that marrying in this year would bring discontinuity in the lineage. This could be due to because in high antiquity, as mentioned before, marriages were held during Spring festivals. According to one text: 'Why marriages must be in Spring? This is because heaven and earth intercourse with each other and is the time yin and yang receiving each other.' Whenever a 'gua nian' was approaching, people would either be married the year before it arrived or after.

If there were two Springs in one year the opinion was split. Say the Chinese New Year falls on the 31st of January, the 'li chun' falls on the 4th of February and the next year the 'li chun' falls on the 31st of January and the Chinese New Year falls on the 10th of February, that means there will be two Springs within that lunar year. In some areas, people were all for it because they liked the idea of double Springs, they believed it would bring double bliss. However, in some areas, people were against the idea because they thought the double Springs had too much to do with sexuality and the thought of over-indulgence in sexual intercourse was just too much for some people to bear.

Most people preferred not to risk getting married in the year of two Springs. In Central and South China, according to the custom of these two areas, one family must not celebrate two weddings in one year. Similar to the idea of the year with two Springs, in the Hunan areas, if there were a few households living under one roof there must not be a daughter marrying out and a daughter-in-law marrying into the same house. This was considered as 'si zhoong si' meaning 'happiness against happiness'.

Among the ethnic people, the Bai, a couple must not marry in the same year of their horoscopes' animals. If the bride was born in the year of the horse then she should not be married in the year of the horse and if the groom was born in the year of the dog then he should not get married in the year of the dog.

As we have looked at the taboos surrounding the 'year' of marriage we now look at the taboos surrounding the 'month'.

According to one text, in ancient times people married from the ninth month onwards till the first month of the following year. In the old days, the Han-Chinese and some ethnic minorities believed that the days after the twenty third of the twelfth month were the auspicious days for getting married. Between the twelfth month and the first month these were not busy months in agriculture and since agriculture was the most important industry in China it is not difficult to see why the custom had taken root. As for those busy months the fifth, seventh and ninth month, the Han-Chinese and the Wa people and some other ethnic minorities, considered it a taboo to marry during these months, saying that these were evil months with ghosts everywhere. For the marriage to go ahead during these months was to bring bad luck to one's family. Actually the truth is, the weather was hot in the fifth, seventh and ninth month, food rot easily, people were more lethargic, domestic animals were often sick at this time and so weddings were avoided during these scorching months. In Taiwan, some people avoided getting married from the fourth month to the ninth month. It is said, getting married in the fourth month brings bad luck because 'shih' meaning 'four' sounds like 'death' (many Chinese still consider this figure a taboo figure). The fifth month is an 'evil month' (mentioned in the Duan Wu Festival) so it will not be a good month for wedding either. There is a local saying in Taiwan, 'sixth month marry a half year wife'. This is because six months is half a year and so people are worried that the marriage might only last half a year. People avoided the seventh month like avoiding the plague because it was when the ghosts were out looking for food. As for the eight month, there was this saying 'eighth month marry the wife of the earth god'. This is because the fifteenth day of the eighth month· was the day where people worshipped the earth god. Also, it was believed that the earth god was dominated by his wife and so if any man married in this month he would be dominated by his wife. As for a wedding in the ninth month, it was not good either because 'ninth' sounds like 'gou' (dog). 'Gou' was and still is used as a term of abuse for people committing adultery, 'gou nan nu' means 'dog male and female'. In Taiwan, the tenth month till the third month in the following year were the less busy months in agriculture. The fourth month to the ninth month were the busy months and during these months the weather was unpredictable as these were the hottest months with typhoons and torrential rain. This kind of weather of course could upset people's normal daily routine. If bad weather suddenly descended on a wedding day, it would affect the mood of the people and bring problems to the people involved. These reasons were good enough to make people feel that it was bad luck to marry during these months.

Certain days would not be considered for a wedding day. The wedding day must be on an even number day because an odd number day was regarded as bad luck. This custom was observed by the Han-Chinese and some other ethnic minorities. There was a saying, 'how shih cheng shuang', meaning, 'good things come in pairs' and so the wedding date had to be an even number date. An odd number date would imply 'singleness'.

In some areas, the Han-Chinese never arranged a date on the seventh day of the seventh month because it had something to do with the legend of the 'ox watcher' and the 'weaver girl'. According to legend, the 'weaver girl' was the daughter of the Jade Emperor of heaven who came down to earth to marry the 'ox watcher'. When the Jade Emperor found out about this romance, he forced his daughter to return to heaven. Only on the seventh day of the seventh month were the two of them allowed to meet each other once a year. All parents wished their children to have happy endings in their marriages, so this day was seen as a taboo to tie the knot. In some rural areas, the fifth, fourteenth and twenty third days of every month were also unlucky days. The Hani people living in the province of Yunnan were especially superstitious of the day when there was an eclipse of the sun and moon as it was considered as unlucky for marriage. Anyone marrying on this day would give birth to a baby with six fingers, had twins or a baby with hare lips, so this day was avoided.

The practice of avoiding certain years, months and days in marriage have now more or less eradicated except in a few areas where people are still cautious about it. In China, in the rural areas, people usually get married during the less busy months. As for the city folks, most people choose public holidays such as the first of May, first of October and before and after the Spring Festival. Public holidays are preferred because during these days most people are free. The old superstitious way of fixing a wedding date no longer has its hold on people. Some older generations still remember the taboos involved in the fixing of their wedding dates but because most young people are refusing to be frightened by superstitious customs, they have no say regarding this matter.

GWOR TA LI

Bringing the gifts, (bride price), to the bride's house was known as 'gwor ta li' literally means 'celebrate big ceremony'. In the old days, this rite was considered as very important. The groom's family usually used this occasion to display its wealth. Gifts were transported in trunks in elaborate work, paraded along the streets in the accompaniment of the matchmaker, musicians and firecrackers were set off.

In the old days, after receiving the gifts, the bride's family laid them out in the courtyard and relatives were invited to view. The representatives of the groom's family would be invited into the living room to perform a little ceremony. During the ceremony, he would place a 'rou yi' on the lap of the bride to be and stick one or two hairpins on her hair. The bride's family had to return some gifts to the groom's family such as cakes and fruit.

In Shandong area, mincemeat must not be included in the food stuff because it was afraid that the bride would acquire 'slowness' and would be slow in doing house chores. The bride's family would not receive everything sent to them; some food stuff would be sent back to the groom's family together with the bride's dowry. In Central China, the custom there was not to keep the cockerel; it was returned to the groom's family with a hen. This hen must be live, and it must not be a white colour.

At the house of the bride, when placing the wedding biscuits on the ancestors' altar, if the joss sticks were not straight, they must not be taken out and put in the urn again. It was important that it was done only once. When the people of the groom, those who brought the gifts, were leaving, the bride's family must not say 'chai lai jor' which literally means 'come and sit again'. This is because putting the joss sticks into the urn again and saying 'come and sit again' might become a reality meaning that the bride might marry again and that would be bad. Of course, this was all to do with the concept of a good marriage.

In Taiwan, before sending the wedding biscuits to relatives and friends, they must be checked for perfection so that the top of the wedding biscuits were not burnt. If there were any burnt marks on them the bride would be teased that she liked to gossip. If the wedding biscuits did not look good the bride would be teased that she was not pretty.

In Hubei areas, three days before the wedding, the groom's family had to bring some pork and wedding biscuits and paid a formal visit to the bride's house. On such an occasion, most of the time the bride was nowhere to be seen.

In Taiwan, it is a taboo for the bride's family to receive a whole pig from the groom's family. According to the custom, most of the meat is taken out and the carcass is returned to the groom's family with some meat left. According to a local saying 'eat your meat but not your bones'. If for some reason the bride's family forget this superstitious rule it will anger the groom's family.

Xibo people celebrate their weddings for three days. On the first day of the wedding the groom takes the food stuff and wedding gifts to the bride's house. The groom also must present two bottles of good wine to his parents-in-law.

On the day before the wedding, the Jing groom would bring the wedding gifts to the bride's house. According to the custom, the groom had to pay a visit to the bride's house in the evening. This visit was known as 'rern chin', it was to let the groom get to know all the relatives of the bride's family. During this meeting, the groom led by an uncle of the bride offered areca nuts and tea to every relative and was formally introduced to them. As most Jing people lived within miles of each other usually a groom was able to return home on that night. If a Jing man married a Zhuang or Han-Chinese woman then he might not observe this 'rern chin' custom but follow Han-Chinese and Zhuang customs.

Among the Chinese in Malaysia, apart from the Christians, most Chinese observed the practice of 'gwor ta li'. Usually, a week before the actual wedding day, the groom brings the rest of the bride price, (the cash is paid earlier), a whole roast pig, wedding biscuits, a couple of live chickens, dried Chinese mushrooms, dried sea-cucumbers, dried ormers, apples and oranges. Some people have one roast pig and one uncooked pig the former is called 'golden pig' and the latter is called 'white pig'. In Guangdong, during the old days, the roast pig was not brought to the bride's house during 'gwor ta li' but on the third day after the wedding only if the bride was found to be a virgin!

Cantonese wedding biscuits are specially made for the Cantonese speakers. They are carried in special round boxes

56

which are later returned to the shops where they are bought. Cantonese wedding biscuits are round in shape, about an inch high, made from a thin puffy pastry, stuffed with bean paste and they come in two colours of pink and yellow. The yellow ones are stuffed with lotus seed paste and the pink ones are stuffed with black bean paste.

Hakka speakers have the same kind of wedding biscuits like the Cantonese whereas the Fujian speakers have quite a few varieties due to regional differences. Some of their biscuits are made from puffed glutinous rice which come in a round shape like a ball and an oblong shape. These are hollow inside and are very sweet and sticky. Some come in the form of a square shape, some are biscuits, and some are actually candy and there are four varieties. These biscuits and candy are wrapped in pink papers, one candy is made with whole peanuts and sugar, one is made with sesame seeds and sugar. One biscuit is made with glutinous rice flour very sweet and sticky and one is made with chopped peanuts and sugar and it is my favourite of all.

Cantonese speakers usually give two wedding biscuits, one pink and one yellow to neighbours and friends to announce the marriage. When neighbours receive the wedding biscuits they will say 'Ah, your daughter is getting married!' Usually, relatives are given more than two wedding biscuits plus a piece of roast pork. These days, a box of Western style cakes is also included to keep up with modernisation. Some Hong Kong people, I am told, are given cards known as 'bing card' meaning 'biscuits' cards' which they take to the nearest shop to collect their own cakes not the traditional Chinese wedding biscuits but Western style cakes.

'Gwor ta li' is usually an exciting and busy day for the bride's family. It is a day where close relatives gather together for a feast. As most Chinese are ancestors' worshippers, the whole roast pig is offered to the ancestors as a sacrificial offering together with the chickens and the wedding biscuits. The Chinese involve their dead ancestors in everything including births and marriages. It is to announce the marriage to the dead ancestors. After the sacrificial worship, the cooked chickens, some of the roast pork, dried mushrooms, sea cucumbers and ormers are eaten during the feast. The rest of the roast pig is cut up into pieces and is distributed among the close relatives.

In Malaysia, the 'li bing' still has a part to play in Chinese weddings. As for the live chickens, they are probably a legacy of ancient times where two live wild geese were given to the bride as betrothal gifts. Unlike the old days, most of the goods are accepted by the bride's family, only a few biscuits are returned to the groom's family.

DOWRY

After celebrating the 'gwor ta li' the next stage was the giving of the dowry by the bride's family for the bride to take with her to the groom's house. The dowry was called 'jia zhuang' which literally means 'marriage ornaments'. In the past, a Manchurian groom was responsible for fixing only an empty house whereas the bride's family was responsible for getting everything from a pair of chopsticks to a bed.

Among the Han-Chinese, a bride's family was not responsible for buying the furniture only the bed linen and things for everyday use from chopsticks to a toilet pot.

There were rules concerning a dowry. It was all right to give more but would attract criticism if certain items were missing from the traditional list. Items included a set of 'rou yi' either made of white jade, green jade or coral. As a symbol of peace and luck it was an indispensable item for the Manchurians. Some Han-Chinese used it, but some preferred the statues of the three deities who were the symbols of 'Joy, Prosperity and

Longevity'. Other items were; a pair of candlestick stands either made of tin or copper, a copper table lamp for the bedroom, a pair of pot plants, a pair of large vases filled with red and green chicken feathers, a large mirror, a pair of containers for storing tea leaves, a whole tea set, ceramic ware for storing tea and oil, vases and a spittoon, a fruit tray with apples and pomegranates, a pair of high-legged trays for storing fresh fruit, a large tray with nine or more compartment with dried fruit such as lichees, gui yuan, raw chestnuts, raw groundnuts, jujubes, sugared lotus stems, sugared melon sticks, dried apples and dried apricots, an earthen jar of Shaoxing yellow wine, a screen with beautiful embroidery of birds, flowers and trees, make-up and make-up kit, a set of different combs, things for oral and facial use, bed linen embroidered with two Mandarin ducks, blankets, door curtains and bead-curtains, clothes of four seasons, pieces of different kinds of fabrics, embroidered shoes, embroidered items such as towels and purses, ashtrays and tobacco boxes, gold and silver jewellery and last of all one or two personal maids. These maids followed the bride to the groom's house to continue to look after the bride as they had done so in her natal home. Although these maids looked after the bride in her husband's house, it was the bride's family who paid for their wages. This practice originated from ancient times. The above dowry list is of course only for the wealthy as for the poor they could only afford a modest dowry.

In 1772 the Manchu emperor Qian Long's daughter married Duke Kong Xian-pei, a member of the Kong family and a descendant of the ancient philosopher Confucius. Included in her dowry were several thousand trunks of clothing and jewellery. Besides these there were also boxes of ginseng, coral, ivory carvings, and miniature landscapes. On top of these, ten eunuchs were also included as part of her dowry, paid for from the tax revenue.

According to Han Suyin, an authoress of many books about China, in Sichuan, women who could make pickles were much praised, a sign of good breeding and eligibility. Daughters of a mother who made excellent pickles were sought after for marriage on the assumption that the special recipes would be passed on from mother to daughter. As pickles were a speciality of Sichuan so it was included in a bride's dowry:

'Pickles were part of the wedding dowry,
taken by the bride to her husband's home,
along with head pins and rings, necklaces,
lacquer boxes, cushions, bed-hangings,
embroidered quilts, bolts of silk and
satin, furs, morning and evening mirror,
clocks, fans, and personal maid servants.
The bridal boxes, carried two by two
on lacquered poles with silver hooks,
also contained jars of pickles, reputedly
made by the bride.'
(see The Crippled Tree)

In the past, many people used to regard the ninth month as unlucky for making the wedding blanket, part of a dowry. Many preferred the tenth month. It was hoped that the bride was blessed with ten sons. If it was made in the ninth month it was generally feared that the bride might give birth to nine girls. This of course had so much to do with the ancient Chinese concept of having sons to continue the lineage. White cotton threads must not be used in making the blanket only reds were used. Widows were not allowed to sew the blanket or women with sons but no daughters or had daughters but no sons.

In some areas, items such as scissors, mirrors and teapots were not included in a dowry because it was believed that the brothers of the bride would die. In Zhejiang, in Hangzhou, toilet pots were indispensable because it could affect the lineage. There were two types of toilet pots one type was for toileting, one type for giving birth. In the past, some women gave birth sitting on a toilet pot. Inside these new toilet pots red dyed eggs and fruit were placed with the symbolical meaning that the family be blessed with many sons and grandsons.

In Shenlongjia, in the west of Hubei, the inhabitants there used to do things different from the rest of the country. For the rest of the country, a groom's family was responsible for buying the furniture for the bridal chamber and the bride's family was responsible for all the nitty gritty things such as bed linen, pillows, blankets and curtains as a dowry but here it was just the opposite.

In the past, furniture was part of the dowry of a young girl from the south of Suzhou. These days, bed linen and electrical goods are also included. Every two blankets are folded together, cakes, sweets, red dyed eggs and a red pouch with money are placed inside it. Inside the toilet pot; rice, beans and eggs are placed and wrapped with a blue flower material. This toilet pot known as 'zi suan tung' used to play an important part in a bride's dowry. When the dowry has arrived at the groom's house this toilet pot will be received by the father of the groom it has the symbolical meaning that the lineage is being perpetuated. Rice and beans are placed inside the toilet pot for the symbolical meaning that there would be a good harvest with the five grains.

In the bridal chamber, the relatives of the groom and neighbours could help themselves with the cakes, red dyed eggs and sweets and money in the red packets taken out from the blankets and the toilet pot.

Among the Xibo people, on the day of sending the dowry to the groom's house, it is the responsibility of the bride's brother and sister-in-law to make sure that everything goes well. Before the cupboard is sent to the groom's house, the mother of the bride will place some money in it. This is to wish the new couple that their cupboard will be filled with silver and gold, prosperity, and happiness. When this is done the sister-in-law of the bride will lock the cupboard and will hand over the key to the groom's mother later.

Today, dowry is still called 'jia zhuang'. In Malaysia, after the bride's family has received the bride price in the form of a large sum of money, they will then use it to buy jewellery such as a few gold necklaces and pendants, bracelets, a few bangles, earrings, rings, pieces of fabrics, usually about ten to twenty to fill the shelves of the wardrobe, new clothes, two sets of bed linen, a couple of blankets and a set of crockery. All these items are given to the bride as her dowry. This is the reason why daughters are called 'maggots in the rice' by some Chinese if not all because a family do not gain anything from the bride price except some food stuff. Unlike the Fujian speakers who ask for a very high bride price, the Cantonese speakers only ask for a modest sum and that is why they called their daughters 'sit poon for' literally means 'losing money goods'.

Unlike the old days in traditional China, these days no fuss is made when taking the dowry to the groom's house, certainly no musicians with gongs and cymbals are taken there by the couple, not on the day before the wedding, weeks or days before.

The dowry of a bride reflects her family's financial situation, and a fat dowry reflects a family's wealth and status. Sometimes, pressure from social opinion forces families to give generously because Chinese are so worried about 'losing face', if they do not give a reasonable dowry to a daughter. For a well-off family, giving a reasonable dowry to a daughter will not hurt much but for a poor family, merely getting by, a dowry is a financial burden.

When the elder brother of my stepmother got married, his Fujian wife brought along the biggest dowry I have ever seen. Included in her dowry were a few acres of rubber estate, new clothes, stacks of fabrics filled the shelves in her wardrobe along with bed linen and bath towels. I have never seen a bride with so much new underwear, especially brassieres. Her jewellery included diamonds, jade and gold necklaces and her bracelets were as thick as ropes. Fujian speakers have always preferred their jewellery to be heavy. They are not so interested in the style but the weight of the gold. Not only her bedroom was filled with new things but also her kitchen was full of new crockery.

On the day of the wedding, friends of the bride and the relatives of the groom, usually women will flock to the bride's bedroom and take a good look at her 'jia zhuang'. As late as the 1970s, some brides in Malaysia still included a toilet pot and a wash bowl painted with a pair of Mandarin ducks, the symbol of wedded bliss. These ducks were used as the symbol because they always swim in pairs. Some old-fashioned families at that time still insisted on having a set of red bed linen with two Mandarin ducks embroidered on them or a dragon and a phoenix. Some people used to buy two sets of bed linen, one set red for the wedding day and one set pink.

BEFORE THE WEDDING

Before the wedding, to make sure that everything ran smoothly there were certain things to be avoided. Tujia women were forbidden to see any strangers a month before their wedding. During this period, they were to refrain from doing house chores. Apart from working on their clothes for their wedding there was one duty required of them; it was to master the 'weeping song' for marriage.

During the wedding, a Tujia bride must chant weeping songs in her dialect. There were songs for her parents, her brothers, her sisters-in-law and the matchmaker. It was also proper that she wept for her own distress and misery. Usually, the duration of weeping was seven to ten days but sometimes it could go on for a month, to such a state that caused dryness in her mouth and she lost her voice and consciousness. Only when she reached this point would she be regarded as a capable woman. Otherwise, she would be disliked by both her family and her husband's family. During this period of weeping, she was entertained by members of her family in a farewell dinner where other people were invited to join in with the crying to keep her company.

According to Ge lao custom, a woman had to extract two front teeth when she was about to marry. The practice was to prevent bringing bad luck to the groom's family. However, according to one text of the Western Jin period, the extraction of two front teeth, top and bottom, was regarded as a sign of beauty. As for the belief that it would bring bad luck to the groom's family if a bride married without extracting two front teeth, this was practised much later.

When a Yi girl was getting married, she had to go through a near starvation diet with nothing but a few eggs and water. This duration of dieting could be from three to five days or a little longer than that from seven to eight days. According to the custom, the longer the girl went on this dieting the better. This way she was seen as someone who knew the rites well. If the girl was seen indulging in overeating before her wedding, she would be the laughingstock of her community.

In the past, the Tanka people, boat people who lived along the coasts of Guangdong in boats, also practised the weeping custom before marriage. These Tanka people are descendants of aborigines in South China and were categorised as 'zhien min' meaning 'low class people' during the Manchu period or perhaps earlier. These people were subjected to various disabilities. They were not allowed to be educated, settled on land nor marry the Han-Chinese. Their disabilities were abolished when the Republic of China came into existence in 1912. Tanka literally means 'egg family'. Ten days before her wedding, a Tanka girl was not allowed to show her face in public. At night, the women gathered to weep. Sometimes sisters formed a group together or a mother and daughter or a few bridesmaids together. Praising the parents' virtue mostly had to do with bringing the bride up and the sorrow of leaving them. Songs were soft and nice to listen could easily make anyone emotional to shed a tear or two.

In the past, the Muslims of China did not allow the bride and groom to meet on the month before their wedding. It is said, this custom is not so strict now. In some of the areas in the North-East, among the Han-Chinese there is a custom of not allowing the bride to visit her groom's family three days before her marriage. This may have to do with the significance of the rite of welcoming the bride. If there is too much communication between the bride and groom before marriage, then the rite of welcoming the bride will lose its significance.

In Hunan, in the Xiang lakes areas, before a wedding, the bride was given a dish of fried eggs with vinegar. The aim was to delay her menstruation until after her wedding day. It was considered a taboo for the bride to be menstruating on her wedding day. There was an old superstitious saying 'chi ma bai tang, jia por ren wang' which literally means, 'riding a horse during the worship of the ancestors, family broken people dead'. This is because the sanitary belt was called a 'chi ma pu' meaning 'riding a horse cloth' by the Chinese. Women's menstruation was regarded as dirty and still is among some Chinese, and women were never allowed to join in the worship of ancestors when they were menstruating.

In Taiwan, things were a little different. 'Fu' obtained from Taoist or Buddhist temples was a piece of yellow strip of paper with red characters written on it and was burned, mixed with

65

water, and given to the bride to be to drink. This was to ensure that she would not menstruate on her wedding day because it was a taboo for a bride to be menstruating on this day.

On the eve of her wedding, a Bai girl has to go through a ceremony known as 'xi jiao li' meaning, 'wash feet ceremony'. In the middle of the living room a pair of scarlet candles are lit, and a basin of clean water is placed for washing feet. When everything is ready the bride will come downstairs accompanied by her close relatives. She will be seated in front of the 'xi shen', meaning 'happy deity' and be ready to have her feet wash. It is to hope that in future, husband and wife will get on well and have a happy life together. Before having her feet washed the bride must answer some questions from the relatives and then tell them what she wishes to have. When she is satisfied that her wishes will be granted, she will happily put her feet into the basin to be washed. The washing is done by the relatives and the water is changed several times about four to five times. This washing business goes on for quite a while, the longer the better because this means that the relatives are sorry to part with her. After the washing the water is thrown out of the front door outside the house, this is to show that 'a daughter who is married out is like water which is splashed out of the door'.

According to the wishes of the bride, relatives will present her with gifts. According to their financial situations, the relatives will give her gifts such as a little hen, a calf and a little goat mainly farm animals. These little animals will follow the bride to her husband's house on her wedding day. These animals will be raised by her and it is hoped that they will breed well and multiply. If these animals did not breed well the bride will be blamed for being lazy that she did not work hard to look after the animals properly. After marriage, the bride will be expected to respect her parents-in-law, get along with her sisters-in-law .and neighbours and to love and help her husband to build up a happy family.

According to Tanka custom, on the eve of the wedding, a meal was eaten by the bride and her friends. This night was called 'wan fan' meaning 'late rice'. On this night, a ceremony was held known as 'pai fan' meaning 'worship rice'. Wine and fruit were laid in front of the family altar together with candles and joss sticks. During this night, only female guests of the bride were invited. Two by two, each holding a fan these girls went forward to the bride's family altar and worshipped the various deities. After this worshipping ceremony the girls sat together in a circle chatting, singing, or playing cards all night.

On the day before the wedding, the Lisu groom accompanied by four young men went to the bride's house for a feast. In the bride's house, green pine needles were scattered all over the floor. During the feast, the groom and his friends were entertained by the matchmaker singing songs to praise the bride and to thank the bride's family for their warm hospitality. At this time, the bride ran off to the hills to show that she was running away from the marriage. After the singing, the matchmaker and the bride's mother would go to the hills to look for the bride. At night, a fire was made outside the bride's house, the matchmaker played the gourd flute and walk round the fire three times. Afterwards everybody held hands and danced round the fire till late at night.

On the eve of the wedding, a special ceremony is held called 'shang tou' meaning, 'comb the hair' ceremony. It is said to ensure good luck to the bride and groom. An auspicious time is selected by a fortune-teller or by themselves looking at the almanac, (many Chinese kept one in the house), for a good day and time for the ceremony, during which the bride and groom to be, had their hair combed by a person in their own homes. This is usually done by a middle-aged woman with sons and daughters. If the woman has only sons but no daughters, it will not do nor just daughters but no sons.

The 'shang tou' ceremony is still practised by the Chinese in Malaysia especially by the Cantonese. I have seen quite a few of these ceremonies. It is still a custom for the bride to be, (the same for the groom in his own house), during the ceremony to wear a white Chinese suit, a top with a Mandarin collar and a pair of trousers similar to a pair of pyjama trousers. Lucky phrases and wishes are uttered by the woman while the hair is being combed and she will say:

'First comb, comb till the end,
(meaning that the marriage will last till the end),
Second comb, white hair and even brows,
(meaning the couple will grow old together),
Third comb, plenty of sons and grandsons'.

After the ceremony, round balls made with glutinous rice flour in sugared water called 'tang yuan' are eaten by everybody present at the ceremony. It has symbolical significance because it means 'a life of unbroken harmony' for the bride and groom.

WEDDING COSTUMES

In ancient times when a man was getting married it was known as 'siao teng ker'. It was like a man who had passed the Confucian examination and landed an official post therefore he was allowed to wear a ceremonial robe and hat. His bride could wear a phoenix coronet and ceremonial robe which symbolised luck and peace. At one time, this custom was popular among the Han-Chinese, Manchurians, Koreans, and a few other ethnic minorities of China. According to a Manchu text, the phoenix coronet was an ancient royal accessory.

In the Han period it was worn only by the great empress dowager and empress dowager when they were visiting the monasteries or temples. The coronet was decorated with the symbol of a phoenix, hence, it got the name 'fung guan', meaning 'phoenix crown'. Some changes were made to this coronet later, some had nine dragons and four phoenixes, some had nine 'hui' and four phoenixes. 'Hui' were the feathers from the tail of a pheasant.

In the period of the Ming, the coronet became part of an empress day wear plus flowery hairpins. In the ordinary society, there were imitations made for ordinary women to wear during their weddings. However, one text mentioned a different explanation that not only the son of an official, but the son of a peasant could also marry in an official ceremonial robe and his bride could wear a phoenix coronet and ceremonial robe, to indicate that her position was that of a wife and not a concubine. From this it shows that if a bride did not marry in a phoenix coronet and court ceremonial robe it would be unlucky and she would be seen as a concubine.

Following the revolution and the collapse of the empire system, the custom of wearing a phoenix coronet and ceremonial robe had disappeared into the history. Today, wearing official ceremonial robes and phoenix coronets are nowhere to be seen anymore except in films, opera shows and cultural exhibitions. Most Han-Chinese men now wear Western suits and their brides wear fashionable Western style wedding gowns with the exception of the brides in Hong Kong who are still wearing 'kua', a long-sleeved top with a Mandarin collar and a skirt, red or pink colour, the traditional wedding costumes of Guangdong since the dawn of the Republic. In China, some brides still wear 'hong long hua', (flowers), because 'long hua' sounds like 'yoong hua', symbolising prosperity.

Unlike the Han-Chinese brides on land, a Tanka bride was not allowed to wear a phoenix coronet nor a ceremonial robe for her wedding. For her wedding, she could only wear an ordinary dress and covered her head and face with a red cloth.

Different ethnic minorities of China have their own distinctive marriage costumes. The costumes must be brand new. If it is an old costume it is considered as unlucky meaning that the bride is not pure. Although there is a custom where brides wear old clothes during weddings. In the South-East of China, there is a custom among the Dong people, where the bride's girlfriends wear new clothes with silver and gold jewellery but the bride looks like a beggar wearing old clothes, straw-sandals and is without any headdress.

Another distinctive custom is that the bride has no dowry to take with her to her husband's house. The idea behind this custom is to let the bride know that she is expected to work hard after she is married. It is said, this custom reflects the traditional virtue of the Dong people.

Most ethnic minorities in many areas consider the marriage costume as very important. Before the bride has her marriage costume made, an auspicious date has to be fixed. The costume must be sewn by women who have prosperity, longevity and have both sons and daughters. This means that only women who have reached a certain age are asked to do this. Widows and pregnant women will not be asked to help. A marriage costume must not have any pockets so that the bride's family's fortune and joy will not be taken away with the bride. The costume must be cut from a single piece of material not two, so that the marriage will last till the end.

Most marriage costumes are red and white is a taboo colour. Red used to be the only colour for a bride among the Han-Chinese and some minorities. Although in cities like Shanghai and Beijing, Han-Chinese brides are wearing fashionable white wedding gowns but in rural areas some brides are still wearing simple Chinese suits a pair of trousers and a top with a Mandarin collar. In Yunnan, among the Yi people, it is a taboo for the groom and bride to wear white. They could only do so after a hundred days later. In old Taiwanese society, brides liked to marry in red. Although the suit worn during the 'combing hair ceremony' had to be in white, this had to do with 'purity'. In the North of the Guangdong area, on her wedding day, the Zhuang bride wears a black wedding costume, her bridesmaid also wears black, each carry a black umbrella all the way to the groom's house. The groom's family is responsible for sewing the bride's costume and is sent to the bride's house by the matchmaker. This custom of wearing a black costume during wedding is associated with the 'si chair', meaning 'happy bird' because it has black feathers. This custom of wearing black in a wedding is seen as a sign of bliss and luck though not sure whether it has something to do with the custom of ancient times where the groom wore black to welcome his bride.

WEDDING MUSIC

In ancient times, there was no music in weddings. It was said, music had too much 'yang' and it was not good for the bride. Actually, it was to let the bride learn her way of becoming a good wife, so that her thinking would not be distracted by the music. This kind of interpretation no doubt has so much to do with Confucian thinking. If music was never used in weddings, then it would not be recorded in the Li-chi at all, so it seems that at one time music was used in weddings before the Confucians opposed it. Although the rules were laid down, in ordinary society people still preferred to follow their own customs. In Honan and Shandong, the wealthy liked their music during weddings.

However, there are some people in rural areas even today who do not play music in their weddings. Some of the minorities like the Yi people in Yunnan do not play music in weddings but in funerals and festivals. These people are said to be following the ancient custom of not having music in weddings.

These days in China, music is part of a wedding. In rural villages, people have their own groups of musicians specially for weddings. Some people use cassette players, playing all kinds of music such as modern and opera songs, as noisy as possible. If a wedding has no music, it will be too quiet and to the Chinese this is just not right.

In a Hui Chinese wedding, music and entertainment in any form is forbidden. This strict rule might have something to do with their Islamic religion.

WEDDING PRESENTS

In ancient times, the custom of giving presents to the bride and groom was not observed. This was confirmed by the Li chi that it was unnecessary to give presents. To the ancient Chinese, marriage was seen as a stage that everybody had to go through and so there was no need to make a fuss about it. Perhaps later the concept of marriage was looked at from a different angle, its significance was raised and so people started to give presents and it became more important than the other rites in life. Later, even the ruling authority had to give in to the people and change the rule. According to a Han text written during the reign of Han Hsien Di, (189-220 AD), he issued an edict saying that marriage was an important part of a person's life so it was all right to give wine and food as presents.

Marriage presents are still a must in China today. Nowadays the practice is called 'chow fern zi' with the presents given by relatives and friends. The price of marriage presents go up all the time and this really is a problem for the people who are poor. Since the practice expected people to give, it would seem rather awkward not to give. In China today, there is a suggestion to reform this ancient practice but currently with not much success.

In Honan, in a place called Yoong Yang, goats and wine are given as marriage presents. It is a taboo if the eyes of the goat are black and if the wine is not pure enough. In Taiwan, ducks must not be given as marriage presents this is because 'duck' sounds like 'capture', so it is unlucky. However, it is all right if ducks are on the wedding menu.

On the wedding day, it does not matter how many people come to bring presents, but people do not like a debtor to turn up on this day. If a debtor turns up it would appear a bad omen for the wedding. When a Bai couple has decided to get married their elders will issue an announcement: 'Today is a happy day, debtors are not allowed to come for their debts'. If anyone broke this rule the person will be punished by the whole village.

FIRECRACKERS

According to a man named Xiong Por Loong, who lived during the Manchu period, 'firecrackers are originally used to frighten away the evil spirits, now it is used in weddings and funerals, this is against the rite'. This reflects that rites cannot really stop people from doing what they wanted to do. In fact, in the old days, people used firecrackers in weddings to frighten off the evil spirits. This is because a wedding was seen as a happy day, and still is today, so all the more, people were afraid that evil spirits were out to make chaos for them. For this reason, firecrackers were used to make some noise to scare off the ghosts.

Since then, every happy occasion, including birthdays of the elderly and the birthdays of the dead ancestors were celebrated with a string of firecrackers outside the front door and as time went by it became a custom. Whenever there is the sound of firecrackers people immediately know that there is a happy occasion going on. If there are no firecrackers during a happy occasion it will make people worry that something is not quite right.

DOUBLE BLISS

Whenever there is a Chinese wedding the characters 'Double Bliss' are everywhere among the possessions of the bride and groom. These two characters came from a story in the Northern Sung period. The story mentioned a scholar by the name of Wang An Shi who went to Kaifeng, the capital, to sit for the imperial examination. To be near to the capital, he decided to stay with his maternal uncle who lived in Honan. When he arrived at the East gate of the city, he saw a pair of tuai lian, (characters on long strip of papers), in front of one of the houses and he stopped to read. After reading it, he remarked 'good tuai lian' and was heard by one of the old servants of the house. 'Ah ha, this top part of the tuai lian has been out here several months now and is waiting for someone to add the bottom half to complete it,' said the old servant. Wang An Shi was told to wait and the servant went into the house to inform his master. As the next day was his examination, Wang An Shi had no time to wait but instead headed for the direction of his uncle's house.

During his oral examination, the examiner read a top half of a tuai lian and told him to complete the bottom half. While thinking, Wang An Shi suddenly remembered the tuai lian he read in front of the house of the Mr Ma yesterday and so he read it out to the examiner. The examiner was more than pleased with his oral examination performance.

After his examination, he went back to his uncle's house. As soon as he stepped into the house, he saw the old servant of Mr Ma waiting for him and said that his master was expecting him at his house. At the house of Mr Ma, Wang An Shi was asked to complete the bottom half of the tuai lian. (There is a history of the tuai lian in Chinese New Year). With no trouble, Wang An Shi wrote down the tuai lian which was put to him by his examiner earlier that day.

When Mr Ma read it, he was very pleased and summoned a maid to take it to his daughter's room to let her read it. After Miss Ma read it, she was very pleased indeed, not only pleased with the writing but also with the person who wrote it. Mr Ma was happy that his only daughter liked Wang An Shi and he said to him that he and his daughter were meant to be husband and wife.

After obtaining the permission from Wang's uncle, they were married on the third day. On the day of the wedding, there were people and noise outside Wang's uncle's house and someone made an announcement that Wang An Shi had passed the imperial examination and was now an imperial official and that the emperor was expecting his audience the next day.

That night, Miss Ma, now his wife congratulated him for receiving his 'ta teng ker' and 'siao teng ker' and said it was a day of double bliss for him. In the past, when a man had passed an imperial examination, it was known as 'ta teng ker' and when a man married it was called 'siao teng ker'. Wang laughed and told his wife that it was her tuai lian that helped him to pass his oral examination. After saying that, he picked up the brush and wrote the characters 'Double Bliss' on a piece of red paper and stuck it on the front door. Since then onwards, the 'Double Bliss' became the symbol of a Chinese Wedding for nearly a thousand years where it was printed in wedding invitation cards, used as posters in a wedding banquet and on many other things associated with a wedding.

THE EXACT TIME OF THE WEDDING

'Hoon' was an ancient term for marriage. According to the definition of one text, 'hoon' was the time when the sun had gone down, about thirty seven minutes. When the sun went down that was the time the 'hoon' had arrived. The Yi-li had this recorded: 'The marriage ceremony of a man and wife are celebrated during hoon'. This is where the term came from and it is also said that it had something to do with the notion of 'yin' and 'yang'. From this it shows that ancient marriage during hoon was to do with yin and yang, the man welcoming the woman. All marriages had to go ahead during the evening otherwise it might be unlucky.

It is said, today this custom of marrying at night still exists but the reasons are not clear. Some people said it is because there used to be a bully or someone with authority in their area who wanted to rob the 'first night' of a new bride and so started this ancient custom again. However, this custom is said to be a remnant of the barbarian period where women were abducted and forced into marriage. According to the Yi-Li, in ancient times, the groom was dressed in black, sat in a black carriage with a torch in front of the carriage.

In Hupei, in the areas of Shenlongjia, the custom of marrying at night still exists, complete with trumpets and cymbals. When it is quiet in the middle of the night, the groom and his men set off firecrackers with the sound of drums and cymbals then set off for the bride's house. According to the people of this area, it is their custom to fetch the bride to the groom's house before the end of the day otherwise things might go wrong. As most of the time the journey is far, the groom's party therefore has to start in the middle of the night in order to arrive at the bride's house and come back on time. Cymbals banging and drums beating of course are to do with merry making and to scare away the wild animals that may be lurking in the dark.

However, according to one source, welcoming the bride at night is due to a geographical reason as high mountains between villages make travelling difficult. On the wedding day, the welcoming party is expected to have lunch at the bride's house and to make it back with the bride for the wedding feast at the groom's house before dark. This explains why the welcoming party starts the journey in the middle of the night.

Setting off to welcome the bride at night seems to meet the need of the people living in Shenlongjia. There are inconveniences in arranging a wedding at night. Towards the end of the Manchu period most people in Beijing were still welcoming the bride at night usually starting the journey about fifteen minutes after the sun had gone down. During the early days of the Republic this custom was still observed by some people, but the majority preferred to welcome the bride in the daytime.

In the areas outside Beijing, the poor peasants there used to welcome the bride at night. Welcoming the bride at night had nothing to do with the ancient custom but because of poverty. These peasants were extremely poor and had to borrow almost everything for the wedding such as a red lantern to hang on the front door, a cotton padded jacket for the groom, four men acting as musicians play the drum, gong and cymbals and four men to carry the sedan chair hired from a nearby small town. Marrying at night was able to avoid attracting spectators because people were ashamed that they could not afford a decent wedding.

In Guangxi, in an area called Jin Siu, the Yao people there welcome the bride at night. At night, the welcoming party, sent by the groom, will start the journey to the bride's house. There will be no music because it is not a custom to do so. When they have arrived at the bride's house there is no ceremony. Accompanied by her maternal uncle or the matchmaker, the bride will pick up her working tools such as a hoe and a sickle and will follow the welcoming party to the groom's house. Every doorway in the groom's house is illuminated with an oil lamp to make sure that it is bright enough for the bride so that she will not kick at the bottom of the door frame but step over it.

Among the Gu Zhoong people in Jin ping in Yunnan, their weddings are celebrated at night. On the night of the wedding, three enormous woks will be set up inside the camp. One wok is used to cook horse and deer meat, one is used to cook boar meat and one is used to cook mutton. Everyone in the camp, whether they are guests or neighbours all put on new headdresses and wait happily for the meal. The bride will be accompanied by a group of young women. On her head she wears a coronet with many silver balls, similar to a Han-Chinese coronet. Her wedding costume is a long tunic gown and there are five colours in the sleeves. Following the bride are two young women, one carrying a straw mattress and one carrying a trunk made of cane with her dowry inside. Relatives and friends will bring gifts such as materials for wrapping the head and silver balls for decorating the head for the bride.

In the old days, people were extremely superstitious about the exact timing for the bride to enter the groom's house. For example, the groom had to fetch his bride between ten o'clock in the morning to two o'clock in the afternoon. This is a problem created by the superstitious custom. It is due to this reason that the trades of the astrologists and fortune-tellers thrived exploiting the ignorance of the people. Today, in Malaysia, many Chinese still look at the almanac for the right time to welcome the bride.

WELCOME THE BRIDE

Welcoming the bride to the groom's house was the last rite, introduced since the Zhou period after the decline of the matriarchal family system. The rite of welcoming the bride was more or less the same everywhere in China. In high antiquity, it was observed by every groom but whether it was the same for an emperor, different texts had different references. According to the Chun Qiu Gong Yang Zhuan, the ancient text of the Spring and Autumn period, the 'son of heaven' like the rest of the peasants observed the rite of welcoming the bride. However, the Chun Qiu Zuo Zhuan mentioned this: 'The son of heaven has no equal, … do not need to observe the rite of welcoming the bride.' Although this rite was originated from high antiquity in the Chun Qiu era, a text of Shandong mentioned that during this period the ordinary people of the state of Qi did not observe this rite.

During the Zhou period, on the wedding day, the groom paid a visit to the bride's house carrying a wild goose with him. Later the groom took the bride to his home and the wedding was celebrated during a ceremonial banquet. This ceremony was also taken to regularise the union of the groom with the 'ying' sisters or other female relatives of the bride which she brought with her as secondary wives for her husband.

During the Northern Sung period, the groom went to the bride's house with an animal cart or a sedan chair, the cart or chair was decorated with red and green silk. After the bride had stepped into the cart or chair the bearers and members of the groom's welcoming party would not move an inch until the bride's family had distributed red pouches, with money inside, to all of them. When they had arrived at the front door of the groom's house the same thing would repeat again nobody would move until the groom's family had given each of them a red pouch.

During the Ming period, the groom paid a visit to the bride's house on a horse. As soon as he stepped into the living room the bride bowed to him twice standing in the south side. After this, the groom performed the ceremony of the goose by throwing it to a member of the bride's family in the middle of the living room. After this ceremony, the groom left for his home alone to inform his parents to prepare to welcome the bride later. Meanwhile, the bride's parents sat in the south side of the living room for a ceremony. During this ceremony, the bride bowed to her parents four times and was given a lecture by both of them telling her to respect and obey her parents-in-law so that they would not lose face. After the lecture, the bride was escorted by members of the groom's family and some members of her family to the groom's house.

Welcoming the bride was considered an important day, it was said, it was the day when 'yang' and 'yin' were combined. Although the day of welcoming the bride was usually fixed on an auspicious day there were things to be avoided on this day. This responsibility usually fell on the groom's family to watch out for anything that might be unlucky.

In the North-East, when Han-Chinese and Mongolians went to welcome their brides, the number of people among the welcoming party had to be an odd number. Smaller groups consisted of seven or nine people and the larger groups had about eleven or thirteen people. It did not matter how many people were in a group so long it was in odd numbers so that when they came back with the bride the number would be even. In contrast, in the Xiang lake areas and in the places where the majority of Han-Chinese lived, the welcoming party had to be an even number but the numbers eight and sixteen were to be avoided they were considered as unlucky numbers. Widows were never asked to join the welcoming party as they were seen as bad luck, only those with living spouses were invited.

On this day, the Hani people sent a middle-aged couple to accompany the groom to the bride's house to welcome the bride. Before the couple were appointed this task, they must satisfy a couple of criteria. Firstly, their parents were both healthy and secondly, nobody had died of any tragic accident in the family.

When a Korean groom went to fetch his bride there were a few superstitious customs he had to observe. When he was leaving his home, sack cloths were placed on the ground and he had to walk on them till he reached his horse. When he had reached his bride's village, he was again given a sack cloth to step on when he got off his horse. It was believed that their storehouse would then be filled with grains that the couple would be free from want all their lives. After getting off his horse the groom was not allowed to enter his bride's house straight away. Instead, he had to borrow the bride's neighbour's house to change into his official ceremonial robe. Only then, he was allowed to enter his bride's house.

According to Miao's custom, the groom had to eat at his bride's neighbour's house while the rest of the people who came with him were given a hearty meal at his bride's house. Miao's custom did not allow a groom to eat at a bride's house.

Among the Boa'an people in Gansu, on the day of welcoming the bride, the family of the bride laid out a meal for the groom's party and the matchmaker. During this time, young men from the bride's village came to create some trouble so that the guests would not be able to eat in peace. It was a custom of the people. Sometimes guests were dragged into the courtyard and their faces were smeared with ash taken from the bottom of a wok, treating them like clowns. There were cases that some of them were even beaten up by the village lads. When they were being mocked, the groom's party had to restrain themselves from being angry. Despite of all this they had to keep their cool and keep smiling. If someone was angry, then it meant that the two families would not be friendly afterwards and be unlucky. Smearing faces with dirt and kicking and punching was a unique way of wishing the couple a happy marriage. Also, it was said, it was to ensure that the children of the new couple knew their maternal uncles.

In the North-West of Sichuan, there is a river known as the Black Water. Along the banks of this river lived a minority group called the Qiang people. The people living in the upstream of the river, in an area called Ma-tang, literally meaning 'horse pond', had a different marriage custom from the people living downstream. The courtship of the former was quick, and a couple could be married within days. The groom had to pay a bride price first and then set the wedding date. After this relatives and friends from both sides were invited for a feast at his house. On this day, the groom either rode a horse or walk to the bride's house followed by his guests. When the bride and groom had arrived at the groom's house, they did not have to go through any ceremony, instead the two of them went straight to their new room and consummate the marriage immediately.

As for the other group of Qiang people living downstream in the Black Tiger village, their young people were not allowed to choose their own spouses. This group of people used to follow the Han-Chinese way of marriage, decided by parents and with the help of a matchmaker. Before the wedding could go ahead the groom's family had to pay a large bride price. Before the groom could take his bride home, he had to hold three wedding feasts. These feasts were held at the bride's village. During the first two feasts, the whole village of the bride was invited. During the third feast only relatives and friends from both sides were invited. From the first wedding feast till the last, there was no sight of the bride because she had to go to a neighbour's house under her parents' order. It was to show that she was too shy to meet her groom. On the day of welcoming the bride, according to the custom, the bride had to hide in a neighbour's house to give the impression that she was not willing to marry the groom. Of course, the groom was all prepared for this, he came with a horse and ten to twenty young men with weapons in their hands to search for the bride. Anyway, it was easy target because the house with a red cloth hanging over the front door would be the house where the bride was hiding. Spotting their target, the groom and his men just walk straight into the house and search for the bride. It was said, the bride had to be taken by force and slung over the horse back and taken to the groom's house. Quite a dramatic way of welcoming the bride. Perhaps one could argue that this was a remnant of the kidnapping of brides in the barbarian period.

Tibetan girls in Qinghai usually married young, at the age of sixteen or seventeen. On the wedding day, a girl would put on a leather outfit with a colourful belt. On it hung many silver boxes. When she walked, these silver boxes made a ding dong sound. On her head, she wore a headdress decorated with amber, greenish gems and red corals. The wedding ceremony was very unique. The bride had three bridesmaids and the groom had three best men. When the bride started to ride forward slowly her three bridesmaids would escort her. At this moment, the three best men would ride to the front of the bride and started to sing. The song was all to do with the groom, about his intelligence and his good personality. When they had finished one line it was the turn of the bridesmaids to do the same for the bride. When this singing session was over the first best man would wave a piece of white silk in the air with his right hand it was to do with luck and peace. After this he would place the piece of silk on the hand of the bridesmaid the one who was standing in the middle of her group and he would beat his horse and rode away from them. The second and third best men would do the same. After this the three bridesmaids would serve wine on trays and at the same time started to sing. Three men from the bride's family would be standing outside the family's tent and welcome the groom into the tent.

Among the Gaoshan hill tribes of Taiwan, (Gaoshan means high mountain), there is a tribe called Lu-Kai. In the past, their wedding ceremony lasted four days. On the first day, the groom's family had to pick lots of areca nuts and send them to the bride's house. In the next morning, the bride's family had to distribute all the areca nuts to every person in the village. At night, the whole village celebrated the marriage. On the third day, the groom's family had to bring good wine, cakes, knives, cooking utensils and blankets for the bride's family. The bride's family would then hand over these presents to their village chief as some sort of bride price. In the afternoon, young men and women of the whole village would come to the bride's house to sing and dance with the new couple. At night, the groom would take his bride home. On the fourth day, guests would visit the groom's house early in the morning. After all the guests had left someone would tie the bride up on her waist and legs with three thick ropes. The bride would then find a place to hide from her groom. It was a custom for the groom to search for his bride and when she was found they would start a dramatic struggle. Finally, the groom would use his knife, cut the ropes and take the bride away. On that night, the groom would ask the bride to consummate with him but there would be another make pretend struggle from the bride trying to avoid consummation with the groom. On the next night, the bride's parents would stand by the bedside and watch on till the couple stopped struggling and the groom carry the bride to the bed. Only then, they would leave for home.

In inner Mongolia, in Yi-ke-zhao, when a groom welcomed his bride, he was dressed like as though he was going to fight in a battle and brought about half a dozen relatives with him. When they arrived at the bride's house, his in-laws would pretend that they did not know anything about the wedding and would not open the door to let them in. Eventually the bride's family opened the door after much persuasion and explanation. After entering the tent, the groom immediately offered his gifts to his in-laws. A delicious meal was prepared for the groom and his relatives. After the meal, the bride would sit with her back to the groom. The groom would kneel behind her back and ask her to tell him her name, but she would not answer him. At this moment, the relatives of the bride would laugh and ridicule the groom. After a while, the bride would tell the groom her name and only then would he get up. This ceremony was called 'tau siao min', meaning, 'beg little name.' On that night, the groom stayed in the bride's tent. At the crack of dawn, the bride rode round her family's tent three times. After that she rode away quickly. At this moment, the groom quickly followed behind the bride. The bride would be heading for the direction of the groom's tent. The relatives of the bride would be following close by. When they had reached the groom's family tent the door would be shut against them. Again, a lot of persuasion was needed before the groom's parents opened the door. After entering the door, the new couple would be taken to an altar. On it a goat was placed, and they prayed to heaven and earth. After this the bride had to perform the ceremony to her parents-in-law, praying to all the various deities and the stove god. When the lama had finally said his last blessing upon the couple would the whole ceremony be over.

In Anhui, on the wedding day, the groom went to the bride's house with a goose. At the bride's house, his in-laws paired his goose with a gander to take back to his house. These two birds were not allowed to be slaughtered for food instead they could die naturally. It was hoped that the couple would live long lives. Perhaps the goose was a legacy of ancient times. When the groom arrived at the bride's house the front door was shut against him. Only after he had paid some cash would the door be opened to him. This custom of paying money or bribe in order to obtain entry into the bride's house is still observed by many people in Hong Kong and the Hong Kong Chinese in Britain, and the Chinese in Malaysia.

In Sichuan, the custom was the same as in Anhui, the groom brought a goose with him when he went to welcome his bride but not just a goose also a gander and they had to be white. It was said, when the bride's family heard the quacking noise, (of the goose and gander and the cymbals), they would know that the groom had arrived.

Among a small group of Yi people known as Sanis, living in the Guishan mountainous area of Yunnan, they too have a similar custom like the Bao-an people. On the day of his wedding, the groom and his relatives must form an even number team between six and twelve people to welcome the bride. Each one of them will carry two baskets of rice, meat, wine, and vegetables on their shoulders using a long pole, one basket in front and one at the back. The groom is escorted by his relatives walking between them. No matter how far the journey is to the bride's house, these men must carry their load without shifting their shoulders or stopping for a rest. This is to signify a lasting marriage. When arriving at the bride's house the door will be shut against them. The groom's party must answer all sorts of questions before they are allowed to enter the front door. At this moment, young men and women will rush out suddenly and smear their faces with black grease which is a mixture of lard and coal ash. This is supposed to be a test of endurance and it is to test whether the groom and his relatives have mild dispositions and temperaments. On the way back to the groom's house the groom and his relatives will carry the same baskets but now they are being filled with stones. As before, they are not allowed to put these baskets of stones down until they have reached a place where the bride's relatives cannot see them anymore. If the groom is not able to carry his baskets of stones away or if he puts them down after a short distance he will be considered as an irresponsible and a bad farmer. For this he will lose his respect.

The Ke-er-ke-zi people have a rather unusual custom welcoming the bride. When the groom and his welcoming party arrive on horses at the bride's family tent, the women welcome them, but the men with ropes in their hands jump at the groom and tie him up. At the same time, the bride is also being tied up by her relatives. The couple is surrounded by the relatives making fun of them. To get them out of this ordeal, the groom's father or brother must beg the bride's relatives for mercy and this includes giving lots of presents to them. Only then will the couple be untied. It is important that no one becomes angry. This kind of welcoming the bride is unusual according to the author Ren Cheng. Perhaps it is a remnant of the kidnapping of brides in the barbarian period, (see Zhong Guo Min Jian Jin Ji).

On the day of the wedding, an Ewenke groom is accompanied by his parents and almost everybody belonging to the same clan to the bride's house, (The Ewenke people still belong to a kind of clan society which is a remnant of primitive society). Walking in front is the elder who carries a picture of a deity. Following close to him is the groom and next are the parents of the groom and the rest of the clan people. Trailing at the back are the people who are carrying deers. In front of the bride's house, the bride's family wait to receive the groom's party. As soon as the new couple meet, they will first kiss the picture of the deity and then hug and kiss each other. This is followed by exchanging gifts. After this, the bride and groom will each pull a deer and walk round the 'cuo luo zi', (a little round dwelling about three metres in height), three times and then everyone enters it to attend the banquet. Unlike other people, the banquet starts before the wedding ceremony.

Some Ewenke people in some areas still practise an ancient marriage custom called 'eloping marriage'. When two Ewenke lovers have decided on a wedding date the young man will inform his parents. Near to his parents' yurt, a new yurt and a new cuo luo zi are built for him. When everything is done, at an appointed time and place, the girl will slip out of her house quietly and elope with the young man on horses' backs. At this time, inside the young man's cuo luo zi, an elderly woman is waiting for them. Inside the dwelling, the old lady will change the girl's eight pigtails into two large braids. Once the girl's hair style is changed the young lovers are supposed to be legally married. Before dawn, the new couple will go to the yurt to worship the ancestors. Afterwards two people will be sent to the bride's house to inform her parents of the elope. The two representatives will offer wine to the bride's parents but they will be very angry and will refuse to drink. After much persuasion they will change their minds as the Chinese saying says, 'Uncooked rice is cooked into rice', and will drink the wine. Relatives and friends of the groom will only congratulate him after the bride's parents have accepted the marriage. Only then the banquet will start with singing and dancing.

Among the Xibo people in Xinjiang, the bride must be welcomed to the groom's house before the first daylight of dawn. When welcoming the bride, the groom sits on a horse while the bride sits in a horse drawn carriage with the bridesmaid and a middle-aged female relative of the groom. Hanging on both sides of the saddle are bags of the five grains, a symbolical meaning that grains are in plentiful supply. In front and at the back of the bride's carriage the groom's welcoming party shouts and cheers all the way to the groom's house.

Weddings are usually held in autumn for the Hani people. An auspicious day is decided by a wizard of the village. On the wedding day, the groom sends a welcoming party of about ten people carrying pigs' heads, pigs' hocks, chicken, sugar, root gingers and three large 'ba ba', (a puff ball snack, hollow inside made with glutinous rice flour), and walk to the bride's house. Outside the village, the bride's family will be waiting to welcome the groom's party. Inside the bride's house, the guests are warmly entertained with pork, chicken, and vegetable dishes. According to Hani custom, the bride will leave for the groom's house only when the sun is setting in the West but there is still enough daylight for the journey. As they walk along, some of the young men and women sing out loudly. Usually the lyrics are, 'The one who went hunting has caught his animal', 'The one who went fishing has caught his fish', and 'The one who looked for a girl has found a girl'. When the bride has arrived at the gate of the groom's camp, she must take off her white dress and put on a new costume decorated with silver jewellery. Only then can she enter the camp.

In the West of Guangxi, lives a group of Yao people. This Yao group live in the mountains. Their marriage customs are different from other Yao groups. On the wedding day, with his bride price in his pocket, the groom is accompanied by a large group of relatives and friends. There will not be a horse or sedan chair for the bride, she is to walk to the groom's house. Along the way home, the groom and his party know that things will not be as easy as it looks. As expected, half-way during the journey suddenly a group of people will spring at them shouting, 'snatch the bride back'. The two groups will then start a fight, not real fight though, just a show. At this moment, the bride and groom will seize the opportunity to leave the war zone and flee for the groom's house. Once the new couple have left the war zone the relatives and friends of both sides will stop the fight and make their way towards the groom's house. By this time, food and wine will be prepared for these people.

GROOMS DID NOT WELCOME THEIR BRIDES

Today, in some parts of China the rite of welcoming the bride is not observed, for example, in the district of Nanchang in Jiangxi in the East of China. However, whether to observe the rite or not is just a matter of customs and people are merely following the customs of their areas.

At the tick of the right time, the so-called auspicious time, probably picked by a fortune teller, the best man of the Tanka groom turned up at the bride's family boat in a boat. Like the Han-Chinese bride, the Tanka bride worshipped her ancestors, kowtowed to her parents and the rest of her elders before she left for her groom's house. Similar to Han-Chinese custom, she was carried to the boat on the back of a 'si niang', meaning 'happy woman'. Those who wanted to accompany the bride were very much dependent upon the amount of boats provided by the groom. Of course, the more boats the better because it was a matter of prestige. Along the journey, firecrackers were set off attracting spectators from other boat people. When the wedding boat arrived at the groom's family boat, the bride was carried by the 'si niang' again.

On his wedding day, a Jing groom did not welcome his bride, instead he sent two of his sisters and two singers a male and a female, to welcome his bride. It was very interesting because the two singers had to sing their way into the bride's village. When they arrived at the entrance of the village, they were denied entry by the bride's relatives who challenged them to sing some songs. This was known as the first 'guan', (guan means gate). After they had passed through this guan they were challenged again once inside the village. After the second guan they still had to face the third and final guan at the entrance of the bride's house. Each time when passed through each guan, they distributed red pouches with money inside, which was to do with luck.

Unlike most brides who either rode on horses, donkeys or in sedan chairs the Jing bride had to go to her groom's house on foot. On her wedding day, the Jing bride wore a red top and black trousers. An umbrella was used to shade her from the sun by her bridesmaid, although possibly it was used to shield her from evil spirits, like the Han-Chinese. Two singers from the bride's family would accompany her to the groom's house. Sometimes the number of singers exceeded ten or more. The two groups of singers sang as they walked to the groom's house. The songs they sang were all to do with praising and wishing the couple well. According to the tradition, she had to walk at a slow pace with the tip of her toe touching her heel of her other foot. On the way, she had to avoid passing by temples and ancestral halls. Passers-by had to make way for her. Even local officials had to dismount from their horses to let her pass first. Nowadays, a Jing bride still walks to her groom's house on foot.

Like the Jing bride, the Li bride also must walk to the groom's house on foot. If she sees a snake on the way, she must not carry on walking, instead she must immediately return home to inform her parents who will then ask a sorcerer to expel the evil before she could go again. If she saw a snake and carried on walking instead of returning, she will only bring bad luck to her husband's parents. When the Li bride arrives at her groom's house she will be warmly welcomed by her groom, his parents, and his relatives. This is followed by a wizard following her, murmuring incantations at the same time wielding a pair of scissors and spreading rice. Finally, the wizard would beat a fresh egg with the scissors to expel ghosts and ensure her a peaceful future with her husband.

In Gansu, a Yugu groom would not welcome his bride. At the crack of dawn, after a good breakfast, the bride and her bridesmaid set out for the groom's house riding on a camel together following by her relatives either riding on camels, horses, or donkeys. There was singing all the way to the groom's house. When the bride's party came near the groom's tent they would be met by some representatives of the groom's family and would be offered hada, (a scarf), wine, lamb's breast and some food stuff made with flour. The leader of the bride's party, her maternal uncle, her bridesmaid and other relatives will then be asked to stop and get off their camels and horses for a little rest but the bride will stay put on her camel. After the little rest and food, they would ride on to the groom's family's tent. When they have arrived at the tent, some of the relatives of the bride would charge their horses at the door of the tent but the groom's family would shout and make lots of noise to frighten the horses so that they would not come near. Afterwards, those riding on camels would do the same, finally followed by the ones on horses and camels who would charge together. After this charging, they would all go round the tent three times. After that, the bride's family would be warmly entertained by the groom and his family with food and wine.

According to Dongxiang custom, a bride is not welcomed by her groom on her wedding day. On that day, she is carried by her brother into the donkey boxcar with her head covered with a square multicoloured cloth. The boxcar is either made with wood or bamboo. Inside a beautiful rug is placed and beautiful patterned fabrics are hung all over the boxcar. On this journey, the bride is accompanied by her uncles, brothers, and sisters.

WEDDING CELEBRATED AT THE BRIDE'S HOUSE

Usually, a Tartar wedding is held at the bride's house. When the groom arrives at the bride's house, his way will be blocked by a colourful rope by children. To pass through this rope he or his relatives will have to throw some money on the ground and then ride round for a while on their horse-drawn cart before obtaining an invitation to enter the house. If there is no invitation, they must throw money again and take another ride. On the third time, they will distribute handkerchiefs, scarves, and scented soaps and usually the door will be opened to them. The groom and his relatives will be warmly welcomed by the bride's family to the wedding banquet and are entertained with singing and dancing. Afterwards the bride and groom share a cup of sugared water. This symbolises that their marriage will be as sweet as the sweetened water till old age. On the next morning, the bride's parents will call on their daughter and son-in-law in the bridal chamber. The new couple will kowtow to their elders to pay their respect. On the third day, the groom will be taken home by his family and will return to the bride's house in the evening. Usually, a Tartar wedding is celebrated for three days. After the wedding, the groom will stay in the bride's house for a couple of months, some even stay as long as one year or even longer till the first baby is born before taking the bride back to his own home.

Among the Ke-er-ke-zi people, they also celebrate a wedding for three days. On the first day, the groom goes to the bride's house with his parents, relatives and friends and brings a live goat, other farm animals and gifts. When they have arrived nearby the parents and the relatives will go straight to the bride's house but not the groom and the best man because according to the custom they have to go to the bride's sister-in-law's house. When the guests are seated the bride's family will start a rite where food is spread from the window in the roof. Fried dough balls, milk candy and fruit candy are placed in a bag and are hooked on to a long pole and taken up to the window at the roof where it is left to fall all over the living room. All the children present will help themselves to the food and sweets. This means that the wedding ceremony has started.

 Goats and other animals are slaughtered to entertain the guests. As the Ke-er-ke-zi people are Muslims the wedding follows Islamic rites.

The imam will recite Islamic scripts, pray and then proclaim the couple as man and wife. After this the imam will cut a salted fried dough ball into two and give it to the new couple to eat. This symbolises that they will love each other till old age. On the second day, the wedding is celebrated with all kinds of traditional Ke-er-ke-zi sports such as horse racing, wrestling, wrestling with goats and chasing young women. Winners are rewarded with gifts. On this day, the parents of both families will exchange gifts. At night, the bride will meet the groom in her sister-in-law's house and will stay there for the night. Like all Muslim weddings, the couple, the bridesmaid, and the best man sit in a makeshift tent inside the house and are surrounded by their guests. Young men will play with different Ke-er-ke-zi musical instruments. There will be singing and dancing and other interesting activities till late at night. On the third day, the groom will bring the bride back to his home. The bride will say goodbye to her family in tears. Some mothers even follow their daughters to their husbands' homes to keep them company for a couple of days. Some even stay for a month.

Like some other Muslim ethnic groups, the Tadjik people in Xinjiang also celebrate the wedding in the bride's house. Relatives and friends from both sides will join in the celebration at the bride's house. According to the traditional practice of the Tadjik people, every woman must bring some white flour, apart from bringing various food stuff, tea leaves and little farm animals. As soon as they have arrived at the bride's house, they will sprinkle the white flour on the walls of the house. This is a way of blessing because white symbolises purity and happiness.

In contrast, the colour white is a taboo colour in weddings for the Han-Chinese in the old days. Both the bride and groom wore two rings on their fingers each ring is tied with a long red and white strip of material. On her head, the bride wears a red silk veil and covers her face with a long see-through veil. Like all

Muslims the wedding is conducted by an Islamic religious leader who reads the Islamic scripts and prays. During this ceremony, the religious leader will sprinkle some white flour at the bride and groom. After this, with both hands he picks up two pieces of lamb's meat, blows his breath over it and gives it to the bride and groom to eat. After the couple have eaten the lamb's meat the bride will grab a handful of white flour and sprinkle it over the groom, thus, bringing the wedding ceremony to a close.

According to the custom of the Dai people, families of both sides must invite their own guests on the wedding day, but the wedding ceremony and banquet are held at the bride's house. During the ceremony, an elder of the groom's family will ask the bride and groom to kneel in front of him but apart. Each of them will stretch out a hand and hold a stick of sugar cane and a banana. Meanwhile, the elder will sing songs of blessings to them. This is followed by another ceremony known as the tying of threads' ceremony. Threads of white and multicolours are tied on to the wrists of the bride and groom. White threads symbolise purity and multicoloured threads symbolise passion. Tying threads means that people wanted to tie the hearts of the bride and groom together and to wish that they will respect and love each other till their old age.

SUNG JIA

When a bride was ready to leave for her groom's house she was usually accompanied by a group of her relatives. In the old days, it was known as 'sung chin', literally meaning, 'send a relative off'. Among the sung chin group there must not be any widows and pregnant women. The former was considered as 'unwhole' perhaps because the other half had died.

In one coastal area, fathers were usually among the group but not the mothers. Also, maternal aunts and the wives of the maternal uncles were not allowed to be among the group either because according to a superstitious belief, the bride might be struck down with a nasty illness. This superstition forbade women to show their faces in public occasions. This was discrimination against women and perhaps women were seen as soft hearted, emotional and might burst into tears when they had to part with the bride, bringing bad luck. This reason alone was good enough to exclude women from sending the bride off. However, in some areas, people did not follow the custom of sending the bride off to the groom's house, the relatives only walked her to the sedan chair or horse.

In the old days, women of wealthy background brought along their 'pei jia ya tou' meaning 'accompany marriage servant girls', who continued to receive salaries from the bride's family. These servant girls never returned with the sung chin group but stayed with the bride in her new home and continued to serve her some even served till old age.

In Malaysia, 'sung chin' is called 'sung jia' meaning 'send a marriage'. On the morning of the wedding, the girlfriends of the bride will come to her house early to accompany her to her groom's house. Usually, the bride has her hair done by a hairdresser in the hair saloon and then has her make-up done by a professional make-up artist or a girlfriend or herself if she is good at make-up. There is a special rite which is performed by the bride's father. After the bride has put on her wedding gown, her father will place the head veil on her head but he does not secure it for her, this is left to the make-up artist or friends.

When the groom has arrived at the bride's house he will remain in the car until the bride's younger brother or a male kin opens the door for him. When he steps out of the car, he will give a red pouch to the bride's brother who has opened the door for him. When the groom and his male friends, usually single men, walk towards the front door they will have no trouble passing through.

Whereas in Hong Kong, a groom will have to pay a bribe to the girlfriends of the bride before they open the door for him to enter. In Hong Kong, usually a groom must pay ninety-nine H.K dollars and ninety-nine cents. Some may even have to pay as much as nine hundred and ninety-nine dollars and ninety-nine cents. It does not matter how much the amount of money is, what really matters is the number 'nine' because it sounds like 'everlasting'.

Once inside the house, the groom and his friends will be seated at a table and will be served with all kinds of fizzy drinks such as root beer, orange juice and coca cola. On the table there will be all kinds of Chinese cakes such as the popular nine-layers' cake, (made from glutinous rice flour with nine thin layers, hence, how the cake got its name), a spongy cake called 'chi tan gao', meaning, 'chicken eggs' cake, (a favourite of the Fujian dialect speakers), agar agar slices, Western cakes, sliced oranges, mini bananas (a little bigger than a thumb), groundnuts and of course the famous melon seeds dyed in red colour. Later the groom will be taken to the bride's room where they will bow to each other three times and he will hand over a bouquet to her.

In Malaysia, the groom brings the bouquet when he welcomes the bride. Before they leave for the groom's house, the new couple will worship the bride's ancestors. After that the girlfriends and female relatives of the bride will accompany the bride to the groom's house. Usually, the groom must provide transport for the bride's party not only to take them to the groom's house but also to take them home later. When they have arrived at the groom's house someone will set off a small chain of firecrackers as a celebration. Like in ancient times, the groom's parents will not be there to welcome the bride nor will the close relatives of the groom. Only distant relatives and friends can watch the bride entering the house. Once inside the groom's house, the bride will be taken straight to the new room where she will be accompanied by a sister or a close friend. At his house, the groom is now the host so he and his men friends will make sure that the bride's girlfriends and relatives are seated and are served with snacks and drinks. After worshipping the groom's ancestors at his family's altar, the bride's friends and relatives will accompany the couple to the studio to have their wedding pictures taken. After this, the job of the sung jia party is finished and they will be given transport back to their homes.

STEPPING INTO THE SEDAN CHAIR

In ancient times, before the sedan chair was invented, a bride was taken to the groom's house in an animal cart. During the Tang period, an animal cart was still used. After the bride was seated in the cart, the groom on his horse back would go round the cart three times and then head for his house. Since the Sung period, the animal cart was replaced by the sedan chair till the Republic. The sedan chair was an ancient transport equipment originated from the animal cart. Ordinary people were not allowed to use the sedan chair for transport. It was a privilege of the elite. However, during weddings the ordinary people were permitted to use the sedan chair as marriage was seen as one of the three most important events in a person's life. Only principal wives could use sedan chairs but not concubines or prostitutes, even marrying for the first time they had to use animals' carts.

In the capital Beijing, it was very important that a bride hired a brand-new sedan chair and that nobody had used it before. It was said, if it were not a new sedan chair the bride's family would refuse to let their daughter to get inside it. It was believed if it was an old chair, the marriage might have some disasters.

Before the bride left for the groom's house many areas in China observed a custom called 'chui qiao tang'. This 'chui qiao tang' was a meal or rather a broth, eaten by the bride, prepared for her by her sister-in-law before she set foot inside the sedan chair. There was quite a bit of fuss involving this meal, the bride could not refuse, and she was not to finish all of it. There was even a song about this meal: 'If I drink it, afraid that poverty will befall natal home, if I do not drink it, afraid that mother-in-law's family will be poor. In that case, I drink half of it and leave the other half, this way, both sides will not be poor'. From this it shows that the 'chui qiao tang' symbolised wealth. Also, it was used to test a daughter's loyalty. To prevent the bride from losing face, there were always people to remind her about the superstition involved.

Before the bride stepped into the sedan chair there was a superstitious custom to be observed, her feet must not touch the ground. In the old days, the Han-Chinese, the Hui, the Manchurians and a few minorities observed this custom. The reason behind this superstition was not to let the bride take away the soil from her parents' home. If she walked, her shoes could have easily collected some soil with her into the sedan chair and she would have taken the soil, the 'prosperity', to her husband's house.

According to one explanation, it was because the bride did not want to leave her natal home. Another said, the custom had to do with V.I.P. status and another said that it was to prevent evil and hope for luck. There were a few ways of stepping into the sedan chair without having to step on the ground. One way was to bring the chair to the bedroom and the bride was carried into the chair on her father's or elder brother's back. In some areas, the bride wore a pair of her father's or elder brother's shoes over her red embroidered shoes and walked to the sedan chair. Once inside the sedan chair she took off her father's shoes, this way, she would not be collecting any soil in her shoes. Some people laid red rugs or straw mattresses on the floor for the bride to walk on them.

Some minorities did not use sedan chairs, the bride was wrapped in a red blanket carried by the maternal uncle or brother all the way to the groom's house. On the way, the bride was not allowed to put her feet on the ground and not to step on water either.

In one area near Xin'an in Zhejiang, there were a few families living in boats on a river. Among these boat people, there was a custom of throwing the bride from one boat to another. If the bride. was accidentally dropped into the water it was regarded as unlucky. If this happened, the bride's family would become the laughingstock of the neighbours and would bring bad luck to the family.

In Zhejiang, in a place called Fu-yang, there was an unusual custom which was not seen elsewhere. The sedan chair must not be put on the ground, it had to be placed on a round bamboo tray. When the groom had arrived with the sedan chair, the 'si niang', a woman whose profession was to help a bride with her make-up and help her to put on her wedding costume, would start to help the bride to do her face, put on her thick red trousers, red skirt, a top jacket and the phoenix coronet. The bride was not to stand on the floor she was given a round shallow tray to stand on. When she was all dressed up her relatives brought a tray of twelve red coloured eggs, dumplings stuffed with meat, fish, pork, sugar, salt, charcoal, and some rice more than three catties. This food was divided into twelve portions, with two dumplings in each portion, wrapped into twelve parcels with papers. All these were dumped into her trousers and one by one they came out from her trouser legs. It was hoped that when she was giving birth it would be as quick and easy as a hen laying her eggs!

This was followed by the father or elder brother of the bride holding a tray of rice and a dish of meatballs and fish balls feeding her with the food. Whilst she was eating it, lucky phrases were uttered, for example, when she was given a mouthful of rice they would utter 'wan zi wan suan', meaning, 'ten thousand sons ten thousand grandsons'. When she was eating a meat ball or fish ball, 'tuan tuan yuan yuan' was uttered, meaning 'together together round round'. When she had finished eating, they had to say, 'nian nian yow yu' which means 'surplus every year'. Of course, she was not to finish everything otherwise there would not be any surplus left every year and the marriage would be doomed to failure. After this, she was given a piece of round shaped meat, but she was not to swallow it until she had arrived at the groom's house. After she had eaten the well-meaning meal, she was carried by her elder brother to the kitchen to worship the stove god. While she was offering prayers, she was not allowed to stand on the floor. She had to either stand on a stool or a chair. When this was over, she was carried into the sedan chair and was escorted to the groom's house by her brother.

In Anhui, the bride would start to cry while she was being carried by her brother to the living room. Rice was scattered at the doorway for the bride to walk over it. The whole family would have a good cry before the bride got into the sedan chair. Weeping during a wedding day was also seen in an area in Hubei. When the sedan chair had arrived, the bride was helped into the chair by an elderly couple who had prosperity and longevity and it was hoped that it would be lucky for the new couple. As she entered the door of the sedan chair the bride started to cry. At this moment, her relatives joined in with the crying.

Many brides of the minorities of China are still observing the custom of 'ku jia', meaning, 'cry marry'. One reason for crying is because the bride does not want to leave her parents to go and live in a new place. Also, the bride is sad to part with her relatives. There are two kinds of 'ku jia', one is real crying and the other is not real crying. If a bride is forced into marrying her groom then her crying is definitely real crying, but for the bride who loves the man she is going to marry then her crying is only for show, for she is only doing what is required of her by tradition. Also, if the bride is not able to cry the rest of her relatives will encourage her to cry, 'Try and cry a little, cry in the mouth but glad in the heart, if you don't cry, it is not very nice.' If she still could not cry the mother will step in and give her a slap or two to make her cry. This is because if the bride did not cry when getting into the sedan chair, she will be seen as silly, not brought up properly and she will not get on well with her husband. According to the Tujia and Hani people, they think that if a bride did not cry then the marriage is unlucky, and the couple will not be happy.

In the past, a Qiang bride was slung over a horse and taken by force to the groom's house. Nowadays, a Qiang bride must be carried out of her natal home by her brother or a male cousin and firecrackers are set off at the same time. She will either ride on a horse or is carried in a sedan chair to the groom's house.

Before stepping into the sedan chair, Han-Chinese custom required the bride to wear a red veil which covered the whole of her head and face. This red veil was a little different from the veils of the Arabian women. This Chinese veil was two by two square feet which covered the head and the face so that people were unable to see the face of the bride. In the past, many minorities also observed this custom. These days, the Han-Chinese have abandoned this custom, but some minorities are still observing this custom.

For example, a Yao bride waxes her hair with beeswax to harden it and puts a wooden box like object with two holes for the eyes to see over her head, covering the whole thing with a red veil. Doing the hair this way was said to be a very ancient custom and was like the woman Nu-Wa. A red veil is used because red is the symbol of luck and could prevent evil. It is said, the veil was a legacy of ancient times where brides were kidnapped. The veil was used to cover the head of the woman so that she would not be able to find her way home later.

Different from Han-Chinese brides, the Islamic brides wear black veils. In the past, all Islamic women wore veils covering their faces except their eyes. Young unmarried girls wore green colour, older women wore white and brides wore black veils. According to Islamic concept, it is shameful for a woman to show her hair, she must cover her hair up. These days this rule is not so strict anymore and many Islamic brides in China are abandoning their veils to show off their permed hair. Although the custom of the veil is seldom seen these days, in the old days it was widely used. From the moment the bride stepped into the sedan chair till she stepped out, worshipped the ancestors and then to the bridal chamber, only then the veil was removed from her by the groom. If the veil was removed too early, it was considered bad luck.

This custom had created many tragic marriages in the past because most marriages were decided by parents and matchmakers who at times did conspire to keep away vital information about the physical appearances of the couple. It was not unusual for a groom to find that he had married an ugly bride when he removed the veil. Many a time, a bride found herself face to face with a blind husband or a husband minus a leg. There was nothing she could do because she had already gone through the ceremony worshipping his ancestors. This constituted the binding part in a Chinese marriage. This moment her situation fitted the Chinese saying, 'Raw rice is already cooked into cooked rice', she was already married to the man and in those days a woman had no choice but to stay put because there was no such thing as divorce for a woman. In the old days, in China, a man could divorce his wife, but a woman could not divorce her husband.

In the past, in Shenlongjia in Hubei, before a bride stepped into the sedan chair she was carried by her brother or her maternal uncle and stood on a flat pole which was placed on the floor. This pole was used for weighing the grains. Standing on the pole, the bride threw a pair of chopsticks on the floor of the living room before stepping into the sedan chair. This was to hope that she would have a baby son soon. In Shanxi today, some people there still observe this chopstick throwing custom. On her wedding day, before she leaves for the groom's house the bride will throw a pair of chopsticks on the floor. When she has arrived at the groom's house, in the afternoon, she must pick up a pair of chopsticks from the floor. This throwing and picking up a pair of chopsticks had three symbolical meanings. The first; the bride was married on that day and would not be living in her natal home anymore; second, the bride had become a member of the groom's family, whether sweet or bitter she had to live in her new family forever, chopsticks were essential to every family; finally, when the bride was picking up the chopsticks during a meal she would remember that she had to budget and to be careful not to waste anything when she was doing the cooking. Looking at this custom, one could see that the virtue of waste not want not was reflected in the marriage custom of this area.

As soon as the bride's sedan chair went out of the front door the bride's family would shut their front door immediately. This was said to prevent the bride, taking her natal family's wealth along with her to her groom's house. In the old days, the Han-Chinese were superstitious about this. In Taiwan today, it is said, some people are still observing this custom.

In Shanxi, some people observed a wishing custom. According to a text in Shanxi, as soon as a daughter left the house for her husband's house her mother would sit in the living room in a red dress. Someone would bring her a tray of sweets and would ask her, 'Is it sweet?' She must answer in a loud voice, 'sweet'. It was to wish that the married daughter would be liked by her parents-in-law. Anyone without a mother would have the practice observed by a father. For anyone without parents, an aunt, uncle or any relative would do. Anyone who did not observe this custom would meet bad luck. From this custom, one could see how parents worried for their daughters whether they were treated well or not. In the past, people used to say, 'che si fu', meaning, 'marry daughter-in-law', and no one said, 'che qi', meaning, 'marry a wife.' This custom was created by a society controlled by parents and so relationships between a wife and husband were not important to the Chinese. What was very important was the attitude of the parents. In the past, so it seemed, a man married so that he could give his mother a daughter-in-law to serve her. After a Tujia bride had left her natal home her elders stood at the front door and shouted, 'Prosperity, come back, prosperity, come back,' all the way from the front door to the living room. This way, they thought, they could chase back the 'prosperity' which was about to follow the bride to her groom's house. This shows that this 'prosperity' was a precious thing, not to be taken away by other people, even one's daughter.

ON THE WAY TO THE GROOMS HOUSE

On the way to the groom's house, it was important that nothing went wrong. Anything that did not go smoothly would be seen as a sign of bad luck for the marriage, so the groom's family would be extra cautious about certain taboos and were also sure of certain ways to break them if encountered with them. There were three things that could go wrong for the bride. First, when getting into the sedan chair, second, when getting out of the sedan chair and third, which direction she was going to sit in the bed or kank. All these of course were taken care of before the actual wedding day by the instruction of the 'feng shui' man, (a man who claimed to know geomancy). These people made their livings out of people's ignorance and fears and said which things they must do. They would not dare to disobey otherwise things might really go wrong.

In the areas populated by Han-Chinese, there was such a custom among them, 'East come West return, do not return in the same route'. The sedan chair must not go and return by the same route. Probably people did not like the idea of returning in the same route in case the marriage broke up and the groom would have to marry again. In the North of Honan, there was a saying in the ordinary society, 'Returning in the same route, husband and wife will not live till old age'. Also, there was this talk of evil spirits and ghosts waiting at the same route to harm the people returning from the groom's house. These reasons of avoiding the same route seemed a little simple but however it satisfied some superstitious people.

During the journey to the groom's house the biggest taboo was 'si zhoong si', meaning, 'happiness against happiness', this meant if a sedan chair met another sedan chair on the way. According to sources, this custom was observed in Honan and Shandong in the North, Jiangxi and Hunan in the central, Yunnan in the West of China and also in Taiwan. This was considered as a taboo among the Han-Chinese, Xibo, She, Miao and Muslims in Xinjiang. Two weddings going on at the same time was considered as unlucky. It was said, the family with less wealth would feel inferior and that was unlucky. As for the other wealthier family this was also unlucky for them because their 'si' would be weakened by the other party. This is because people liked to have all the 'si' to themselves and did not want to share it with other people but at times there was no way to avoid another wedding going on at the same time. If it did happen there were several things people could do. In the past, if two sedan chairs happened to be passing by at the same time, a competition of speed would follow, the one who was ahead would get all the prosperity.

Among the Miao people, if there were two brides marrying into the same village, then, according to custom, the one who got in first would have all the prosperity. Most of the time, people would avoid getting married on the same day. If it was unavoidable, then everybody would try to get into the village first. When two wedding carriages of the Xibo people met they were not allowed to stop and let the other past first they had to brush past each other quickly. Presumably if one stopped for the other then the prosperity would have gone over to the other bride. In a district in Jiangxi, this was also a taboo. If two sedan chairs met, then the bearers of each chair would try to lift their chairs as high as possible. According to the people of the area, the family of the sedan chair which was being hoisted highest would prosper later. For this reason alone, it was enough for both sides to get into a fight.

There was another way of breaking the taboo, that was to let the brides exchange their gold rings, (probably not wedding rings), or one of the relatives exchange a new handkerchief or a new towel. This way, both sides would receive the blessings from each other, and the verge of a fight was averted, and unluckiness was avoided. This way of exchanging things instead of a fight was also popular in the Hunan area. Brides of that area exchanged handkerchiefs or red hair strings.

When a Muslim bride was on her way to the groom's house it was also a taboo to see another wedding party. If it happened, the only way to solve the problem was to let the two brides exchange their belts. In Taiwan, one way to solve this taboo was to ask the brides to exchange the flowers in their hair. If this was not done, serious tragedy might befall one of them. This way of exchanging things was like getting the other person to be on one's side and it was like joining forces together to break the taboo.

If two She brides happened to be marrying on the same day or going the same route, they must first discuss among themselves who was going first because according to their custom two brides should not go together. Usually, the bride who had a longer journey to go, was permitted to go first. The one who was going later would not go by the same route because it would be 'walking over old road', considered as unlucky. The way to solve the problem was to let a yellow cow walk in front of the wedding party. The horns of the cow were decorated with red cloth and red flowers. The road where the cow had walked over was considered as 'new road' so it was all right for the bride to walk over it. It was even considered to be lucky and that the couple would lead a happy life together.

Another thing to avoid during this journey was a funeral procession. In Taiwan, it was considered unlucky if a wedding party met a funeral procession. This was seen as 'unluckiness against happiness'. In the areas populated by Han-Chinese, this was also a taboo. However, there were also people who were not worried about this because there was a coffin in a funeral and 'guan chai', meaning, 'coffin' which sounds like 'official's wealth'. Therefore, some people thought it was lucky to run into a funeral. However, some people were not happy because a funeral reminded people of death and crying, so it should not be mixed up with the happy atmosphere of a wedding. Most people avoided funerals like avoiding the plague. If people already knew that there was to be a funeral, then they would change the wedding date. If, however, there was no time to avoid a funeral then people would think of 'official's wealth' and would not feel so bad about it.

Among the red turban Yao people in Yunnan, a bride must avoid water on her way to her groom's house. If there was a stream on the way someone would carry her on the back so that her feet would not get wet. The marriage carriage of the Xibo bride was not allowed to stop on the way. The Han-Chinese were also superstitious about the sedan chair being placed on the ground during the journey. Whether it was the bride, the sedan chair or carriage, the aim was to make sure that everything must be done by the people concerned to prevent any unlucky thing that might happen.

As soon as the sedan chair was on the way 'ku jia', had to stop otherwise it would be unlucky. Brides were always said to possess some kind of 'bad air' in them. For this reason, it was a taboo to peep at a bride in her sedan chair. This was why a bride's sedan chair was covered with drapes so that people could not see her. Whenever a bride passed by people were always excited to go out to the streets to look at her but what they actually saw, was only the sedan chair. There was also some silly talk that if someone saw a bride the person would become blind or would catch the 'bad air' from her and die. These kinds of superstitious beliefs separated the bride from the other ordinary people. The bride was seen to have a kind of power that could harm anybody who came near her and could offend the deities.

According to a text about the marriage custom in Luoyang, two people walk in front of the bride's sedan chair each holding a red blanket or rug. Each time they passed by a temple, huge stone, or a large tree they covered the sedan chair with the blankets. This perhaps had something to do with the old concept that women were dirty, especially a new bride. From this it shows that people believed that their deities were not sitting in temples but that they were peeping at people behind large stones and trees. Red blankets were used as a barrier between the bride and the deities perhaps because people were afraid that the bride might offend the deities or perhaps they were afraid that evil spirits might create chaos for the wedding party.

During the journey to the groom's house, the Pumi bride is not allowed to look back at all. The reason is perhaps the groom's family wanted the bride to look forward to her new life in her new home. It is a taboo for the bride to ride to her husband's house on a mule and wear a white wedding costume. The Tujia bride rides on a pony or a donkey but not on a 'san ma' meaning 'castrated horse'. The idea is the same as the Pumi bride not riding on a mule because mules and castrated horses are not able to have offspring and so people do not want the brides to have any contact with these animals. White wedding costumes are considered as a taboo because white is linked to funerals.

Face to face with a pregnant woman on a wedding day was a taboo for the She bride. Pregnant women were said to have 'blood flame light' that would wash away the 'si' from the bride. Also, evil spirits would follow the bride to the groom's house. This superstitious belief was to warn all brides not to come into contact with pregnant women on their wedding day, if they did, they may be pregnant too. Also, it was believed, if a bride were seen by a pregnant woman, she would be separated from her husband on the day of the pregnant woman's labour. There was always a way to prevent bad luck. Before a bride set off for the groom's house, she was to carry some 'gui yuan', small brownish black fruit, in a small tray. Whenever she saw something unlucky, she would throw some 'gui yuan'. This would frighten the evil spirits away.

On this day, nobody liked bad weather. Some people in some areas dreaded the rain during the wedding day. In Taiwan, if it were raining on the wedding day, the groom would be someone who liked his liquor. If there was thunderous rain this meant that the groom was a very heavy drinker. As for the Shui and Zhuang minorities, they dreaded lightning on a wedding day, they believed it was a sign of bad luck. If lightning struck on a wedding day, it was believed that either the husband or the wife will die young.

The Ta Khan Er bride had to arrive at the groom's house before dusk. When the carriage was approaching the groom's house it must move towards the Eastern direction. As for the Bai bride, she had to follow the clouds, if her groom's house was in the opposite direction then she had to go round to the back of the house and then turn round and came back to the front of the house. In the old days, the marriage carriage of the Xibo had to return to the groom's house before dawn. All this exact timing of when to arrive at the groom's house was of course, the legacies of high antiquity. These days, many people do not take these things so seriously anymore.

STEPPING OUT OF THE SEDAN CHAIR

In traditional China, when a Han-Chinese bride's sedan chair had arrived at the groom's house, the sedan chair had to be put in the right place and the bride was invited out of the chair by two young women. In many areas, at this moment, firecrackers were set off to celebrate the wedding and to get rid of the 'bad air' brought by the bride. Before the bride entered the door imminently, there were ways to make her obedient to her husband and her parents-in-law. In Zhejiang area, when a bride's sedan chair had arrived, it was left there for a while before someone came to invite the bride to come out. This practice was said to dampen the 'fire' in the bride so that she would not dare to go against the hierarchy, and would not, dare not obey orders. In some areas, the sedan chair had to pass under a pair of trousers that belonged to the mother-in-law. In Anhui, when the bride had arrived at the groom's house the door was shut against her sometimes as long as an hour. Until someone invited her to step out of the sedan chair, she was to remain seated inside. According to the practice, it was to suppress the temperament of the bride so that she would not be rash in doing chores in her married life.

In the district of Fan-yu in Guangdong, when the bride was stepping out of the sedan chair, the groom actually hit her head with a fan before going into the bridal chamber! When a Tibetan bride arrived at the groom's house according to Tibetan custom, she was greeted with a shout from the relatives of the groom, all of them shouting at the same time. At this moment, the bride was given another shock when grains were thrown at her, supposed to scare the evil spirits away.

Among the Manchurians and Yugu people, they had a different way of getting rid of evil from a bride. When the bride had arrived at the groom's house, the sedan chair was carried passed between two fires which were set up for the occasion. After this the groom would aim his bow and arrow at the door of the sedan chair and would shoot three arrows at the door. When the bride stepped out of the sedan chair she had to step over a saddle. These customs were legacies of traditional Manchurian practices. In ancient times, Manchurians were hunters and so they were inseparable from their bows and arrows. Armours and bows were used as betrothal gifts by the Ruzhen people, the ancestors of the Manchurians. These ancestors of the Manchurians used to engage in tribal warfare taking each other's belongings, animals, and also kidnapping people as slaves. Women who were kidnapped were forced into marriage. Shooting three arrows at the door of the sedan chair was to show the power of the groom. It was to pretend that he had used force to take the bride as his wife. The practice of stepping over a saddle shows that in the past a bride was kidnapped and was tied on to a horse and brought all the way back to a tribal community then untied from the back of a horse. As for the fire, it shows that hunters used to marry in the wild.

According to texts recorded during the latter days of the Ming dynasty and in the early period of the Manchu dynasty, all mentioned that the Ruzhen people used to build 'tatan', (a dwelling), burned a fire either by burning grass or wood and arranged a feast to welcome the bride. As brides were usually from other communities they were escorted by their fathers and brothers. The Yugu people also had the practice of shooting three arrows at the door of the sedan chair by the groom. It was to do with prosperity and to drive away the evil spirits. According to Yugu tradition, when the bride had arrived at the groom's house, she had to walk between two fires outside the front door. At this moment, the groom armed with his bow and arrows and shot three arrows at the bride though of course not exactly shooting at her body. At this moment, the bride unveiled herself and threw it away and the groom broke the bow and arrows into halves and threw them into the fire.

In Taiwan, when the bride was about to step out of the sedan chair the groom would come forward and give the door a kick. The idea was to show the bride who was the boss so that she would know her place and be obedient to him otherwise there might be trouble in their married life. At this time, the parents of the groom should not be present just in case the groom missed kicking the door and accidentally kicked one of his parents which would be bad luck. However, no matter what explanation, parents-in-law were not supposed to be present when a bride stepped out of the sedan chair. This was similar to the days of high antiquity where the bride was only formally introduced to the parents-in-law the next morning. This custom was also observed by the Bai people.

However, in Shandong, in a nearby island called Xiang-tao, the custom there was just the opposite. When the sedan chair arrived, the father of the groom opened the door of the chair and flung the curtain to the top of the chair. The father-in-law met the daughter-in-law not only on the wedding day but also saw the bride going into the house, the two things which were taboo to many people in many areas.

In Yangzhou, as soon as the door of the sedan chair was opened, the bride quickly scattered some money out of the door. Like Xiang-tao, the parents-in-law welcomed the daughter-in-law into the house. If the bride did not observe the custom of scattering money she would be seen by her mother-in-law as a woman with a life of begging for rice. This means that she was only good for eating but not good for earning money for the family.

When the bride was stepping out of the sedan chair, the same as when she was stepping into it, her feet were not allowed to touch the ground. In the past, Han-Chinese, Muslims, Manchurians and the Zhuang people observed this custom. Some people laid red blankets or rugs, wood planks or mat on the ground for the bride to walk on it till she reached the bridal chamber and sat on the bed or kank.

In Shandong, when a bride stepped out of the sedan chair, she was given a wooden chair to sit and was carried all the way inside the house. In Jiangsu area, people placed red blankets or sack cloths on the ground for the bride to walk on it. In Anhui, rice sack cloths were used. During the Northern Sung period, when the bride stepped out of the sedan chair, a green material or rug was laid on the ground for her to walk on it. At this moment, someone would carry a basket filled with grains, beans, fruit, and money and scattered these outside the front door. These things would soon be picked up by children of the neighbourhood outside the front door. The meaning behind this custom was to thank the deities and the bride for bringing wealth to the family.

There were many areas where brides not only were forbidden to walk on the ground but also not allowed to see the sky. This was why a bamboo tray, or an umbrella was used to shade the bride. In the North in Honan area, a bride had to keep her eyes shut when she stepped out of the sedan chair. Nearly all the brides with their heads covered with veils were carried into the grooms' houses. Brides were not allowed to see the sky and step on the ground because people were afraid that the 'bad air' in their bodies might offend the deities or the other way round. Shading the bride with an umbrella is still being practised by some Hong Kong Chinese in Britain but is not observed by the Chinese in Malaysia.

There was another explanation as to why a bride was not allowed to step on the ground. It was to make sure that the bride knew her place in her new home. However, according to another explanation, the reasons for not allowing the bride to see the sky or step on the ground were all part of making sure that she was taken into the house carefully.

In the Beijing area, a bride must not be empty handed when she was stepping out of the sedan chair. Either a bride would hold an apple or a vase and then step over a saddle which was part of the rite. This saddle was either placed in front of the sedan chair or in front of the door of the bridal chamber. An apple or vase was used because these two things sound like 'ping', meaning something like, 'smooth' and saddle sounds like 'an', meaning, 'peace'. 'Ping An' means 'peace'. Stepping over the saddle was observed by the Han-Chinese since the Tang period and lasted till the end of the Manchu dynasty. According to one source, it was originated from the Xianbei people, a tribe who used to live in Mongolia, where their brides rode on horses.

In Guangxi, the Zhuang people of Liujiang observed the custom of throwing five grains at the new bride. This custom was also observed in Honan and Kaifeng in the North, only that soya beans were also used with other grains. In Nanyang, wheat was used to throw at the bride. The meaning was the same as the other areas, it was to wish the new bride a happy marriage with her husband. It was believed if a marriage was to be happy, it must be spread with grains. Only then the life of the new couple would be prosperous with five grains filling their storage house and with luck and peace. When the Zhuang bride stepped out of the buffalo cart or sedan chair and walked towards the door of the groom's house, that was the moment when grains were scattered at her head. Spreading the grains was a very important task. Only a woman with living parents and with sons and daughters was picked to do the job. During the spreading, she had to make sure that the number of times were even and not odd and she must not drop the bag of grains. From this it shows that only a very careful and responsible person would be picked.

In Heilongjiang, a Her-jer couple celebrate their wedding at dawn because it symbolises prosperity, together they will bow to heaven and earth. When the bride enters the bridal chamber, relatives and friends will throw sorghum, soya beans, corns, mung beans and millet over her head as a kind of blessing. At the same time, firecrackers are set off, drums and gongs are beaten in the hope to drive away evil spirits and to secure a peaceful family life and many sons for the couple.

This custom of spreading grains is also observed by the Hui Chinese, Salar, Bao an, Kazak, Ke er ke zi, Ozbek and Russians in China. Before she leaves her parents' home, the Bao an bride will scatter grains of wheat, bean, rice, corn and tea, wishing happiness to her parents and to repay their kindness. The Kazak and Ke er ke zi brides will spread fruit and wheat flour before they leave their parents' homes. After entering the bamboo house, the Dong bride will be sprinkled with millet by her mother-in-law before she is led to the bridal chamber.

In Yunnan, the Pumi bride was not allowed to enter the groom's house on the wedding day. If both the bride and groom lived in the same village or lived near each other, the groom could fetch her to his house before sunrise, then she did not have to stay the night in the hut outside his village. Before the wedding, a little hut was built in a quiet spot near the groom's village, with essential things such as food, beddings and other things needed to stay the night. While the bride was staying for the night, relatives of the groom and people of the village would come to visit the bride and keep her company. Before she went to bed one of the elders would light some joss sticks and say a few words of blessings but there was no special ceremony. The reason why the bride had to stay the night near the village was because this way it was as though both her and her groom belonged to the same village.

This custom was said to be a legacy of ancient times when people of the same family name intermarried with each other. People could marry anyone except their own parents, brothers, sisters, and their own children. People could marry their first cousins or even their uncles. When an elder brother died the younger brother could marry the sister-in-law. This kind of marriage system was said to stop the women from marrying out and to possess them as property or as labourers. Until very recently the Nu, Bulang and Lisu people were still practising this marriage system.

ENTERING THE DOOR

In traditional China, Han-Chinese were extremely superstitious, many deities were worshipped in their homes. In front of the house were the two door gods Shen To and Yue Lay, (mentioned in the Chinese New Year), in the kitchen there was the stove god, in the bedroom there was the bed god and last but not least there was the window god. Since different deities were useful to the family in different ways people had to treat them with respect. All these various domestic deities were very important therefore, the bride was not allowed to step on the foot of the door frame because it would anger the god of the door frame. The Chinese were always sensitive about the bottom of the door frame because it was seen as the line between the outside and inside of the house. Even when someone was visiting during an ordinary day he or she had to be careful not to step on the bottom of the door frame because it would be seen as a lack of respect for the owner of the house.

On the wedding day, a bride had to be extra careful especially she was believed to have some kind of 'bad air' in her so if she stepped on the bottom of the door frame it would be unlucky. If she had stepped on the door frame it would be like stepping on her husband's family, 'wei feng', 'power and prestige' and worst still it might cause one of the parents-in-law to die. Therefore, in Taiwan, there was a saying, 'Step over the door frame, live till a hundred and two'. This saying was to remind the bride to step over the door frame, not on it or accidentally kick it. However, not all women are obedient and submissive to tradition. Stepping on the door frame almost became a practice for the Tujia bride. When she enters the groom's house a Tujia bride will purposely step or kick the door frame to show that she is not going to give in to tradition. This is an act of defiance and it shows that women themselves wanted emancipation.

According to Xibo custom, when the bride stepped out of the carriage, a red rug was laid on the ground for her to walk on it. In front of the house, she and her groom worshipped heaven and earth. After this ceremony, the groom entered the front-door and knelt facing outside the house. Meanwhile, the bride knelt at the front door from the outside facing the groom. At this moment, the groom used a horsewhip to remove the red veil from the bride. After this the bride was led into the house.

In the past, the Dong people celebrated their weddings at night. When the bride was entering the groom's house with her bridesmaid, according to the custom, not only the groom and his family had to hide from her but they must not see her entering the door otherwise it would bring quarrels to the family. After the bride had entered the house she was not allowed to walk about the house. She would be given a bucket, the symbol of hard work, by an elderly woman, who herself had many children and grandchildren. With the bucket in her hand the bride was told to go to the living room and place it on the left side of the ancestral altar. After this she was to enter the bridal chamber and sat by the wooden column. Only after the bridesmaid had entered the bridal chamber, was she free to walk about the house.

There was an unusual marriage custom in a place known as Rudong in Shandong. When the bride had arrived at the groom's house, every time she walked pass a door in the house, she had to put her left foot first. This is because the people of this area believed that walking in such a way there was hope that the bride would give birth to a son.

WORSHIP HEAVEN AND EARTH

'Pai tian Di', meaning, 'worship heaven and earth' was the term for wedding ceremony of the Han-Chinese and other minorities of China. Usually, it was held at the groom's house in front of his ancestors' tablets. The bride and groom, under the guidance of the 'li guan', meaning, 'official of rites', performed the rites of marriage laid down in ancient times. There were three stages in this worship: the first stage was worship heaven and earth; the second stage was to kowtow to the parents of the groom and the last stage was for the bride and groom to bow to each other. If the parents-in-law were still fairly young, say, in their early forties there was no kowtow for them. It was generally believed that only those who were advance in years could receive the kowtow rites from the younger generation otherwise it would be considered as unworthy. For those who were not old enough usually they abstained from receiving the kowtow rites, otherwise they might not be able to receive the prosperity, so, the solution was to ask the bride and groom to worship the domestic deities in place of the parents. In the past, the new couple were required to prostrate themselves before the ancestors' tablets and the groom offered drinks to the dead ancestors but not the bride.

At the times of high antiquity, the ancestors were not worshipped during the wedding ceremony and the parents-in-law were not present either. It was not until the next morning that the bride was formally introduced to her parents-in-law by her husband. If the parents-in-law were deceased, then after a period of three months the groom introduced his bride to his dead parents during a ceremony in which he presented a piece of paper with the characters of the surname of his new wife. If unfortunately, the new bride died before she was introduced to her dead parents-in-law, then she would not be considered as a member of the grooms' family. Worst of all, her body would not be permitted to be buried in her husband's ancestral grave but would be buried elsewhere with other women with similar situations.

Various texts mentioned the consummation of the bride and groom on the night of the wedding and only on the following morning the bride was formally introduced to her parents-in-law. As it was said, the relationship between a husband and wife should exist first before the relationship between parents-in-law and a daughter-in-law. Even today, in a She wedding, it is a taboo for the daughter-in-law to see the parents-in-law during the wedding ceremony. At this time, the parents of the groom must hide in a neighbour's house and will only return home after the ceremony is over and after worshipping the stove god. After the ceremony, the parents are invited back to the house. After worshipping heaven and earth the bride and groom are now man and wife. The matchmaker or a 'how min ren', meaning, 'good life person', usually an elderly woman with many children and grandchildren, will lead the new couple to the bridal chamber.

In Beijing, the bride did not perform the kowtow ceremony to her parents-in-law until the next day after her wedding. In the past, women's lives were revolved around the stove therefore the first to be worshipped was the stove god in the kitchen. Both the groom and bride had to kneel down on their knees and knock their heads on the ground to the stove god. After that paper ingots and paper money were burned in the courtyard. If the groom's family had an ancestral hall and many generations of ancestors, it was worshipped next. Next to worship were the last three generations of ancestors. Usually, the altar was installed in the family's living room.

In this ceremony, the bride was formally introduced to the groom's dead ancestors. Three bowls of jiao zi were offered as sacrificial food to the ancestors as well as joss sticks and candles. Some people wrote down the following, 'The son of So and So is married on such a day. The name of the new daughter-in-law. The new daughter-in-law pays her respect to her husband's ancestors to ask for your blessings and protection', on a piece of paper and burned it outside the front door when the ceremony was over. After this it was time to perform the family's kowtow ceremony. All the groom's family and relatives took their turns in the living room to receive the kowtow from the new couple according to hierarchy. Each member of the family received a cup of tea from the bride and each gave her a red pouch with money or a gift such as a fan, a purse, a ring, make-up or a handkerchief wrapped in red papers. Not just receiving, the new couple had to give money in red pouches or little gifts to the younger generation. After this ceremony, the new couple retreated to their new room.

One minority group, the Lisu people, have a long history in China, mostly living in the Sichuan area. According to an old text of the Tang period, the ancestors of the Lisu were known as Su-man, ('man' means 'barbarian'). Inbreeding has greatly altered the physique of these people, as a result they are small. As soon as a Lisu bride entered the door of her groom's house, she was led to the altar to worship his ancestors. While the bride and groom were worshipping at the same time the matchmaker of the groom's family and the matchmaker of the bride's family would start to sing to each other. Afterwards, the new couple accompanied by the bridesmaid and best man stood on a straw mat, and a round tray was placed in front of them. This was a unique custom of the Lisu people starting with the parents of the groom walking past the new couple, throwing silver coins or notes into the round tray and then standing on one side of the room. This was followed by the rest of the relatives and friends. This money was known as 'si qian', meaning, 'happy money' and was all given to the bride and groom as a wedding gift. When this was over the two matchmakers of both families sang a song again which had something to do with silver money, copper money, the love of the parents, brothers, and sisters.

After this another unique practice to be observed was known as 'get a new name'. The matchmaker of the groom's family was responsible for giving the new names to the bride and groom. Names that were used before marriage were no longer being used because from now on the new couple must be addressed by their new names. Generally, women were given names which had something to do with flowers, musical instruments, birds and grass whereas men were given names which had to do with trees, mountains and villages such as 'Kai Tai' and vegetables such as 'Ah Pu'. This ceremony ended with a song by the two matchmakers. This was followed by a dance known as the 'united dance' participated by young men and women.

In the North-East, the Ewenke people celebrate a wedding at night out in the wild, sitting in a round circle. At the start of the wedding ceremony, an elder will fill two cups of wine made with the bark of the Birch tree and the bride and groom will perform the ceremony to the fire god by pouring the wine into the fire.

After this the new couple will offer wine to both parents. When this is over the couple will hug and kiss each other. This will be followed with singing and dancing everyone holding hands in a large circle till late at night. The songs are about blessing the marriage.

Like most Westerners, the Russians in China follow the Western style wedding of the West. During the marriage of a Russian bride and groom, both will exchange rings. It is said, even the Russians have their taboos during a wedding. The groom must be careful to place the ring on the second finger of the left hand and not on the right hand. Wearing a ring on the second finger of the left hand indicates that the person is married. Like the old days, many Chinese, (non-Christians), are still wearing their rings differently from Westerners, that is, the groom wears it on his left hand and the bride wears it on her right hand, known as 'nan zuo nu u'.

During the wedding ceremony, the Han-Chinese did not like children and those in mourning to be present. This is because children were unpredictable and might cry during the ceremony. A wedding was a happy occasion so it would be unlucky if there were children crying and ruining the happy atmosphere. As for those in mourning, they reminded people of funerals and so it was unlucky.

Among the Elunchun people, they also had certain taboos about weddings. Widows were not invited to a wedding. Anybody who belonged to the same horoscope as the bride and groom were also banned from the wedding ceremony. Barren women were not allowed to attend the wedding and especially not to be present in the living room where the wedding ceremony was held.

In an area in Honan, the person who helped the bride during the ceremony was called 'chan ker'. This task was usually given to a woman who had to be clever and good in what she was doing.

Any person with a horoscope that did not go along with the horoscope of the bride would not be considered for the task. For example, if the bride's horoscope was a hare then the horoscope of the person must not be a dog, if the bride's horoscope was a pig then the horoscope of the person must not be a tiger.

In the past, among the Cantonese dialect speakers, a 'tai cum chare' was indispensable for the smooth running of a wedding. Those who took up this profession were usually middle-aged women. Wealthy people especially liked to hire such a woman to take care of marriage rites in a wedding. Right from the moment when the bride entered the groom's house, the 'tai cum chare' was there to assist the bride in the proper performance of her ritual obligations. It was her duty to see that the rites were carried out properly. These women are now more or less a dying species because the younger generation do not care to hire such a person because it is old-fashioned and costly.

Nowadays, people just ask one of their female relatives or a friend to help with the marriage rites and it does not have to cost the groom much except some money in a red pouch. Nowadays, only the rich can afford to hire such a person during a wedding not because they are old-fashioned, but it has something to do with prestige. As a 'tai cum chare' do not come cheap it must be really something to be able to afford one. The number of people who accompanied the bride and groom had to be in even numbers, odd numbers were taboo.

According to the Naxi and Tujia people it was bad omen if the red wedding candles were blown out during the ceremony. At the start of the wedding ceremony, the Tujia people and the Naxi people made sure that the candles were lit by two responsible women. Only women with sons and daughters, were hard working and were good at house chores were considered for this task. Their task was to light the two red candles in front of the deities in the living room. If the flames of the candles were not strong or if one of the candles went out half-way during the ceremony, then it was believed that the couple would face some tragedies and that they would not live together till old age.

WEDDING BANQUET

Before the new couple retreated to the bridal chamber the groom's family celebrated the wedding with a banquet that very night. This practice was called 'chi si jiu', meaning, 'eat happy wine'. As it was a happy occasion certain people such as widows, pregnant women, and people still in mourning were not invited, otherwise it would be unlucky. One minority, the Bai people believed that if widows and pregnant women were present at the banquet, in future even when the bride had her own children, they would die young.

At the banquet, men and women were segregated, men were seated together at one table and women at another. (In Taiwan, some people are still observing the practice of segregating men and women in banquets). Special hospitality was given to the relatives of the bride. It was afraid that if the bride's relatives were not looked after properly, they might find something to pick on afterwards and this would sour the relationship between the two families. In the past, the groom had to move from table to table to toast to the guests. During the banquet, the guests were not allowed to start eating until the groom had drank three cups of wine. This was the custom of the Korean minority in China.

Most banquets had elaborate dishes, some served eighteen dishes, some twenty four, and some thirty six. The dishes had to be in even numbers and odd numbers were taboo. In Taiwan, it was a taboo to put duck on the menu of the wedding banquet because 'duck' sounds like 'capture' which reminded people of prisoners being captured and taken to jail. As the word was unlucky, this dish was not to be included in the menu of the banquet. Spring onion was another taboo food not to be eaten during a wedding feast especially to be avoided by the groom because it sounds like 'wash' and therefore it was also an unlucky word. There was also another talk that spring onion symbolised 'yang' and because a man was full of yang so a groom must not eat that otherwise a disaster might happen to him.

In Taiwan, it was said, on the night of the Lantern Festival sometimes single women trespassed onto other people's vegetable gardens to pluck spring onions because they believed by doing that they would be able to marry good husbands. From this it seemed that spring onions actually symbolised the groom and so it was a taboo to eat spring onions during a wedding banquet. Another dish, a rice porridge with mixed vegetables, melon seeds and shrimps, was also excluded from a wedding menu because it was usually eaten during funerals. In some areas, it was a taboo to eat 'man tou', a dumpling made with flour and yeast with no fillings. In a wedding banquet it was a taboo because it was white colour. Some people thought of a solution by putting a red spot on a 'man tou'. During the banquet, when the fish was on the table after eating the top part, it should be turned over, but the bones must not be broken. Broken fish bones meant that the marriage of the bride and groom would break up later.

During a Tanka banquet, the groom's family entertained their guests with every kind of seafood. It was said, even the people living on land looked on with envy. Later that night, the men friends of the groom grouped together and entertained the guests reading literature and singing like the 'pai fan' ceremony of the bride's girl friends on the eve of the wedding.

In Sichuan, the wedding feast of the Qiang people was very simple. There were no tables and no chairs, and everyone sat on the floor on a mat in a circle with a large tub of wine in the middle. Each person was given a small bamboo stick and drank from the same tub. When everyone had eaten enough rice and drank enough wine they would start to sing and dance with the men on one side and the women on the other. This dance would be followed with a dance by the bride and groom.

Wedding banquets were for the wealthy people and those who could afford it. Among the peasants outside Beijing, on the night of the wedding, the family of the groom could only afford to eat an ordinary meal with the new couple and the person who accompanied the bride to the groom's house. After the simple meal, the new couple would follow the groom's parents to the family grave to perform the ceremony to the ancestors. This ceremony was equivalent to the ceremony at the ancestral hall of the rich.

Before the banquet begins, a Hani bride and groom must share and eat an egg and a pig's hock together and drink wine. After this they will kowtow to the groom's parents and relatives. At the start of the banquet the bride will offer wine to all the guests. Songs are sung to the new couple by young people with lyrics which have something to do with love and faithfulness.

In Jin Siu in Guangxi, the Yao people there entertain their own family with a very simple meal of only a chicken and a few catties of pork as a wedding meal. There is no formal wedding ceremony for the bride and groom to go through. Everybody eats and drinks together and says something to congratulate the new couple, thus, bringing the wedding to an end. The next morning the new bride will carry her working tools and walk side by side with her husband to work in the fields, only then will everybody in the village know that they are married. This kind of simple wedding makes economic sense because it does not affect production therefore it is still practised by the Yao people in Guangxi.

According to Yugu tradition, a bride and groom have to offer wine and bow to all their guests who attend the wedding banquet. Throughout the banquet, singers sing love songs. Every guest is given a hada and a portion of mutton to take home. Usually, a goat is divided into twelve portions and the best parts are given to the important guests.

In Jin ping in Yunnan, during a wedding banquet the Gu-zhoong people entertain their guests with horse meat, deer meat, boar and mutton and palm wine. During the banquet, the bride and groom together will pour wine from a bamboo stick, (this bamboo stick is filled with wine), to all the elders.

When the banquet was over, people had to be careful when they were collecting the dishes not to put the plates on top of each other so that there would not be trouble in this marriage. If a guest accidentally broke a plate during the banquet, it would be seen as a bad omen. Some people who knew how to put things right again would collect the broken pieces and put them in the middle of the stone mortar, this meant that 'what was broken was being mended again'. This was a way to 'save' the bad luck.

Unlike the Western wedding reception, in Malaysia, a Chinese wedding banquet is a noisy event. It is quiet to start with but could become very noisy when the wedding party starts to do the round. It is a custom that the bride and groom and his family go round to each table to greet their guests, to hold their glasses to their guests and say, 'yum sing', in Cantonese, meaning something like 'bottoms up'. At this moment, it is typical of the host family to say to the ten guests of each table, 'chiu fu um tow', in Cantonese, meaning that they have been neglecting their guests. This remark is usually repeated at each table. Usually, there are about thirteen courses in a Chinese banquet in Malaysia including the dessert, the usual number of courses for wedding banquets. Normally, the first dish is a cold dish which is consisted of ham; the famous 'rotten eggs', (blackish in colour which have been cooked by chemical reaction induced by lime. These eggs are not a hundred years old as said, the colour certainly cheats the imagination, they are only one or two months old); ormers; white boiled chicken; straw mushrooms; duck and crab. Other dishes will include the famous suckling pig; sea-slug (sea-cucumber); Chinese mushrooms; fish; deep fried chicken; sharks' fins soup; birds' nest' soup; vegetables dishes; fried rice and lichees in syrup.

BRIDAL CHAMBER

'Doong fang' was the Chinese name equivalent to bridal chamber. Literally it means 'cave room' though not sure why it was so called. In later periods, it was called 'xin fang', meaning, 'new room'. The bridal chamber was usually decorated elaborately. Flowers were not used for decoration because they withered easily so it was considered unlucky. However, one flower known as 'lien chiow hua', a red flower, was an exception. It was used because the name of the flower sounds like 'lien chow gui zi' which roughly means, 'continually bring a son'. In Taiwan, 'lien chiow hua' were also used to decorate the bridal chamber. People in Taiwan particularly liked the flowers because of the red colour and so it was used widely. Other flowers, flowers of the pomegranate were also popular for decorating the bridal chamber for its symbolical meaning because the pomegranate fruit has many seeds and people hoped that the new couple would have many sons and grandsons.

In the South of Suzhou, many old customs are still perpetuated by the peasants. On the morning of the wedding, a middle-aged woman will make the wedding bed. Bundles of glutinous rice straws about twelve to twenty are spread all over the bed.

At the top of the bed, a long sugar cane is placed. This has the symbolical meaning of soft glutinous and sweet honey.

Two straw mats are placed on top of the glutinous rice straws. On top of the straw mats two blankets are placed. On top of all these, two bearers' poles, two cutting grass tools, two weighing scale sticks, two trays of steamed, 'si gao' meaning, 'happy cakes' with red and green characters such as 'gold and jade fills the living room' and 'longevity and prosperity' and two trays of round flour balls made with glutinous rice with six small ones and six large ones in each tray. These round balls had the symbolical meaning of family union, and the wish to have many sons and grandsons.

Inside the new room, the most important thing was the direction of the bed. Not only was the bed proof of the relationship of a man and wife but also a significant place where the lineage of the family continued. In the past, the Han-Chinese observed the rite of placing the bed in the right direction of the new bedroom. To perform this rite, a hundred and eight coins were needed. These coins were known as 'tung qian', meaning 'bronze money'. Eight coins were placed under the bed, it symbolised that the Eight Characters of the bride and groom were compatible to each other. As for the other hundred coins, they were divided up, half were placed at the head of the bed and the other half at the foot. It was said to have the symbolical meaning of 'tung sin tung ti', translating as 'same heart same body'. An auspicious date and time were set for this rite. It was also ensured that the position of the bed was compatible to the Eight Characters of the couple and did not clash with the position of the window and the altar of the deities. People were superstitious about the corners or angles of tables, chairs and wardrobe facing the bed.

After placing the bed in the favourable position, there was another important thing to do, that was to worship the 'chuang mu', meaning, 'bed mother', the deity who looked after the bed.

When the decoration in the new room was finished no ordinary people could enter it such as widows, pregnant women and anyone who was born in the year of the tiger. No one could sit on the bed or touch the things because people were superstitious that it might bring bad luck to the new bride.

At night, before the wedding day, a small boy was asked to sleep with the groom on the new bed to keep him company until the actual wedding night. Although in Taiwan, this was interpreted differently, a young boy was asked to accompany the groom to be for the night so that the bride would give birth to a male baby in the future. It was said, this practice was observed by most people. Right from the time when the wedding bed was placed in the right position people were superstitious to leave the new room empty and it was a taboo to let one person slept on the new bed that explained why a small boy was asked to sleep with the groom. In the past, in some areas, among the Han-Chinese, before setting off to welcome the bride, the family would ask a boy to go into the new room with a gong and banged three times to make some noise. If this was not done, it was afraid that something might happen on the way.

In Zhejiang, in a place called Fu-yang, after the wedding ceremony, the bride had to walk on sacks on the way to the bridal chamber. The sacks were not laid on the floor beforehand they were laid by someone standing next to the bride. As soon as she stepped on one sack another one was laid in front of her and carried on until she reached the bed in the new room. The person who was doing it had to be fast handed. There was a symbolical meaning in this known as 'chuan thai qwai' meaning, 'carry on the lineage quickly'.

In Hangzhou, when the bride was on her way to the bridal chamber she was escorted by people in front and behind her. The person leading the way in front of her carried a lamp called 'zi suan teng' meaning, 'sons' and grandsons' lamp'. Those behind her were holding a rice sack and a 'tow', a thing for measuring rice. These were placed on the area where she had walked on and repeated all the way till she reached the bed in the new room. The symbolical meaning for this practice was 'carry on the generations' because 'sack' sounds like 'generation'.

In the South of Suzhou, after the ceremony to the ancestors and the parents of the groom, the groom would escort the bride into the bridal chamber, each holding one end of a red and green long cloth with a knotted flower in the middle. Inside the bedroom, the groom had a little task to do, that was to lift the head veil off the bride, looked on by his mother or his grandmother. With his back to the bride and with two long sugar canes and two weighing scales' sticks resting on his shoulders the groom lifted the head veil and threw it on top of the bed. (In the past, a Chinese bed had a box-like wooden top). According to the custom, if the head veil were lifted high, the bride would soon have a baby. After this the groom's mother set a meal before the new couple and both were expected to eat a little. It was known as 'chien nian fan', meaning, 'thousand year rice'.

Usually, it was the groom who lifted the head veil off the bride but in the Xiang-tao island of Shandong, this task was given to the father of the groom. After the new couple had entered the bridal chamber, the groom's father and the groom knelt to the deities in the bedroom and knocked their heads on the ground. After this the groom's father walked out of the new room to the North side of the house and stood by the door facing inward. At this moment, the groom escorted the bride walking on red rugs stood in front of the groom's father. With a weighing scales' stick in his hand, the groom's father lifted the head veil from the bride and flung it to the top of the eaves. This little task required practise beforehand because the veil must not fall to the ground otherwise it would be unlucky, and the marriage ceremony was not considered as perfect. For a perfect ending to the marriage ceremony, the groom's father had to start practising to perfect this task about ten days before the wedding.

Among the Bai people in Yunnan as soon as the bride arrived at the groom's house both the bride and groom would rush into the bridal chamber to grab the pillows. It was believed that whoever managed to snatch the pillows and sit on the bed, would be the head of the family.

In Yoong-ning, in Yunnan, a Naxi couple also observed the custom of rushing into the bridal chamber first on their wedding day. It was believed, the one who got in first would be the one to dominate the other. After worshipping heaven and earth the Tujia bride and groom would rush into the bridal chamber to sit on the bed. There was a rule about this and the bride and groom were required to observe one thing, 'nan zuo nu u' where the groom sat on the left and the bride on the right and both of them must not cross over the middle line. Sometimes a bride sat on the middle of the bed and was pushed back to her side of the bed by the groom. While this pushing and struggling was going on the groom would pull down the bride's veil and brought the struggling to an end. According to the author Ren Cheng, this custom of wanting to sit on the bed first reflected the time of high antiquity and the fight between the mothers and fathers when patriarchal family system replaced matriarchal family system.

Later on it was taken on as a kind of game the bride and groom played on their wedding day but some people believed that if they did not sit on the bed first then they would be dominated by their spouses. However, most of the time the bride and groom were not too serious about this. Usually, at this moment, they would rather be loving to each other than to fight. Most of the time, if the bride and groom were fighting to sit on the bed first, it was only an act, they were merely following the custom of ancient times.

In Jian, in Jiangxi, there was an unusual custom in this area. The custom required a bride to wear a thick padded jacket on her wedding day. In Winter, the thick jacket would have served the right purpose but in Summer it was real suffering for a bride having to coop up in a sedan chair. Not only she would be sweating profusely, but her make-up would also be ruined. However, there was a reason why the bride needed to wear a thick padded jacket. After the new couple had worshipped the ancestors, the bride was carried into the bridal chamber by an elder. At this time, every relative old and young could hit the bride's back with a stick. For this reason, the bride had to wear a thick jacket to avoid being hurt. As to why the relatives hit the bride with a stick, it was said, to drive away the evil spirits that might be lurking around the bride.

Among the Han-Chinese, they practised a custom called 'roll bed'. Dried fruit such as gui yuan, (a small round brownish black fruit), lichees, jujubes, (Chinese dark red dates), chestnuts and groundnuts were scattered at the four corners of the bride's bed. After this someone would put a male toddler on the bed and let him crawl for a while and this was known as 'roll bed'. People did not mind if the child urinated on the bed because this was a good omen that the new couple would have many sons and grandsons. Today, in Malaysia, some Chinese still observe this custom.

Sometimes during the banquet or an hour later, in the bridal chamber, the bride and groom drank wine together as it was an ancient custom. In ancient times, a 'pao gua' was cut into two halves, filled with wine and the bride and groom drank from it. This custom originated from the Zhou period. This pao gua was said to be very bitter in taste not for normal consumption. Even the wine became bitter when poured into it. Drinking from one half of a pao gua had the symbolical meaning that the husband and wife were joined as one body. As for the bitterness of the pao guo, it meant that the couple not only shared all the good things but also the bad things in life.

During the Tang period, a gourd replaced the pao guo. The gourd was cut into half and tied together with five coloured threads. One little boy would hold one half of the gourd and another boy would hold the other. The two halves of the gourd would be filled with wine and the two boys would give them to the bride and groom. If the groom was a good drinker, he would have the gourd filled three times. If a gourd was not available, then two silver or gold goblets were used. The two goblets were also tied with five coloured threads.

During the Sung period, this custom underwent some changes and goblets replaced the gourd. The two wedding goblets were tied together with red strings. In the bridal chamber, the bride and groom exchanged the wedding goblets and locks of their hair were knotted together. When the new couple had finished drinking the wine the goblets were thrown at the bedside as a kind of vetting. If both the goblets laid flat or both were in an upright position then it was bad omen, and the marriage was considered not compatible. If one goblet was upright and the other lay flat then it was lucky and it symbolised that heaven was compatible with earth, yin compatible with yang and the marriage would be a happy one.

In the past, in the North, green materials were used in the bridal chamber. This originated from an ancient practice known as, 'sit inside the tent'. During the Manchu period, there were two different forms. Once inside the bridal chamber, the bride was made to sit on the kank, (the kank was made of earth with an opening at the side where people in the North slept instead of beds. Firewood was burned through the opening to keep the kank warm. This idea was like the Romans warming the floors in Winter). Some people made sure that the bride stepped over cloth and gaoliang, (a plant used to make spirit) because 'pu', (cloth), sounds like 'step' and 'gao' sounds like 'high', the symbolical meaning of 'step step high rise'.

The other form was, after the bride had walk over a red rug, she sat in the kank with her groom, he pressed his left side of his gown on her right side of her gown. This means that they had already shared the same bed. Some people put up a tent in the kank and let the new couple sit there for a while to show that they were already sleeping together. At this time, someone would start scattering dried fruit such as gui yuan, lichees, chestnuts, jujubes and groundnuts inside the tent and at the same time would utter lucky phrases, 'many sons and grandsons', and 'live till a ripe old age together'. After this someone would take away the tent and the groom would use a new weighing scales' stick, wrapped with red paper, to remove the red veil from the bride. If the groom was cunning, he would sit on the veil so that he could dominate the bride forever. Usually someone from the bride's family would not let the groom do that and would quickly say, 'high rise' which meant the new couple were permitted to look at each other for the first time.

This 'sit tent' custom originated from the times of Han Wu Di of the Han dynasty. During the wedding of Han Wu Di and Li Fu Ren, he received her into the 'zhang', meaning 'tent', (similar to a mosquito net, only that it was made of good quality see through material beautifully made), to sit facing each other and to drink from the pao gua together (During the Zhou period, every emperor had three Fu Ren meaning consorts. Li was the maiden name of Han Wu Di's consort). At this moment, the ladies of the palace scattered dried fruit and flowers into the tent, the more they scattered the more sons the royal couple would have. Since then, this rite took off as a custom and had perpetuated till the early period of the last century.

In the past, in Beijing, after worshipping heaven and earth, the new couple retreated to the new room. Both sat in the kank with the edges of their gowns tied together in a knot. Someone in charge then placed a cloth on the knot and poured the contents of the vase, (the bride brought with her when she stepped out of the sedan chair), usually containing big and small grains and some gold and silver rou-yi. This symbolised that the new couple had received prosperity. This custom was said to have originated from the peasants where people celebrated for a good harvest during a wedding.

In the new room, the bride and groom ate a meal together. Again, the number of dishes had to be in even number as an odd number was taboo. Usually, there were six meat dishes and six vegetarian dishes. In some areas, the Han Chinese let the bride eat some not quite cooked jiao zi. (While she was eating, she would be asked, 'sen pu sen?' 'Sen' means 'raw' or 'not cooked'. It was important that the bride replied 'sen' and not 'pu sen', because it also means 'give birth'. The former had the symbolical meaning of 'giving birth' and the latter 'not giving birth'. It was a way to obtain some verbal luck from the bride. These jiao zi were dumplings stuffed with meat and vegetables, small in size, similar to the Cantonese 'wanton'. Jiao zi are still very popular among the Northerners in China today.

In the Beijing area, jiao zi were usually provided by the bride's family. These jiao zi were usually served in two bowls, fourteen in each bowl The groom's family was responsible for providing noodles known as 'long life noodles'. At this time, the new couple would sit in the kank with their legs crossed and were served with jiao zi and noodles. The woman in charge would feed them and would utter lucky phrases like 'sons and daughters pack the living room' and at this time a young boy would ask from outside the bedroom window, 'sen pu sen?'

Usually, the groom or the woman in charge would quickly say 'sen' signifying that the bride would like to give birth to many children.

According to Manchurian custom, sometimes a roast goat, usually leg only, was brought to the bridal chamber after the couple had their drink. A woman would feed some of the meat to the groom and bride. At this moment, a shaman woman would start to dance a ritual shaman dance outside the window in the courtyard, it was a way to congratulate the new couple.

Among the Her-jer people, symbolical meanings were important in a wedding. In the bridal chamber, the groom had to eat a pig's head and the bride had to eat a pig's tail. This had to do with the symbolical meaning 'yow tou yow wei, bai tou tao lau' meaning 'head and tail, white heads till old' which really means, 'there is a beginning and an ending, the two will grow old together'.

Faraway in Hainan island near Hong Kong, the Miao bride and groom were given liver with rice. Some prayers were said by the matchmaker over this food before giving it to the bridesmaid and best man who then fed the bride and groom. It was said, only the bride and groom had the right to eat this kind of liver and rice. Also, it must be eaten at a set time and rice must not be dropped on to the floor otherwise the couple would divorce later.

After performing the rites to heaven and earth and the ceremony to the parents-in-law and other elders of the groom's family, the Jing bride was led to the new room. Singers of both families sat in the living room and sang all night till dawn. On her wedding day, the bride abstained from eating food at the groom's house. Food was brought from her family to her by her sisters during the ceremony. The bride was fed by her sisters and they stayed the night.

138

According to Chinese history, the ancestors of the Hui Chinese were merchants from Central Asia. Physically they are no different from the Han Chinese though sometimes their faces reveal some Western blood. Most of them speak Chinese only but some of them understand some Arabic. The Hui Chinese have a different practice from the rest of the people in China. When a Hui bride has entered the bridal chamber, it is not her husband but her mother-in-law who takes off her veil. While she sits in the bridal chamber, her father-in-law holds a banquet in the living room to celebrate the wedding. When the banquet is over, only then the bride and groom start to have their meal together. After the meal, they will take a bath. When the bride has finished her bath, she must sprinkle some of the bath water at the four corners of the bridal chamber. After that, the new couple will sit on the bed and listen to a lecture by the Islamic religious leader. It is only after listening to this religious talk that they are man and wife.

As the new room was the new place for a bride to reside after arriving at her husband's house there were taboos to be avoided by her. After she sat on the bed or kank she was not to laugh or move about otherwise it was unlucky. In the North-East of China, the bride was not allowed to get off the kank herself, she was given a helping hand by her husband's younger brother. When he was helping her, he had to give her a slap on her back, to test whether she had a good temper or not. As for the Manchurians, when a brother of the groom helped the bride out of the kank, she had to say 'siao shu, (meaning 'little brother-in-law'), give you a hand, got a donkey and a horse'.

The Mongolians also observed the custom of making the bride sit in the tent, it was known as 'chor fu', meaning, 'sit on prosperity'. For the Han-Chinese it was known as 'chor chai', meaning, 'sit on fortune'. The poor bride was expected to sit on the red blanket with her legs crossed most of the time. It was a taboo if she needed to uncross them and if she did, she would be criticised by the relatives of the groom that she was unfaithful.

Before getting into the bed to sleep, the groom had to make sure that he had put his shoes in a place where the bride would not be able to step on them. If his wife stepped on his shoes, then for the rest of his life he would feel small in front of her. This was something that the bride had to be very careful as well. If she stepped on her husband's shoes, it would be seen as a great insult to him. Also, she was not to put her clothes on top of her husband's clothes otherwise her husband would be dominated by her all his life. These practices were observed by the Han-Chinese in certain areas and had very much to do with 'ta nan ren ju yi', meaning, 'big male chauvinistic mentality'. As to why women were not allowed to put their clothes next to their husbands' clothes this went back to ancient times. This was one of the many classical codes laid down by the Book of Odes, it said:

'Man and woman do not use the same clothes-rack, a wife shall not make bold to hang her garments on her husband's clothes-horse, neither shall she place them in the same chests...
till they have reached their seventieth year, then there is no objection any more to their storing their personal apparel together.'
(see Sexual Life in Ancient China)

This explains why even today many Chinese men are still unable to get this traditional mentality out of their heads. Nowadays, of course, a husband and wife put their clothes in the same wardrobe, but a Chinese man is still very taboo if he walks under women's clothes especially underwear or if a woman accidentally step over his legs. This shows that women are still seen as 'dirty' and 'inferior'. Otherwise, why should a man get

140

so worked up when he walks underneath women's clothing or when a woman steps over his leg? If this kind of mentality goes on Chinese women will never achieve equality.

Within the first month of their marriage the bride and groom had to sleep in the new room because it was a taboo if the new room was empty for a day or two, for example, if the bride went to her parents' home for a few days after the wedding. If the bride was visiting her parents on the third day after the wedding she was expected to return to her husband's house before dusk to prevent the taboo of 'empty room'. If the new room was empty for a day or two during the first month of marriage it was considered as unlucky.

HAPPY SWEETS

Guests who attend a wedding are given sweets by the bride and groom. This custom is said to have come from the red dyed eggs' custom of the Jiangnan area, of the areas South of Jiangsu. This is an old custom which came from a story from the famous ancient story book 'Romance Of The Three Kingdoms', written in the fourteenth century.

According to the story, the governor of Eastern Wu, Zhou Yu, was trying to set a trap to detain Liu Bei, Duke of Shu, (a descendant of the Han emperor of the Han dynasty), to force him to return some territory by staging a 'chow chin' competition. Chow chin was a kind of competition to attract eligible bachelors for a son-in-law. Usually, a notice was given to attract potential suitors to engage in a fight using swords or a non-violent competition such as testing their knowledge on a classical theme. The winner would be rewarded with a wife.

However, Liu Bei's prime minister Zhu Guo Liang knew that it was a trap and he too came up with a plan. Zhu Guo Liang advised Liu Bei to prepare a large amount of boiled eggs dyed in red colour to take with him to Eastern Wu. When the two of them arrived at Eastern Wu, they distributed the eggs to everyone they met from court officials to soldiers and even ordinary people. Everyone who received the eggs was told that it was an important custom of the palace and so those who received it felt very honoured indeed. News travelled fast and soon most people heard the news that the Eastern Wu princess was to be married to Duke Liu Bei of Shu. Under pressure, Zhou Yu had to let the princess marry Liu Bei. From then onwards the Jiangnan area adopted the custom of distributing red dyed eggs during a wedding. Later, probably sometime during the last century, the red dyed eggs were replaced by sweets. This custom is still observed by the Chinese in China and in Taiwan but not by the Chinese in Malaysia.

TEASING THE BRIDE

One of the legacies inherited from ancient times is the custom of 'nao fang' or 'toor si fu'. The former means 'make a row in the bridal chamber' and the latter means 'make fun of the daughter-in-law'. Although the terms are different, it is the same thing, also known as 'Teasing the bride'. According to Van Gulik's book 'Sexual Life in Ancient China', the earliest references to this custom were recorded by Ko Hung in his book 'Pao-pu-tzu'. Ko Hung was a Taoist philosopher who lived during the third century AD during the period of the Three Kingdoms. The following was Ko Hung's description of nao fang:

'Among the vulgar people prevails the rule of teasing the bride. Right before the assembled guests, and in front of the relatives of the young couple, people will ask them coarse questions, and reprove them with lascivious address, their low and offensive behaviour is beyond words. They will even urge the pair on by beating them with whips, hang them up by their feet, flushed with wine those people will stop at nothing. They sometimes even wound the bride and groom so that their blood flows, or that their bones are broken.' (See Sexual Life in Ancient China).

According to Van Gulik, this custom may be a remnant of old ceremonies intended to scare off evil spirits that might want to harm the bride and groom when they exposed themselves during consummation, but as ancient Chinese believed that sexual intercourse was an oct ordained by nature and the sacred social order and so those who engaged in it should not be exposing themselves to any dangers from evil forces. Van Gulik went on to say that there was the possibility that the custom originated with the aborigines that inhabited the South-East and East of China it was only during the last centuries B.C. that they were assimilated with the Han-Chinese people. (See Sexual Life in Ancient China).

There is a Chinese saying, 'Pu ta pu nao, pu rui nao', meaning, 'Do not fight, do not row, is not lively'. 'Rui' literally means 'hot' and 'nao' means 'row'. From this it shows that the Chinese could not stand silence in a wedding and 'noiseless' or 'no noise' was a taboo during a wedding. Some people said 'nao fang' or 'toor si fu' was a way used to congratulate a new couple. This custom was popular among the Han-Chinese. Although the ancient Chinese believed that sexual intercourse was an act ordained by nature that did not stop people from believing that there were evil spirits who were going to do harm to a new married couple. It was believed that nao fang could increase the yang in the atmosphere because the Chinese believed evil forces were full of yin. There was even a saying 'if the people do not make a row then the ghosts will'. Another reason of making a row was to give the new bride a chance to meet the rest of the extended family or maybe the relatives of the groom were worried that the bride might feel lonely on her first day in her husband's house therefore everybody came to crack a joke or two with her to make her laugh.

Usually, nao fang started on the wedding night. At this time, people old and young gathered themselves in the bridal chamber wishing the bride and groom a happy marriage. During this time, no matter who said anything that was embarrassing or ridiculous, the bride and groom must not be angry as it was a taboo. There was even a saying 'Three days no big and no small'. This means that it did not matter what generations people belonged to, old and young could equally join in the nao fang for three days. Again, widows, pregnant women, infant babies, those in mourning, those born in the year of the tiger and those whose Eight Characters were not compatible to the Eight Characters of the bride and groom were not allowed to join in the nao fang. It was believed that this group of people might cause the new couple to quarrel and might bring them bad luck. In Taiwan, the paternal great aunt known as 'gu por', paternal aunt 'gu mu' and the groom's younger sister 'siao gu', meaning 'little aunt', were forbidden to engage in nao fang because 'gu' sounds like 'lone' and it reminded people of 'lonely' or 'loneliness'.

According to one text, it said, in the Zhejiang area, nao fang was like a dramatic show, male guests dressed up as women, some as ghosts and demons just to make fun of the bride. Some cracked jokes, some put up some sign language. They were aiming to make the bride laugh. Nao fang, of course, was noisy but no matter how bad, the groom's family usually would not complain because it was believed that the noisier the better, more prosperity would come to the family. Usually, during nao fang, the guests tried to embarrass the new couple by asking them about the history of their romance. One common game was to make the new couple ate an apple together which was hanging on a string. Sometimes, a couple was made to walk over a wooden plank supported by two chairs. One embarrassing one was to make the groom eat melon seeds out of the mouth of the bride. Usually, the games were tolerable, and no one was hurt.

144

In some areas, some people used nao fang as an opportunity to mock and abuse the bride. In Shuntak, an area in Guangdong, the poor bride was made to stand in the middle of the room surrounded by the nao fang hooligans. All sorts of awkward questions were put forward to her and she was mocked and laughed. If she did not do according to what she was told to do firecrackers were thrown at her. Often it was not uncommon that a bride suffered burns to her arms and legs by firecrackers and her clothes were ruined. Nao fang was such an ordeal as if the bride were an ancient prisoner who was being tortured for her crime. As if that was not bad enough, while the bride was being mocked the groom was not allowed in the room.

In the South-East, the nao fang was even worse, the bride was slapped left and right in her face by the nao fang hooligans. It was said, the beating was to ensure wealth the more beating the more wealth. Sometimes, it went out of hand and led to a quarrel or fight between the host family and the guests and worst still it led to injury and even death. To the bride, this kind of uncivilised nao fang practice was really an ordeal and it was quite a disaster.

Here are two accounts of how brides were mocked and physically abused during nao fang in traditional China and communist China:

'In our region from the first to the fourth night after a wedding, people come to 'disturb the bridal chamber'. Recently after a young couple were wed, a crowd of young people went to do so after the bride and bridegroom were already asleep, kicking in the door and bursting in. They picked up the bride to give her a plane ride, then threw her down again, crushing her shoulder. When she begged for mercy, they made her perform a number of indecent acts and say some coarse words. (see Chinese Family and Kinship).

'The groom's family were terribly happy and busied themselves looking after the guests, the groom himself being overjoyed. But although the bride was beautifully made up, her face was not a happy one, and this led us to wonder whether she could be dissatisfied with the match. But when we asked our neighbours, they said the couple were very fond of each other, so it all seemed very odd. In the evening, the ceremony began. The bride was led out by a middle-aged woman. First, she worshipped the ancestors, then she stood facing the door of the house. A fifty-year-old man was pushed forward from the crowd. He stripped off his shirt and bared his chest. Then he drank several cups of wine and began to prance around with his eyes on the bride. He was chanting and singing, and the other people joined in, with gongs and drums beginning to beat too. He smacked himself on the legs and body and then gave the bride a sharp box on the ears with his right hand, followed by his left, at which the crowd burst out laughing. As soon as a man got tired the next would take his place, and this went on for an hour. The bride's face was beaten till it was red and swollen, and her eyes were brimming with tears, but she did not dare to cry out. This was a special custom of the area. It had apparently been said for many years that the beating was to ensure wealth, the so-called 'beating for wealth', the more you are beaten the wealthier you get, 'without a beating you don't get wealthy'. (see Chinese Family and Kinship).

In Anhui, in a place called Liu-an, the nao fang custom was not too civilised either because the bride was pushed about by the guests who came to nao fang, touching her hands and her legs. There was even this stupid idea that the longer nao fang went on the better because it showed that the bride was liked by the groom's family.

In Nanchang, Jiangxi, within the first three days of a wedding everybody whether old men with hair as white as snow or young

146

children joined in the fun of nao fang. Within these three days the old could act silly and the young could let loose and did not have to worry about their elders watching over them. The teasing was quite civilised like trying all sorts of tricks to make the bride laugh, for example, a man dressed up as an old woman saying her prayers to Buddha.

On the wedding night, among the Dong Xiang people, the climax of the night for the guests was teasing the bride in the bridal chamber. The Dong Xiang people had their own unique custom of teasing the bride. Inside the bridal chamber, the bride sat in the corner still covered with the veil surrounded by her own female relatives. Not long afterwards, young men flocked into the new room each of them holding a pillow in their hands. As they sang praising songs to the bride, at the same time they threw the pillows at her. The female relatives of the bride were there as a defence to prevent the pillows from hitting the bride. If the young men tried to climb on to the kank they would be pushed down by the women. As soon as the bride was hit the game was over because she had to remove her veil and stand on the kank to let everybody take a good look at her. After this the guests went through her belongings looking at the dowry she brought with her.

Everywhere brides were teased on their wedding nights but in Fuchien in a place called San-yuan, the custom of nao fang was very different because the groom was the target of teasing not the bride. Usually, the people who came to nao fang put black or red paint on the groom's face to make him look like a clown and then made him sit on a chair, lifted him up and mocked at him.

Today, teasing the bride is still practised by many Hong Kong Chinese and some Chinese in Malaysia, especially in the rural areas. Nowadays, the teasing is rather harmless such as asking the new couple to eat an apple on a string together. All for a bit of fun without involving touching or physical abuse.

The custom of teasing the bride sometimes led to tragedies therefore in some areas it was opposed, for example, in some areas in Shandong. This custom was also opposed by one Manchurian tribe known as the Cha-ke-la people. Before dark, the area where the new couple was going to sleep was swept clean, the farm animals such as the chickens, geese, ducks and even the domestic animal the dog were kept away from this area. It was to give the bride and groom a quiet space to enjoy their beautiful night together without having to put up with dirty and noisy animals.

In some areas, populated by Han-Chinese, there was a custom known as 'ting xin fang' meaning ' listen new room'. It was quite a worry if no one was listening at the door of the new room. It was said, 'if people do not listen then the ghosts will'. Sometimes, if the parents-in-law saw that no one was listening at the door of the new room they made a dummy, for example, put some clothes on a broom and placed it against the door to deceive the evil spirits thinking that someone was listening at the door of the bride and groom's bedroom so that they would not bother to disturb the couple.

THE WEDDING NIGHT

On the wedding night, it was a taboo if the wedding candles were blown out early. Ideally, people liked the two candles to stay burning all night. It was said the one who blew the candles off would be the one to die first and because of this the bride and groom would not dare to blow out the candles. In some areas, among the Han-Chinese, there was the practice of 'shou hua zhoo' meaning 'guard flower candles'. On the wedding night, the bride and groom stayed up all night, making sure that the two wedding candles did not go out. There was a saying 'If the candle on the left goes out first then the groom will die first but if the candle on the right goes out first then the bride will die first'.

Usually, when one candle went out the other would be put out at the same time it was to hope that the two would die together at the same time. This was called 'tung sen si', meaning, 'together live and die'. As for the Manchurians it was considered unlucky to blow out the candles by mouth, a fan was used instead.

As the Chinese said, 'doong fang hua zhoo yeh', literally meaning, 'bridal chamber flower candles' night', it was usually the night when the new couple spent their first night together. However, some ethnic minorities of China saw that as a taboo, for examples, the Pumi, Miao, Bai, Yi, Nu, Hani, Mulao and Yao people. Some of them refrained from spending the first night together and some of them the first three nights, some even longer. It was said, the reason was to 'duai ker' similar to a singing courtship, it was to test the groom's talent and his love for his bride. Some brides went home to their parents and only returned after the third day.

There was a strange custom that prevailed among the Pai-wan people, one of the hill tribes of Taiwan. On the wedding night, the matchmaker stayed in the bridal chamber with the bride and groom all night. It was said, she was there to find out whether the couple love each other or not. There was another very ancient custom. It was said, the bride had her knickers sewn up on her wedding night. Not only that, but she also even brought along a girl friend to stay the night and the three of them, the bride, the groom and the girl friend actually slept on the same bed! At this time, the groom had to use his power of persuasion to talk his bride into having consummation with him as man and wife.

According to Ewenke custom, after the wedding ceremony at night the groom must spend his wedding night in the bride's house. The next morning the bride will gather her herd of deers and her relatives will accompany the new couple to the groom's house, thus, bringing the wedding to an end.

Like the Ewenke people, the Tadjik bride and groom also have to spend their first wedding night at the bride's house. The next day the new couple will ride a horse together and are accompanied by relatives to the groom's house.

In the past, on the wedding night, if the groom discovered that his bride was not a virgin there would be trouble for her and her family. According to the Chinese author Chen Dong Yuan in his book, 'Zhong guo funu shenghuo shi', he said the Chinese stressed the importance of virginity in a bride ever since the Sung dynasty and because men considered that as very important therefore the women themselves went along with it and virginity became a proof of purity.

During the Manchu period, there were cases where brides were sent home to their natal homes because they were not virgins. In the North of China, the people were especially uncompromising about this matter. In the South, the brides were not sent home to their parents even if their husbands found out that they were not virgins. Having said that, most men accused their brides of being 'un-pure' if they did not see blood on their wedding nights. One wonders how many marriages suffered psychological scars due to ignorance, especially in the Manchu period where there were no modern doctors to examine whether a bride was a virgin or not. The author went on to say that even in his day, (the book is written in the 1920s), the matter was still seen as very important in a marriage.

In those days, a bride was put to the test on her wedding night whether she was a virgin or not. According to one Manchu text, there was a reference about a Cantonese wedding in Guangdong. It said, on the wedding night the si niang, (a woman who helped the bride and groom), helped the groom to take his shoes off and handed him a white handkerchief. The white handkerchief was of course used to wipe off the blood after sexual intercourse. If there was blood, then the bride was

150

thought to be a virgin and roast pigs were sent to the bride's family later. During the consummation of the bride and groom, the groom's parents, relatives, and guests actually stood outside the room waiting anxiously to hear whether the bride was a virgin or not. Later, the groom came out of the bridal chamber holding a tray covered with a red cloth, inside was the white handkerchief called 'si pur', meaning, 'happy handkerchief'. Those standing outside the bedroom especially the parents were elated when they saw blood in the handkerchief. Guests would surge forward to congratulate the groom but would only do so after they had seen the blood in the handkerchief, just in case the bride was not a virgin and it would be an embarrassment to the groom and his family. From this it shows that the virginity of a woman was not a matter between her and her husband but was a public affair.

If the bride was a virgin, her parents would receive a roast pig on the third day of her marriage when she visited them as this was the custom. Rich families could afford to give several roast pigs. In the old days, the parents of a bride would start to worry if there was no sight of the roast pig coming from the groom's family. After the bride's family had received the roast pig or pigs, they were placed in front of the bride's ancestors' tablets before cutting them up and distributing to all relatives. According to the author Ren Cheng, he said one could see that the practice of examining the virginity of the bride witnessed by relatives and outsiders had become a public display of personal morality. He went on to say, sadly, the groom did not see that as an insult to his honour and the bride did not consider that as an insult to her moral character. All this, he said, was the result of feudal backward traditional values which had severely distorted people's thinking. (see Zhong Guo Min Jian Jin Ji)

In the Beijing area, if the bride were not a virgin she would be called 'broken goods'. In those days, blood in the sheets, (to be

151

precise, it was blood in a handkerchief), was the only way to determine that the bride was a virgin. If the bride was found to be a virgin the next morning the groom's family would send someone to the bride's family to 'pao si', meaning, 'report happy' which was to report the good news that the bride was a virgin. Usually, a red envelope with a written statement was presented to the bride's family which said something like, 'Due to your good education, your daughter is a real lady'. However, some people preferred another way of reporting the news in a box with the blood- stained handkerchief presented to the bride's family. If the bride was a virgin even the neighbours would know because the person who reported the news would shout 'pao si coming' as he was approaching the bride's house. Only after receiving the good news, the bride's family went to attend the feast at the groom's house otherwise they would not dare.

Some people used another method, instead of 'pao si', they put up beautiful ribbons as decorations to show that the bride was a virgin. When the bride's family came to the groom's house, seeing the decorations they would at once know that their daughter was a virgin and so they could go in and attend the feast, if not they would have to turn back and go home.

As late as the Republic of China, many Chinese brides still had to go through the horror of the virgin test. Here is an account of a real story by the authoress Han Su-yin in her book, 'Birdless Summer':

'In spite of the new emancipation, a young girl, a university graduate, who had just married a university lecturer. The morning after the marriage, the mother-in-law went to the newlywed's bedroom to inspect the sheets of the bridal bed. (Until very recently, even in Singapore, that supposedly modern city, a special towel was provided for this purpose and brought ceremoniously to the mother by her daughter-in-law on the morning after the wedding night). Finding no blood upon the sheet, the mother-in-law became indignant, raised a great shouting and ordered her son to divorce his wife on the grounds of un-chastity. The bride protested that she was a virgin, her parents supported her, and accused the other family of slander. Finally, it was decided to have the bride examined by a woman doctor... and found the hymen still intact. But it was impossible to convince the mother-in-law. And though her son himself said he was well content, that he loved his wife and entirely believed her, yet it was impossible for the young couple to stay with the family as was the custom, they had to go elsewhere.' (see Birdless Summer).

THE MORNING AFTER THE WEDDING

On the following morning, sometimes on the third morning, the bride had to perform a ceremony to her parents-in-law. In some areas, in Guangdong, there was a practice where the bride offered tea to her parents-in-law. During this tea ceremony, the bride had to go down on her knees, kneeling all the way to the table, which was in the living room, prostrate several times at the front of the table and then kneel all the way to the back of the table and repeat the ritual back and forth many times for more than an hour. Most brides could not withstand this kind of torture and cried their hearts out. There was no reference that the grooms were given this kind of torture.

This practice of offering tea to the parents-in-law is still observed by all Cantonese speakers in Malaysia but unlike in traditional China it is done on the day of the wedding. This tea ceremony is very important to the Cantonese people especially if the parents-in-law are old-fashioned. In a previous sub-heading 'Costumes', I have mentioned that kuas are worn by the brides in Hong Kong throughout the wedding day but in Malaysia a kua is worn only during a tea ceremony. In Malaysia, Cantonese brides are married in Western style white bridal gowns and only change into their kuas in the afternoon to perform a ceremony called 'cham cha' meaning 'pour tea' to their parents-in-law and their elders.

The kua is a very elaborate costume usually hired rather than bought as it is very expensive due to the much-detailed workmanship with the symbols of a dragon and phoenix and flowers embroidered on satin or silk. Red and pink are the two usual colours but in Hong Kong, brides also wear cream colour. Since it is only worn once for the tea offering ceremony, most Cantonese brides prefer to spend their money on other things rather than on one expensive item. Some Cantonese brides ask their dressmakers to make a cheaper version and then wear it every year to offer tea to their parents-in-law on their birthdays.

In the afternoon of the wedding day when the new couple came back from the photographer's studio the bride will change into a kua for the tea offering ceremony. This is usually a family affair only relatives are present. Two chairs will be placed in the living room. As always it begins in the hierarchical order the oldest members will be offered tea first. If the elder has lost his or her spouse, then he or she will take the tea alone. This is a very trying time for the bride and groom because the couple must kneel on the floor until all the elders have been offered tea. However, there is one consolation because every time they offer tea to the elders, they will receive a red pouch either with money or a piece of jewellery inside. This money and jewellery will go to the bride to add to her personal possession. This ceremony no doubt has gone through some changes. All the feudal rites such as prostration have been swept aside and it is much simpler now.

On the following morning after her wedding a Hui Chinese bride had to go through a simple ceremony of greeting her parents-in-law known as 'zhing an', literally meaning, 'invite peace'. In this ceremony, the bride knelt and offered tea to her parents-in-law. Meanwhile, the groom went to his parents-in-law's house to pay a visit and probably had to go through a simple ceremony as well.

When morning arrived, the Jing bride had to prepare hot water for the groom's family for washing their faces. Each family member would receive a brand-new face towel. Each elder of the family had to give a red pouch to the bride when he or she received the new towel. Only after this, the wedding ceremony was officially over. This traditional wedding ceremony was observed before the 1950s but since then many changes have taken place.

In the South of Suzhou, the people there observed a custom different from other areas. On the morning after the wedding, the groom's family used a hundred jin, (one jin is 1/2 kilogrammes), of glutinous rice flour to make into little round balls. Relatives and neighbours were invited to the house to enjoy these round balls. Those who were old and frail, had round balls sent to them to eat at home. Eating these round balls shows the close friendship between neighbours where every family of the area was blessed and united together.

In one area in Guangdong, on the next morning the bride had to get up early and cook a bowl of sweet rice for her parents-in-law and brothers and sisters-in-law. Everyone was expected to eat only a mouthful of rice. It was said, the sugar used for cooking the sweet rice had to be brought from the bride's family. It was also said, when the bride was cooking the rice, she had to spit some of her saliva into the rice! Of course, this was done discreetly without letting anybody see the disgusting act. Those who ate the rice, of course, knew that there was saliva in the rice, but they would keep quiet about it. It was said, those who ate the sweet rice with the bride's saliva would get along with the bride afterwards.

HUI NIANG JIA

On the third day of her marriage, the bride paid a visit to her parents' house accompanied by her husband. This visit was called 'qui ning' or 'hui niang jia', meaning, 'return to mother's house'. As the bride was now someone's daughter-in-law she was required to return to her husband's house before dusk to avoid the 'empty room' taboo. In one area in Honan, when the bride was returning home to visit her parents she had to go by the same route where three days ago she was carried in a sedan chair to her husband's house. There was a saying 'Three days do not pass by two routes'. Perhaps walking by another route was unlucky.

Unlike the Han-Chinese bride, the Hui Chinese bride did not visit her parents on the third day of her marriage. In fact, she was only allowed to visit her parents after one month. According to the custom of the Xibo people, a bride went to visit her parents on the ninth day after her wedding.

Some brides, due to deep-rooted superstitious beliefs, did not visit their parents until after a hundred and twenty days. Some even had to wait for three years before they could visit their parents. In some of the areas in Zhejiang, if the life of a bride was said to be 'against her family', for example, she could reduce her family to poverty, then she would not be allowed to get into the sedan chair from her parents' home. On her wedding day, she was to dress in rags looking like a beggar when the groom came to welcome her. She was then taken to a temple and then changed into her wedding costume; it was called 'cheir jia', meaning, 'borrow marry'. On her wedding day, her parents were not there to see her off, everything was taken care of by the groom's family. She was not to set foot in her parents' house until four months later. For the bride, whose life was said to be 'li wor', meaning, 'separate nest' she did not visit her natal home until after four months or three years later. 'Li wor' means that the couple would separate.

Usually, after the first month, the bride could visit her parents freely. During her visit, she could stay at her parents' house for a few days. Like the rest of the other practices and customs, there were taboos concerning the duration. In Honan, if the bride was visiting her parents on the eighth day of the month then she had to stay eight days, this way, it was said, 'eight and eight' and there was prosperity for both families. This is because the number 'eight' sounds like 'prosperity'. If the bride went home on the ninth day of the month then she had to stay nine days, it was said, 'nine and nine, two sides have', obviously it had to do with 'have prosperity' because 'nine' sounds like 'have'. If the bride followed, according to the practice then it would be lucky for both families otherwise it was unlucky. Having said that, some areas were against the bride staying for eight days. There was a saying which said, 'stay seven days but not eight days, stay eight days the bride's family will become poor'. This perhaps may have something to do with the concept that the daughter was married out and therefore should not stay at her parents' house too long.

Among the Yi people, it was a taboo for the bride and groom to speak to each other on their way to visit the bride's parents. Throughout the journey they were to remain like strangers to each other. Quite the opposite, the Han-Chinese bride and groom laughed and talked to each other and there was even a song called 'Hui niang jia'.

Presents for the bride's family had to be in even numbers because odd numbers were taboo. According to the custom, the bride's parents were not supposed to accept all the presents, some had to be returned to the groom's family.

In Honan, there were certain days of the year where the bride was not allowed to visit her parents. These were, the first day of the first month, the fifteenth day of the first month and the twenty fourth day of the twelfth month. The first day of the first month was the Chinese New Year and a married out daughter was according to the Chinese saying, 'water being splashed out of the home' and so she should not visit her natal home on this day. Also, the Chinese New Year was a time for family reunion, a married out daughter was not considered a member of the family anymore and so it was not right for a married out daughter to spend this day with her parents. Although the fifteenth day of the first month was the Lantern Festival, a time of celebration, it was a taboo for the bride to visit her parents at this time because there were some sayings which said, 'If a bride has seen the lanterns in her parents' house they will be poor' or 'if the bride has seen the lanterns in her parents' house her father-in-law will die'. Also, this day was the first full moon of the year, a day of reunion, therefore, if a bride had gone home to her parents, it was feared there would be no reunion in her husband's family. The bride was not allowed to visit her parents on the twenty fourth of the twelfth month because it was the day of worshipping the stove god.

In the face of all these superstitions therefore a bride was only allowed to visit her parents on the second day of Chinese New Year and the sixteenth day of the first month. This is the reason why most married women visit their natal homes on the second day of the Chinese New Year.

In the North of Shanxi, the bride was invited home to her parents on the sixth day of the sixth month, it was a practice of this area. According to the people of this area, it was to cultivate good relationship between the two families. Not only was the bride invited but also her husband. In Honan, this practice was also observed but it had more to do with after the harvesting. As the local saying puts it 'after collecting the grains, when everything was done, no daughter who does not visit

158

her mother. If a daughter does not visit her mother, either her father-in-law or her mother-in-law will die'.

Brides were expected to observe the taboos of hui niang jia so that they would not visit their parents if the date were not right, if not, it was believed, something unlucky would happen. However, if it was all right to visit their natal homes then they had to go, if not, something bad would also happen.

If the bride and groom were invited to stay the night or a few nights, there were also taboos to be avoided. Among the Han Chinese and Manchurians, it was a taboo to let the new couple sleep together in her parents' house. Usually, the Manchurians let a son-in-law slept in a room in the West of the house. Other guests were not allowed to sleep in that side of the house. It was believed that if the bride and groom slept together in her parents' house her family's fortune would decrease. According to the author Ren Cheng, this kind of thinking has something to do with the ancient concept that sex was dirty and might offend the deities, (see Zhong Guo Min Jian Jin Ji). Also, the bride's family and the groom's family were two separate families and the former certainly did not want their daughter and son-in-law to use their house as the place to conceive the next generation for the other family. People were afraid that if the next generation was actually conceived in the maternal grandparents' home, then the prosperity would follow the baby back to the paternal grandparents' home, and as a result poverty would fall on the bride's family.

In Honan, in the Lin district area, among the Han-Chinese these taboos were observed but however there were people in the same district who were not bothered by the taboo and the bride and groom were allowed to sleep in the same room in her parents' house.

In Rudong, in Shandong, according to the custom, during hui niang jia, a bride had to bring some food from her natal home for her parents-in-law. If there were more than enough it would be distributed among the neighbours.

In the Beijing area, on the third day, the bride's family would send someone to the groom's house to fetch the bride and groom to spend the day with the bride's family. Some people sent the bride's brother to fetch the groom; it was brother-in-law welcoming the brother-in-law. At the bride's house the new couple had to kowtow to the bride's parents, similar to the ceremony performed at the groom's house a couple of days earlier. These endless kowtows exhausted the new couple. Afterwards a feast was laid out for the new couple with the men at one table and the women at another. After the feast, the groom would return to his home first and the bride would stay on to have a little chat with her parents then would return before sunset.

In one area in Shanxi, the groom was offered a bowl of fine noodles when he paid a visit to the bride's house with his bride. Fine noodles were very common food but there was a reason why it was used to treat a groom during this visit to the bride's house. These fine noodles were tied into little bundles to make it difficult for the groom to pick them up with his chopsticks. Although the noodles looked delicious, they were actually very hot, sour, and salty. If the new son-in-law started to tuck in straight away, he would be in for a shock and would make a fool of himself. Usually, the person who cooked the noodles was the bride's sister-in-law. This custom of making fun of the new son-in-law had three intentions: first, to let him know that the bride had many people on her side so that he would not dare to bully his wife; second, it was to laugh at him; third, it was to test his intelligence. If he was smart, he would give the first bowl of noodles to the elder of the family, the second bowl to the person sitting next to him and would only accept the third bowl. Only the first bowl of noodles offered to him was made with extra chilies, vinegar, and salt but the rest were free from extra ingredients.

Among the peasants in the South of Suzhou, on the third day after the wedding, the bride's mother put on new clothes and shoes to go to the groom's house to fetch her daughter to her house. At the groom's house the bride's mother would be asked to stay for a meal. After the meal, the bride followed her mother to her natal home. In the afternoon, about four o'clock, the groom carried pork, fish, and cakes to the bride's house. After a meal at the bride's house the new couple returned to the groom's house, thus, bringing all the wedding activities to an end.

On the third day, the Qiang bride is escorted by her groom to her natal home to visit her parents. During this time, her relatives will make fun of her husband. One of the most popular jokes is to make him eat his food with a pair of long chopsticks about four 'chi' long, (one chi is equivalent to 1ft 1 inch), with the potatoes tied at the end. On the table, dishes of meat and vegetables are placed. Also, on the table are several oil lamps. When the groom picks up the food, he must not drop it in the oil lamps otherwise the oil will splash on to his face making him more embarrassed. Worst of all, he will be punished for his carelessness and failure. Punishment will include being tossed in the air, dropping him on the floor or making him drunk.

In Malaysia, due to geographical reasons, nowadays, the old practice of hui niang jia is not observed on the third day anymore but is observed on the wedding day when the groom is welcoming the bride at the bride's house. There are different ways of doing this. A groom could come to the bride's house, take her out in the wedding car, tell the driver to drive round the surrounding area or block of houses and then come back to the bride's house to worship her ancestors. After this, he takes her to his house. Another way that will save more time is that the groom comes to the bride's house, worships her ancestors with her and then takes her to his house.

CHOW NU SHI

Apart from the traditional marriage system other forms of marriage also existed alongside it. As we have seen, in traditional marriage it was usually the woman marrying the man who went to live in his house but there were cases where the groom was married into his wife's family. This was called 'chow nu shi', meaning, 'bring in a son-in-law'. In high antiquity, this practice was nothing new, as mentioned before, men were the ones who were married off to their wives' families. One famous 'chow nu shi' was Yu The Great. According to a text of the Han period, during the Qin period, men of poor families were married into their wives' families because they could not afford to pay a bride price, therefore they used their 'bodies' as bride prices. If a man had agreed to be a married in son-in-law, he was required to shave off his hair as it was a custom of the Qin period. The head shaving was a form of punishment and any man who agreed to be a married in son-in-law was looked down by people.

However, in high antiquity, it was the norm, men were married into their wives' families. During the matriarchal system, a man was expected to adopt his wife's family name and so were his children. One example was Yu The Great, before his marriage, his surname was Yi, his mother's family name, after his marriage he adopted his wife's family name Tu-san. There were no records about welcoming ceremonies in high antiquity. If there were, it would be the bride welcoming the groom to her house. In the patriarchal society, a man usually did not like the idea of marrying into his wife's family.

In today's society if a woman takes in a husband, people will say, 'tao chant men', which means something like 'turn over the door' which really means it is against the current custom. Here is an account of a man who agreed to be a married in son-in-law in communist China, not without criticism:

'The masses of people in Ni-wan commune, Tou-men county joyously ran about passing the words, 'uncle Chin-hsi is taking a son-in-law'. When news of this spread, a small number of people still influenced by feudal ideas began to criticise. Some said, 'A fine young man like him can find a wife without difficulty. Why should he have to join the family of his wife? What a shame!' When Ho Hua-shen's father heard these erroneous views, he also thought that, as it had been a practice for women to marry into their husbands' families since ancient times, his son would be looked down upon and meet bad luck if he did as planned. Ho Hua-shen studied conscientiously the relevant writings of Chairman Mao and the ten new things of Hsiao-chin-chuang and came to realise that times have changed, and men and women are equal.

'If women could go and settle in their husbands' families, then men could also go and settle in their wives' families'.

Revolutionary young men must take the lead to break with traditional concepts like 'men are superior and women inferior'. Therefore, he patiently tried to enlighten his father, saying, 'As long as we act in accordance with Chairman Mao's instructions, the cadres and masses will give us support'. He also said, 'If it is unlucky for a man to join his wife's family, what kind of luck did you have when you followed the old practice and took a wife into your family before liberation? This refreshed his father's memory of the miserable past. In the end he supported his son's decision to settle in his bride's house. Ho Hua-shen and Huang Ping-tsai then went ahead with their wedding preparations. They both agreed to have their wedding the new way, not accepting betrothal money or presents or giving a feast, (see Chinese Civilisation and Society).

Among some minorities, the practice of bringing in a son-in-law is rather common, for example, for the Men-ba people of Tibet, half of their marriages are in this form. The people there think that there should not be any difference between 'marrying out' and 'marrying in'. These people think that people should not look down on a man who decides to join his wife's family because a son-in-law is also capable of looking after a business so should be able to inherit his wife's family's fortune and to look after his parents-in-law during their old age. Compared to an ordinary wedding, the wedding rites of bringing in a son-in-law are much simpler. On the wedding day, the groom is accompanied by his best man to his bride's house where a ceremony is held.

Bringing in a son-in-law is also practised by the Zhuang people. During the wedding, the groom's family do not accept any presents from the bride's family nor bring any dowry. All marriage expenses are being paid by the bride's family. On the day of his exit to his bride's house, there will be no ceremony in his parents' house nor any banquet, but the bride's family must slaughter chickens and ducks to entertain guests. On this day, the groom will be given his wife's family name, and also given a new name by his father-in-law. Whether in his wife's home or in society, a Zhuang son-in-law is not looked down upon, his position is highly respected. In his wife's home, he is treated like a son. His wife's brothers treat him like one of their brothers and they are careful not to address him as brother-in-law.

In Taiwan, some Gaoshan people belong to the matriarchal society and men are married into their wives' families. That explains why some Gaoshan people prefer to have daughters rather than sons. Having a daughter means that the family 'have earn' but having a son means that the family have 'no earn'. Perhaps this is because a son is married off which means that his family is at a loss, but a daughter brings in a son-in-law, a helper for the family.

Among the Ah-mei hill tribe in the east of Taiwan, the matriarchal system is still perpetuated here. Although the Ah-mei people belong to the monogamy marriage system, the bring in a son-in-law system is still the practice among these people. On the wedding day, the groom is accompanied by his parents, maternal uncle, and brother to the bride's house. Half-way before they arrived at the bride's house they will be welcomed by the bride and her girlfriends. Once they have entered the bride's house, the groom will be welcomed by the bride's parents and sisters and perform the wedding ceremony. After marriage, the groom is regarded as a member of the bride's family, but he has no authority, his welfare is decided by his wife. In his wife's family, he is like a long-term worker with no power in decision making. All matters concerning production are decided by his wife and if he tries to take over, he might run the risk of being kicked out of his wife's house. Although he has no power in his wife's house, in his mother's house however, he has a lot of power. If he is the eldest son, he has a say to influence decisions concerning his mother's family and in outside matters the power to decide who gets what concerning the family's fortune. In his mother's family, he is the maternal uncle of his sisters' children therefore he has a say in decision making.

In Yunnan, a similar practice is seen among the Dai people and Bu-lang people where men live with their wives' families after marriage. The practice is said to be a legacy of high antiquity where men went to live with their wives' families. Here in Yunnan, the Lahu people practise two kinds of marriages either a man joins his wife's family, or his wife joins his family. In the case of a husband joining his wife's family, the wedding is held in the bride's house. The bride comes to welcome the groom to her house. On the wedding day, the groom will take all his personal belongings including his farming tools, is accompanied by attendants and will follow the bride and her bridesmaids to her house.

In Shenlongjia, if a man had agreed to the practice of bringing in a son-in-law then he had to adopt the surname of his wife's family. All his children also had to adopt the surname of their mother. However, during his grandchildren's generation, that is the third generation, it would be reverted to his own surname. Nowadays, it is said, bringing in a son-in-law is still being practised by some people in this area, but a man does not have to adopt his wife's family name anymore.

In Jin-siu, in Guangxi, there is a group of Yao people known as Pan Yao. In the past, they used to live a nomadic life moving from mountain to mountain therefore they were also called Gwor Shan Yao. If there were three families living together it was called a camp, five families together were called a village, the most were over twenty families living together. Traditionally, the marriage system of the Pan Yao was to bring in a son-in-law and children were given their mother's family name. On the day of the wedding, the groom was escorted by all members of his family to the bride's house. In the bride's house musicians played different instruments. The groom did not travel in a sedan chair but walk with an open umbrella. When the groom's party had arrived at the bride's house front door, they had to sprinkle water to get rid of evil spirits.

At night, the bride's house was illuminated with lamps and fire was set up outside the house which brightened the whole place up. Several square tables were put together to form a long table for the wedding feast. In the midst of cheers and music, the bride and groom performed the wedding ceremony. Usually, the eldest maternal uncle or the eldest paternal uncle conducted the ceremony. The kowtow ceremony was performed in hierarchical order. The grandparents were the first to receive the kowtow from the new couple, next the parents, then the maternal uncles and aunts, then the eldest brothers and their wives, the eldest sisters and their husbands and eldest maternal cousins and their spouses. According to the Pan Yao's custom, the groom had to bend at the waist, kneel, and knock his head on the floor repeating this twelve times as one rite. The groom also offered wine to the people he kowtowed to. The bride, however, did not have to perform the same rite as the groom, she only had to curtsy each time the groom went down on his knees. The people who received the kowtow would present little gifts to the new couple. After the ceremony, there was singing for three days and three nights, engaged by all the people of the whole village and the host did not have to take the trouble to entertain everyone because the people entertained themselves. After the marriage, the new couple shared the responsibility of looking after the parents of both families. If the groom's parents needed help, the couple would go back to lend a hand helping with the farming or house chores. Nowadays, the Pan Yao are still practising chow nu shi and the children still adopt the mother's surname.

Among the Gaoshan people of Taiwan, there is a tribe known as the Bunong. These people have four kinds of marriages. The first kind is called exchange marriage. When a young man and woman have been through a free courtship and have decided to get married their parents will meet and discuss the wedding. This kind of marriage is very simple because there is no bride price and no dowry but exchanging each other's son and daughter.

The second kind of marriage is the traditional marriage like most of the people of China, that is, the groom has to pay a handsome bride price, usually in kind such as cattle, pigs, wine and blankets. The bride also must give a dowry.

If a Bunong man has no financial means to marry in the traditional way or if the girl's family do not have a son then he will choose the third kind of marriage, chow nu shi which he will join his wife's family.

The fourth kind of marriage is the kidnapping type of marriage. If a man loves a woman and if he is unable to pay a bride price or perhaps the girl has rejected his proposal, then he might consider this kind of marriage. First, he will gather all his relatives together and wait for the woman to pass by the usual route. As soon as she appears, they will kidnap her to his house. However, before they enter the door of the man's house, he will have to see whether the woman is willing to be his wife or not. If she is willing then she will enter the door willingly, if not she will refuse to enter. If this happens the man will not force her and will let her go home.

In the past, in Taiwan, some rich widows brought husbands into their families. This practice was similar to bringing in a son-in-law. The only difference was that these women were married before. These husbands were called names such as 'chieh jiao fu', meaning, 'receive leg husband'. Usually, a woman brought in a husband because she needed a man to provide for her and to bring up her first husband's children. For the man who agreed to this kind of practice, he was always looked down upon because as a brought in husband he did not have much authority within the family. There used to be a Taiwanese saying which goes like this, 'As long as there is a bowl of rice to eat, will not be a chow nu shi.'

Nowadays, among the Han-Chinese, Bai, Jingpo and a few other minorities, there is still a taboo about the practice of bringing in a son-in-law. These days, to be a married in son-in-law does not necessarily means that a man is poor anymore, it is more to do with carrying on the lineage or to solve the shortage of labour in the bride's family. There is a saying, 'A son-in-law is half a son'. According to the marriage law, a married couple is required to live together and so it should not matter if a new

168

couple are living in his parents' home or her parents' home. This form of marriage is also protected by the law of the country and so should be given the same status as a woman marrying into a man's family. However, the practice of bringing in a son-in-law is still unusual and is in the minority. Among the Han-Chinese and most of the minorities, a woman marrying into the man's family is still the norm and in the majority.

POLYANDROUS AND POLYGAMY

Although most of China's ethnic minorities have entered the class society and monogamy is now the norm, some groups of people who are still under the last phase of the primitive society have preserved their primitive marriage practices such as polyandrous and polygamy. Changes in marriage practices always fall behind economic development because of the relative stability of these marriages and this seems to explain why some ethnic groups within class societies are still practising certain marriage practices characteristic of a primitive society. Polygamy is a way of life among the Muslim people all over the world because according to Islamic law, a Muslim man could have four wives. In China, polygamy not only exists among the Muslim minorities, most of them live in Xinjiang, but among the Tibetans, Pumi, Men-ba and Loba people polygamy coexists besides monogamous marriages.

There are two periods in a Muslim marriage, the first period is the preparation period, and the second period is the actual wedding. During the preparation period, there are seven stages which the two families must go through. The first stage is, both parents have to check the status, personality and occupation of each other. Only when they are satisfied will they proceed any further. The second stage is to ask a matchmaker to communicate between the two families. Finding out the names of the young man and woman is the third stage. There is a rule to this, the name of the young man is given to the young woman's family first before they can find out about the name of the young woman and then the two will be given a chance to meet. After this, the man's family will pick an elder from the family to oversee the wedding. The fifth stage is signing a document to show that both sides are seriously going ahead with the marriage. The sixth stage is the bride price which requires a large sum of money from the young man's family for the young woman's family. After this, the man's family will ask the matchmaker to pay a visit to the young woman's family to fix a wedding date.

During the wedding period, there are four stages to go through. The first stage is the wedding ceremony, and it is done three days before the wedding. On this day, the groom and his family are dressed up to welcome the guests. An imam will conduct the ceremony. When the bride's family have arrived, they are seated opposite the groom's family. After the two families have greeted each other a table is placed in the room. At this time, the groom and bride will kneel beside the table. On the other side of the table, the imam recites the Islamic scripture and prays while the rest of the guests stand and watch quietly. After this, the imam will write down the names of the bride and groom and their fathers' names on a special strip of paper to finish off the wedding ceremony.

The second stage of the wedding is when the bride's family send the dowry to the groom's house. This is done before the day of welcoming the bride.

Welcoming the bride to the groom's house is the third stage. On this day, the groom rides to the bride's house in a car. As soon as he has arrived the bride's parents will welcome him into the house, and he will be seated in the living room. When the bride comes out of her room, he will escort her to the car and take her home. During that night, the groom's parents let the couple sit in the living room opposite each other. Rose water and soup are served to them. When they have finished eating, an elder will give them a lecture of how to be a good husband and a good wife. During this time, they are asked questions about the Koran, only when they have given the right answers will the elder allow them to take off their wedding costumes and consummate the marriage as man and wife.

Polygamy was also practised among the Qiang people in the past, during the Republic period. At that time there were more women than men among the Qiangs due to the result of an earthquake in the Summer of 1931 which killed many men and in 1935 where many men were either killed or being captured by the communists during the Chinese civil war. Many men were killed at the time of the earthquake because most of them were in bed smoking their opium and were buried in the ruins. Qiang women, must work in the fields while their menfolk walk around idle all day. Young men in those days married young and their wives were usually a lot older than them. At that time, a young man barely turned fifteen already had two or three wives.

In Tibet, polyandrous marriages are seen in noble and land-owning families where brothers share one wife between them. The purpose is to prevent the land and wealth from splitting up and so ensure the social status and privileges of the brothers. Among the poorer labourers, apart from brothers sharing one wife, there are uncles and nephews sharing one wife and also friends sharing one wife. This way, there is an advantage because the serfs could avoid the taxes levied on small separate households. On the wedding day, only the eldest brother will perform the ceremony with the bride. If one of the brothers is having sexual intercourse with the wife during the daytime, a skirt is hung outside the door of the bedroom to let the other brothers know that they must not enter the bedroom.

When three brothers share one wife, they also share all the children as well. To the children, the eldest brother is known as 'ta tae', meaning, 'eldest father' to them, the second brother is 'zhoong tae', meanmg, 'middle father' and the third brother is 'siao tae', meaning, 'little father'.

MARRIAGE CUSTOMS OF THE WOMEN OF GUANGDONG

In Fan-yu, in Guangdong, at one time there existed a peculiar custom among some of the woman known as 'Bet lok ka', meaning that they were not living in their husbands' homes. As most of the women here were capable of earning their own living, they were reluctant to get married. However, when they were advanced in years, due to parental pressures they were forced to marry. After marriage, they tried to avoid having sexual intercourse with their husbands.

After a woman was married, a few days later she went home to visit her parents. Some women maintained this bet lok ka situation for many years but did not dare to go against tradition not to produce offspring to carry on the lineage for their husbands. There were others who rather bought concubines for their husbands so that they could be free to do what they like.

At one time, there was a strange and peculiar custom which prevailed in Shun Tek in Guangdong. At one time, Shun Tek was famous for its silk industry. Many young women were engaged in the silk industry; nearly most of them lived like nuns and preferred to be single all their lives. It was said, the people of this area believed that only virgins could do all the work efficiently and due to this superstitious belief nearly all of them were virgins all their lives giving their precious lives to silk making. These women were given the name of 'lao gu por', meaning, 'old aunt grandmother' and the house they lived was called 'gu por oak', meaning, 'aunt grandmother's house'.

Since these women had all dismissed the idea of marriage, they formed a sisters' league, a kind of society where members were all single women. One requirement of this society was that each member had to go through a rite known as 'Saw Hei' which in Cantonese means, 'comb the hair up'. This rite was held in a temple in front of the deities, a rooster was killed, and each member had to drink its blood. Each member had to take an oath of sisterhood and vow never to marry, live a life of celibacy and then undo her plaits and comb her hair up into a different style so that no man would ever bother her again and she would be able to attend to her work without any hassle from men.

When they were advanced in years, they adopted young girls to carry on their life commitment in silk making and so these girls also inherited the old spinsters' house. Later, due to new development in textiles, real silk was threatened by man-made silk so the livelihood of these lao gu por were also threatened and so the whole lot of them left for Hong Kong. Some went as far as Singapore and Malaysia in search of new occupation, engaging themselves in domestic work as servants. As they were hard working women, most people liked to employ them as servants. It is said, there are still quite a few gu por oak in Guangdong and Hong Kong.

This bet lok ka practice was also practised among some women in Shun Tek. There were quite a few reasons why the women of these areas of Guangdong practised this custom. Sexual life was seen as 'shameful' and 'dirty' which was one reason. Other reasons included the uncivilised way of examining the bride's virginity on her wedding day and the restrictions on a married woman. All these women of Shun Tek belonged to some sort of society such as the 'Kam Lan Hui', meaning, 'Golden Orchid Society' in Cantonese, and were a group of unmarried women sworn to sisterhood to live a celibate life. According to the practice, a member could not break away from the rest of the

173

group and go to live with her husband unless all of them had agreed to do the same. Also, this bet lok ka practice was due to the women themselves who longed to pursue freedom. Due to this practice, these Shun Tek women were able to live a freer life without marriage restrictions, able to enjoy a social life and to earn a living. Although these women lived away from their husbands, they did visit their husbands during festivals. With the Chinese feelings on marriage, these practices of 'bet lok ka' and 'Saw Hei' were not only contradictory to the Chinese institutions but also quite a challenge and one must really admire these women of Shun Tek and Fan-yu for their courage to put up such a fight.

Some minorities also practised a similar practice. After her marriage, a Bouyi bride was free to visit fairs and join in the activities. In Guangxi, in a place called Loong-lin, a Zhuang bride not only could join in a singing courtship but also be given a portion of land in which she could manage the productivity and the financial output of her land. According to the custom, after her marriage, the Yi bride lived with her own parents until she gave birth to a baby, only then would she live with her husband. If she could not have a child after many years of marriage, her husband could divorce her on the ground of not being able to produce a son to carry on the family name after her husband's death and a Li woman would go back to live with her parents or brothers.

If a Li woman was ill, her parents would pray to their ancestors to heal her. If she were seriously ill, she would be taken back to her parents' home to die there and after her death she would be buried in her family's ancestral grave. Any possessions she had would be divided among her own brothers. From this it shows that this practice of bet lok ka was a challenge to the traditional system that a woman had to live with her husband. According to the author Ren Cheng, this practice reflected a matriarchal system still struggling stubbornly against a patriarchal system, (see Zhong Guo Min Jian Jin Ji). To this day, it is said, there are some areas where some people are still holding on to this practice.

On the day of her wedding, a Mu-lao bride was accompanied to the groom's house by a group of girlfriends. In the bridal chamber, instead of a bed, a table was placed where the bride and her girlfriends ate their meals and spent all night keeping the bride company. On the next day, after eating their afternoon meals these girls escorted the bride back to her parents' house. Unlike other new brides and grooms, the Mu-lao newlyweds did not spend their first night together. In fact, the bride continued to live with her parents after marriage. The couple continued to live apart until the following Spring festival where the groom would fetch the bride back to his house to celebrate the festival. However, she was not back for good, only stayed one night and then left for her parents' home the next morning. During festivals or whenever an extra pair of hands were needed, she would come back to her husband's house to help but would only stay a couple of days. Only when she had given birth to a child would she actually settle in her husband's house.

HAKKA WEDDING

Among the Hakka people in the East of Guangdong a strange marriage practice existed in the old days. Many Hakka young men went abroad to work in South-East Asia in Singapore and Malaysia, known as Nanyang, meaning, South Ocean to the Chinese. When they had earned enough money, they wanted to marry and settle down, but they did not want to marry the native women. Most men wanted to marry someone from their own village in Guangdong but going home was not cheap nor easy because of the long journey, it did not seem to make economic sense. When a man decided to find a wife, he wrote a letter to his parents, enclosed a photograph, and asked them to find him a wife. With the help of a matchmaker, a suitable woman was found, but the problem was, how to get the daughter-in-law into the house while the son was abroad? To get round this problem, the Hakka people came up with a clever idea. As the marriage rites were indispensable therefore the rites of worshipping heaven and earth and the ancestors fell on the shoulders of a cockerel. Perhaps it could be argued that it was a marriage by proxy. Only a healthy cockerel would be chosen to represent the groom, he was given good feed, good treatment and a red strip of red paper was tied round his body to let people know that he was to represent the groom. On the wedding day, the cockerel took the place of the absent groom, he was taken to the bride's house to welcome her and later performed all the rites with her.

In the past, in East Zhejiang, if a man were out fishing and could not get home to get married due to bad weather at sea, his sister would perform the wedding ceremony for him. After the ceremony, his sister held a big red cockerel and walked the bride into the bridal chamber. This red cockerel was kept in a cage with a long red strip of material tied round its neck. Every day he was fed with rice and vegetables till the groom came back and he would be released. This was known as, 'Sister perform the ceremony, the cockerel accompany the bride in the bridal chamber'.

KIDNAPPING MARRIAGE

Kidnapping the bride was an old practice which actually existed in a few areas in China among the Han-Chinese, for example, in a place in Jiangsu. Usually, it happened when a family was poor and lacked the financial means to pay for a handsome bride price. The method involved could not be simpler. All a man had to do was to get a few relatives and friends, seven or eight men and paid a visit to the girl's house. While they were there they waited for an opportunity and then snatched the girl and left for the man's house. There was nothing the girl's family could do about this because it was the practice of this area.

In nearby Jiangxi, kidnapping marriage was common in an area among the poor but not that poor. These people still owned some land, but they could not afford a large sum of bride price and the other expenses of a wedding. To achieve the aim in marriage this method was used. However, even kidnapping marriage had rules to be followed such as finding the right family with the same financial situation. Some families did not want their daughters to marry into very poor families. Under this circumstance, some poor men resorted to the kidnapping kind of marriage. This kind of kidnapping usually took place at certain time of the year on the twelfth month of the year. Every year between the twelfth month and the first month, those with unmarried daughters took extra care to protect them from kidnappers and the girls themselves hid in their rooms every day. If the man had the approval and support of the girl then he could bribe the girl's family, that would make his work easier.

If the girl's family were against the idea, then it would be difficult for him to achieve his aim. Before embarking on such a mission, a strategy had to be worked out first. The man's family had to make sure that they gathered enough people to help him and check the number of people in the girl's house. On the day of the kidnapping, the man and his friends tried to divert the attention of the men of the girl's family. When there was an opportunity, the would-be groom snatched the girl from her room, wrapped her up in a bed sheet and carried her on his back all the way home. Both sides were not allowed to use weapons during the fight, but fist fights were permitted. As long as a girl was snatched out of the front door then the kidnapping was a success because under this circumstance the girl's family would consider that their daughter was the 'water splashed out of the home' and usually they would not bother to chase after the kidnappers.

There is another kind of kidnapping marriage, an old practice which is prevalent among the Jingpo people of Yunnan. What makes this one different from the two examples above is that the kidnapping day is selected by the matchmaker and that means the groom is not a total stranger to the bride. On the day of the kidnapping, the young man will get support from a group of friends, hide themselves near the young woman's house, lure her out and then carry her off to his house. The next step is to ask the matchmaker to pay a visit to the young woman's parents to propose marriage who usually will not object.

VISITING MARRIAGE

In Yunnan province, in a place called Yoong-ning, the Naxi people there practise a very different form of marriage from the rest of the people in China. This marriage is called 'Visiting Marriage' because the man and the woman are not actually married but only having sexual intercourse at the woman's house regularly. Both partners refer to each other as 'Ah Xiao' or 'Ah Zhu' which means 'lover' therefore it is called 'Lovers' Marriage'. This form of marriage is rather free and there are no fixed formalities, the main concern is the mutual love between the couple. At first, the man visits the woman secretly in the fields. If both of them wish to carry on their relationship, they will ask the woman's parents for approval and if they agree then he will bring his quilts and spend the night with her at her home. At dawn, however, he returns to his own home to work in the fields. Although this form of marriage is rather free there are taboos to be observed, no such marriage is allowed between close matrilineal relatives. In general, there is no change in their economic and social status because they are both living independently of each other. It is said, this kind of relationship is not stable because the two lovers have no economic tie but only a sexual bond between them.

Not surprisingly, a Naxi man or woman will have quite a few lovers throughout his or her life. It is said, the Naxi people in Yoong-ning prefer to have daughters rather than sons. Perhaps that explains why they have a matriarchy society as it is the daughters who have the right of inheritance not the sons and women are the heads of families. As soon as a girl has reached the age of eighteen, she will register as a legal heir to inherit any property. It is also said, children in these areas do not know who their real fathers are because of the many lovers their mothers have and they are given their mothers' surnames.

In the North-West of China, live the Mor-sor people, a Naxi group. When a boy and a girl has reached the age of thirteen, they must go through a coming of age ceremony where a girl will wear a skirt and a boy will wear a pair of trousers. This signifies that their childhood is over and from now on they have the right to participate in social activities in society as adults. When a girl has reached the age of fifteen or sixteen and a boy has reached the age of seventeen or eighteen, they will start courting the opposite sex. When two young lovers have established a relationship, to show their love for each other the girl will give a bracelet for the young man and he in return will give her a belt. Later, every year the young man will give her a silk blouse, a handkerchief, a belt, and a bracelet. On top of these, he must give some brown sugar and tea leaves to her parents and her maternal uncle. Whenever he visits the girl's family, he must make himself useful as a handyman, helping out with domestic chores.

Like the Naxi people of Yoong-ning, the Mor-sor people here are still practising an ancient legacy, a remnant of the matriarchal system where men do not bring in wives and women are not married off to their husbands. Among the Morsor people, the relationship of a man and a woman is established on a 'friendship relationship'. This friendship relationship is equivalent to a marriage relationship. However, both the young man and the young woman will continue to live in their parents' homes. Every night he spends the night with her in her house and leaves the next morning for his own home. Once the friendship is established the couple must go through a simple ceremony.

At the start, the man has to send a go-between bringing a jar of wine, a cotton costume, some tea leaves in a bamboo container, some pork and some puffed balls called ba ba, (a snack made with glutinous rice flour, hollow inside). After worshipping the woman's ancestors, the woman's family will use the pork and wine to entertain their relatives and neighbours. On the morning of the wedding, the man will send a young man to call the bride's name in front of her house. At this moment, he will be surrounded by young ladies, friends of the bride, who will shout and beat him up, though not a real beating. If at this time, the go-between is present he too will not be able to escape this symbolical beating. Usually, the man will pick an elderly woman to be head of his welcoming party and another ten to twenty women. When they have arrived at the bride's house, they must walk through the front door where two skirts are hanging, one belongs to the bride and one belongs to her mother. At this moment, the bride and her girlfriends will sprinkle or splash water at the welcoming party. However, they must not be angry but instead they must show that they are happy. During the cheering noises, the bride will get on the horse, bought for her by the groom, and will head for the groom's house with the welcoming party and a few of her siblings.

Once they have arrived at the groom's house, someone will blow a spiral shell, a homemade cannon is fired, and a trumpet is sounded. Amid the sound of drums, an elderly man will conduct the worshipping of the ancestors, read out a list of blessings to the couple and rub some oil on their eyes. After this both the couple must eat lamb's kidneys and drink wine from the same cup, a symbolical meaning that the couple shares the same heart. After this ceremony, the couple will kowtow to the elders and will receive gifts from them. This will be followed by a banquet to entertain the relatives and friends. This kind of marriage relationship is easy come, easy go. Some people could manage such a marriage for decades but some only for a couple of nights.

During a lifetime, a Mor-sor could have many sexual relationships and could walk away from a relationship easily if one party has no wish to continue the relationship. Any children as a result of a relationship will be brought up by the mother and the father only play a very small part, for example, taking the child or children to his home to worship his ancestors once in a while. This is like high antiquity during the matriarchal society where children only knew their mothers but not their fathers.

RENT A WIFE

In Wei-an, in Jiangsu, at one time, there existed a practice called 'zu qi', meaning, 'rent a wife'. This usually happened among the very poor people with the woman who hired herself out or the man who rented her. Usually, the duration was a year or two and the custody of any children born during this period was given to the man who rented the wife. As to how much was paid to the so called 'wife' during the hire period, it was negotiated by a go-between and both parties had to sign a contract. Men who resorted to renting wives were mostly very poor and this was one way to get a wife even though it was only for a short period. This way, a man could hope that he might be blessed with one or two children to carry on the lineage of his family.

'Rent a wife' was also practised in two areas in Zhejiang in a place called Jin-hua and another place called Shien-ju. Lack of an heir, a son to carry on the lineage, was the main reason why it was practised. There was a slight difference in the circumstance of the men in these two areas in Zhejiang and the men in Jiangsu. The former was rich, but the latter was poor. Any man without an heir and who was advanced in years and if his wife was against the idea of him taking a concubine then might see this practice as an answer for an heir to carry on his family's lineage.

If a man adopted a son it would not do because his name could not be included in the genealogy of the family, it had to be a blood heir. Poverty was the reason why some poor men agreed to rent their wives out, especially when there were many mouths to feed in the family. Although this marriage practice was very different from a traditional marriage, due to the fact that its main aim was to have children to carry on the lineage of a family therefore a matchmaker was needed to negotiate the deal and both parties had to sign a contract. The content of the contract usually stated the name of the person who rented out his wife, the name of the person who was renting her, the duration and the amount of money paid. During the whole period of renting, the 'rent husband' could visit the 'rent wife' in her house frequently and have sexual intercourse with her and any children she bore for him belonged to him and he raised them in his house. When the hiring time was up the two went their separate ways but during Chinese New Year and other festivals there were social visits between the two families. If the 'rent mother' in her old age was still poor sometimes a 'rent son' did his filial duty and took his biological mother to his home.

There was a difference between Jin-hua and Shien-ju, the women of the former had husbands, but the women of the latter were mostly widows. In Shien-ju, the women were usually rented out for five years, but some were rented out for as long as fifteen years. Unlike the arrangement in Jin-hua, there was no contact between the two families once the contract was over. When the rented husband came to stay, if the rented wife had a lover, then he had to go away while the rented husband was around.

This wife renting practice was still practised in China as late as the war with Japan in 1937 because there was a reference by Han Su-yin, the authoress of 'Birdless Summer'. In the book, she mentioned that the wife of a Kuomingtang officer was a 'borrowed wife'. It seems that there was no difference between 'borrowed' and 'rented' because the women were hired and not married to the men. Here is an extract of the tragic death of this woman by Han Su-yin: 'And there is the other benevolent brother's story…

His wife had a child and had gone with the baby for a few days to visit her own family. While there, she went to the theatre with a female cousin, the husband of the latter and their three children. During the intermission, the woman cousin took the children to the toilet, leaving her husband and the woman alone in a theatre full of people, for a few minutes. Somehow, the story went about that this woman had gone to the theatre, alone with a man. It took only some weeks for the tale to reach the dimensions of a full-blown scandal.

One evening while playing mah-jong, the officer won a good deal of the game. 'You may be lucky in gambling, but do you know that a green hat sits on your head?' Said one of his friends to him. 'What do you mean?' 'What, he does not know that his wife is so fond of the theatre?'

The officer returns home, tears his wife's hair, breaks her teeth, and puts her in a cage. These wooden cages, made with bamboo and barbed wire, were only big enough to stand in. They were used in the concentration camps for communists and by the

183

feudal landlords to torture the peasants who could not pay their rents. Into this cage, he drove his wife and put the cage out in the street, for all to see. It took the woman some days to die of hunger; meanwhile no one dared to rescue her, no one dared to feed her, her baby was not allowed near her. Her family tried to go to court but they were not wealthy or influential. 'She is only a borrowed wife', says the officer, 'and she has thrown my face away'.

CHILD BRIDES

'Tung yang shi', meaning, 'child bride' was one of the aspects of marriage which existed in some periods of Chinese history. This aspect of marriage was generally despised. In Honan province, the practice was common, most child brides were physically abused by their mothers-in-law, yet most people did not bother to intervene because they did not see anything wrong in it. It was not easy for a poor man to marry without the financial means and so in this area a poor man had to wait until he had saved enough money to buy a wife, (I used the word 'buy' not 'marry because girls in traditional China were 'sold' like goods), by then the man was nearly middle-aged or even older.

Rich people never let their daughter marry an aging poor man. Only a poor family with many daughters would consider this kind of man for a son-in-law. There was a reason as to why a man would rather marry a child bride and not a grown woman, it was because the bride price for the former was less than the latter. For the rich people, it was just the opposite, they preferred older brides so that they were mature enough to look after their little child grooms.

In Fuchien, a child daughter-in-law was known as 'sim-pu-kia', ('Sim-pu' means 'daughter-in-law' and 'kia' means 'child'). Usually, an infant girl or a young girl would be bought by a

184

family who would take the responsibility of raising her and when she had reached a marriageable age they would marry her to one of their sons. This was known as 'yuan fang' in Mandarin meaning 'consummation'. At one time, the practice was quite common in Taiwan:

'For both the men's family and the women's uterine family, the sim-pua form of marriage had real advantages over other marriage types. The cost of raising a child, often a child who replaced one born to the family, was not comparable to the ruinous expense of bride price, engagement cakes and feasts required by the major marriage. When the couple were old enough to marry, their bow to the ancestors need only be acknowledged by a simple family feast. Both wealthy and poor families saw advantages in the sim-pua form of marriage beyond those of economy, they valued the safety of having a daughter for a daughter-in-law. No outsider had to be brought into the family. The family did not need to depend on the word of a go-between and the dubious judgments of relations about the character, honesty, industry, health and good nature of the woman who was to spend the rest of her life in their house and take care of them in their old age,' (see Chinese Family and Kinship).

During a conversation with a Taiwanese friend of mine who is studying in Britain, she said, 'Ah, the sim-pu-kia form of marriage has already died out now. Twenty or thirty years ago it was common, nowadays, I have not heard about this practice, not in Tainan, the South of Taiwan, where I live anyway.'

At one time, some Chinese in Malaysia still purchased sim-pu-kia. I have a real story about the life of a sim-pu-kia in Malaysia. When I first met Kim Lian and Ah Mun, (both are fictitious names), they were both in their twenties. I later learnt that they were the adopted children of my father's landlord. Kim Lian had fair skin like a European and a clear complexion with a height of no more than five foot in a plump body shape. Ah Mun was of average height for a Chinese fellow with a high bridge nose, in a darker complexion, caused by staying out too long in the sun, had a strong physique due to hard work. Not long after coming back to live with my family from Penang where I used to live with my uncle and his family, I was told about the relationship between Kim Lian and Ah Mun that the family actually bought Kim Lian thinking of bringing her up to be their daughter-in-law. However, when they both had reached adulthood, Ah Mun objected to the arrangement though he never gave the real reason to his adopted parents. I was told that they did not like each other. Obviously, they were not attracted to each other they preferred to remain as brother and sister. Neighbours used to gossip to each other, "Why didn't Ah Mun want Kim Lian for a wife? Oh, I think probably because Kim Lian is not pretty enough." Both the original backgrounds of Kim Lian and Ah Mun were hushed up.

All I know is Kim Lian's mother lived in Singapore. One day her natural mother even paid her a visit, much to the adopted mother's hostility. Chinese people are not as broad minded as Westerners, they are afraid that if they allow any contact between their adopted children and their natural parents then they will go back to them. I think that if adopted parents treat their children well, then they should not be afraid that they will go back to their natural parents but in the case of Kim Lian I was not surprised. When she saw her natural mother, she was very close to going back with her to Singapore if it was not for the persuasion of some neighbours. They said, if she went back with her mother it would be unfair to her adopted parents who had gone through all the trouble of bringing her up. Kim Lian, torn between her natural mother and her adopted parents eventually gave in to social opinion, did not want to be blamed for deserting her adopted parents. Why did her mother give her away when she was a baby? She told Kim Lian that it was her husband's idea not hers, (she was his concubine), that she regretted the decision. Disappointed, Kim Lian's natural mother left for Singapore without her.

As there was no hope of Ah Mun marrying Kim Lian, the adopted mother decided to let her take up an apprenticeship in dressmaking in Kuala Lumpur. Taking up an apprenticeship in dressmaking was only a secondary reason as the primary reason was to hope that she would find herself a husband in the big city. Indeed, it did not take her long to find a boyfriend and she was married within two years after leaving home. Fortunately for Kim Lian she was not forced to marry a man she did not love. Years later, Ah Mun too married a woman from Singapore and settled down near his adopted parents.

It seemed that the practice of sim-pu-kia was rather popular among the Fuchien dialect speakers. I have not heard any other dialect speakers who practised this practice.

At one time, in Swatow, in Guangdong, some people exchanged their daughters when they were young and when they were grown up, they were married to the sons of the families who adopted them. There was an advantage in this arrangement because a family could save a lump sum of money on the bride price and other expenses.

MARRY AN ANCESTOR TABLET

According to the thesis of Chen Dong Yuan in his book, 'A History Of The Life Of Chinese Women', the practice of marriage of the dead originated from the Wei period, (The Three Kingdoms), a thousand and seven hundred years before the Republic of China in 1912. After the death of his beloved son, Zhoong, who was only thirteen at the time, the ruler of Wei, Wei Wu Di was saddened by his loss. In the past, if a man died before his marriage it was seen as an unfortunate thing in life. As a consequence of the death of his young son dying before his marriage, Wei Wu Di came up with a plan to marry him to a girl who had died earlier. The dead daughter of a woman named Jen Shi was chosen as the dead bride for Prince Zhoong and their bodies were buried together. This was the first record of the marriage of the dead. Since then onwards, there were many references in the texts of the Tang, Sung and up to the Manchu period.

In Taiwan, in the past, if a man could not afford to marry a wife, he would marry a dead girl's tablet. In so doing, he would be given a sum of dowry by the dead girl's family and with the money he could then marry a living wife, but the dead girl would be given the position of a principal wife and the living wife could only take the position of a secondary wife. When a young girl died unmarried, it was afraid that her dead spirit might haunt her family. In order to prevent this happening, her family would try to marry off her tablet, (after a person has passed away, an ancestor tablet is installed in the home), which was usually installed in a temple because she was not married. Of course, the family had to pay some money to the temple's keeper regularly for looking after the tablet. Only a married person's ancestor tablet was allowed to be installed in the home. This way, the dead girl's spirit would be worshipped by the living husband's family and his descendants and it was hoped that she would leave her natal family alone.

Every festival, her birthday, and the date of her death, she had to be worshipped and offered sacrifices otherwise she would not let her husband's family live in peace. On the day of her husband's wedding, the matchmaker would represent her husband's family to worship her in her natal home and then her tablet would be carried in a black sedan chair to her husband's house and placed in his family's altar. At this moment, she had become one of his dead ancestors. After this the red sedan chair of the secondary wife was carried into the groom's house and the bride performed her duty as a secondary wife to the dead principal wife.

If a boy died before he was married, his family would try to find him a living wife by paying out a large sum of bride price. The difference in these two examples is that the living wife of the dead boy was not allowed to marry another husband but she was expected to spend the rest of her life as a widow looking after the tablet of a husband she never had. Comparing these two practices, the latter was a cruel practice because it condemned a woman to a life of widowhood whereas a man of the former practice was able to live a normal life with a companion.

There were other cases of marrying a tablet. If a couple were betrothed to each other and the girl died before her wedding then the boy would marry her tablet, if not, her ghost might haunt him for life. Of course, after marrying her tablet he could always take another secondary wife and many concubines, as long as he kept up the sacrifices to the dead wife then he would not have any trouble from her spirit. The wedding ceremony was the same as the case above, the black sedan chair would be carried into the boy's house first and then the red sedan chair with the living wife would be carried in later.

If a boy died before his wedding, the girl could marry his tablet. On the day of his funeral, she would dress in her bridal costume and would be carried in a sedan chair to his house. When she arrived, she would enquire about the boy's illness and the boy's family would say that he had recovered from his illness. After this conversation, she would change into mourning clothes and join the funeral procession. If the girl had no wish to marry the boy's tablet, then she was free to marry someone else later, but she must attend his funeral as according to the practice.

If the couple died before their wedding, then their families could arrange for their tablets to be married. The boy's family would arrange for a day for the tablet of the girl to be carried to the boy's house. The two tablets would be placed among the other ancestors' tablets on the altar. During the ceremony, the dead couple would be told that the brother of the dead boy would let one of his sons to be his adopted son and carry on his lineage.

BETROTHED IN THE WOMB

At one time, a couple was betrothed when they were in their mothers' wombs. This kind of marriage arrangement usually happened when two families were close friends and they decided that if one had a boy and the other a girl the two would be married. This marriage custom was popular in many areas in China and in Taiwan at one time. Usually, when two women were pregnant at the same time, they made a verbal agreement. If one of them had a girl and the other a boy then they would be husband and wife. If they both had girls then the two girls would be 'chet pai', which means they would swear sisterhood together. If both had boys then the two would swear brotherhood together. When the boy and girl were old enough to marry, but if unfortunately, the boy died before the wedding, then the girl was left with a choice either to marry his tablet or marry someone else.

CONCLUSION

All the marriage customs and taboos mentioned above at one time existed all over traditional China. For thousands of years before China's revolution in 1911, the Chinese had lived and developed under these marriage customs. From looking at Chinese history, the Chinese had placed great importance in marriage which was one of the three great events of life: birth, marriage, and death.

Without the marriage union of a man and woman there would be no future generations. As the Chinese stressed, there were three un-Xiao, without an heir, (a son), was the biggest of the three, and so under this kind of mentality, marriage was a route that every individual had to go through. To a large extent, the aim of marriage was to obtain an heir, a son, to perpetuate the lineage but no importance was placed on the love of a man and woman. All the marriage rituals were designed to show society the validity of a marriage, but nothing was stressed to show the genuine love of a man and woman, it was insignificant. As society in China today is moving toward modernism perhaps the young men and women there, to some extent, have a say in their own marriage.

The change in marriage systems also led to changes of the trappings and superstitions surrounding Chinese marriage such as the disappearance of the sedan chair and the rest of the taboos associated with it. The influence of Western style wedding outfits also has swept away the heavy phoenix coronet and ceremonial costumes and the taboos associated with it. Freedom in courtship more or less put the ancient occupation of the matchmaker out of business but having said that the occupation has survived in a different form, for example, the modern Introduction Agency or Marriage Bureau.

As the Chinese author Ren Cheng puts it, in China today, new wind is sweeping the cities, gone are the old traditional ways of marriage. They have no roots in the thinking of young people, only the old generation still recall what marriage was like in the old days with all the taboos to be observed but it is only talk because they have neither the will nor the power to ask the younger generation to go back to the old ways, (see Zhong Guo Min Jian Jin Ji). However, he said, the strength of the old practices have their stubbornness and die hard. Although on the surface these old practices no longer exist, in reality they still do, for example, looking for an auspicious date for the wedding, trying to avoid taboos and wishing for luck have surfaced in the new marriage customs. The forms may have changed but actually they are the same. Anyway, modern marriages could not just sweep away all the old practices, there are always a few that refuses to die or rather some people will not let them die.

Different forms of marriages of the Han-Chinese such as Child Bride, Marry an Ancestor Tablet, Rent a Wife and a few others have been eradicated in China since 1949. These forms of marriage have worked in the past because society was largely feudal. Among the minorities who are still living under the last phase of the primitive society, certain marriage practices such as polyandrous, polygamy and Visiting Marriage have been preserved. In accordance with the Constitution of China, the Chinese government respect the marriage customs of the minorities. Instead of abolishing them, they have adopted the policy of educating these people with those backward elements of their marriage customs.

BIRTH CUSTOMS

INTRODUCTION

In ancient times, people had no idea how a baby was conceived.
All they saw were the changes in a woman's body, that her
stomach was getting bigger by the day and later giving birth
to a baby. All that was a big mystery and people thought it was
the work of the gods. There were many legends about women's
pregnancies, that they were caused by gods and demons,
for examples, that they had something to do with a dragon,
phoenix, big bird, qi lun (a half dragon half lion creature), giant,
falling star, sun, moon or a rainbow. According to Chinese
myth, Fu-Xi was conceived because his mother had walk on
some footprints; that the mothers of Shennong and Yao were
pregnant by the power of the dragons, (dragons were perceived
as gods and possessed tremendous power), and that the mother
of Yu The Great was pregnant because she ate a certain kind
of plant. This conception was the reason why in high antiquity
during the matriarchal society, children did not know their
fathers but only their mothers. Pregnancy was also believed by
people to be due to fate, due to some superpower. Later, this
superpower was seen as 'tai shen', meaning, the 'god of
the foetus'.

The job of the god of foetus was to look after the baby specially
and it stayed with the expectant mother throughout her
pregnancy. Although he was greatly respected, he was also
feared by people because he had the power to protect and to
harm the baby. When the god of foetus was protecting the baby,
people respected him but when he was harming the baby then
people were afraid of him. When people were afraid of him, they
called him 'sha' not 'tai shen'. It was said, tai shen and tai sha
were the same thing, not to be offended.

As people believed that the god of foetus possessed the power
to harm the baby, they were careful not to do anything to upset

193

him. There was even such a belief that the god of foetus could communicate with the soul of the foetus. At certain times, it moved to certain parts of the mother's body or rest himself on certain objects in the bedroom. People had to be careful not to harm him because it was like harming the baby or worst might even cause the mother to have a miscarriage, leading to the death of the baby.

Every month he moved from one position to another in the mother's body. To the Yao people, he was known as 'tai huan', meaning, 'the soul of the foetus', perhaps they meant that he was the soul of the baby. According to the belief, if the baby was conceived in the first and seventh month, the soul of the foetus would be in the front door so it was a taboo to do any repair work on the front door or to dig the ground at the door; second month and eight month, it was in the courtyard so it was a taboo to put heavy things in the courtyard; third and ninth month, it was in the rice mortar and so it was a taboo to move the rice mortar; fourth month and tenth month, it was in the kitchen so it was a taboo to splash water in the kitchen; fifth month and eleventh month, it was in the bedroom so it was a taboo to move things or to do any repair work in the bedroom; sixth month and twelfth month, it was in the mother's stomach so it was a taboo to soak the pregnant mother's clothes in hot water. If these taboos were not observed it would lead to a miscarriage, still birth or the baby born with a physical handicap. In the past, the Han-Chinese, Tujia and She people all observed these taboos. It is said, nowadays in China, not many people believe in the god of foetus except perhaps in some remote areas there are people who still observe these taboos.

TABOOS IN THE BEDROOM

In the bedroom, there were many taboos to be observed by the family of the pregnant woman. Any bricks or stones in the bedroom were not to be moved and no damage must come to it as it was afraid that the god of foetus might be moved in the process. As it was believed the god of foetus could move itself, change its position every month but it was a taboo to help it to move just in case it was harmed during the move.

Nails were taboo in the bedroom and there must not be any nails on the walls, furniture, door, and windows. According to the custom, it was thought that it would hurt the god of foetus. If unfortunately, the god of foetus was nailed in the process, it might result in retarding the growth of the foetus.

In Hubei, it was a taboo to hang portraits in the bedroom of a pregnant woman. It was said, if the pregnant woman were looking at the person in the picture, her foetus would look like the person in the picture. This was known as 'huan tai', meaning, 'change foetus'. According to a text of the Manchu period, in Hubei, this taboo was strictly observed by pregnant women. The people there believed that if a pregnant woman saw the image of another person in a picture it would go into her womb and change her own foetus and place itself in the womb so that the foetus would look like the image. Consequently, in the bedroom of a pregnant woman, pictures were either hidden away, got rid of or the eyes of the images were pricked with pins so that it could not huan tai.

Scissors, needles, and threads were not to be used in the bedroom just in case some clothing was cut and the god of foetus happened to be there and get hurt by the cutting. If the god of foetus were hurt the baby would be born without ears or with folding ears that would not live, or the baby would be born blind.

If things were tied in the bedroom, it was said, the pregnant woman would give birth to a baby with fingers that could not be straightened or a strange baby with crooked hands and legs.

Another belief was the baby would be born with the umbilical cord round the neck.

If a woman put a lid on a bottle, it was said, her baby would be born with blocked mouth, nose, ears, and anus. This had to do with the belief that if a pregnant woman put a lid on a bottle, it was as though she was putting a lid on the mouth, nose, ears, and anus of her foetus. This taboo was observed in Zhejiang in a place called Wenzhou.

The pregnant woman must not use cold water for bathing because cold water would harm the foetus. During a bath, she had to make sure that the bath water was warm enough.

The pregnant woman must not have any threads and ropes hung over her shoulders as it was afraid that the umbilical cord might be hanging over the baby's neck during the birth.

It was believed that the foetus in the mother's womb was sucking a thing which was similar to a nipple. The pregnant woman must not lift her hands up to take, touch or hang anything as it was believed this 'nipple' would come off the mouth of the foetus, so it would starve or cause the mother to have a miscarriage.

Any person with the horoscope of a tiger was not welcomed in the bedroom. Although the person born with the horoscope of a tiger was not a real tiger in the real sense but many people believed that a person born in the year of that animal actually possessed the characteristics of that animal and that was why a person born in the year of a tiger was seen as a tiger that might harm the foetus in the mother's womb.

Among the Elunchun people, a pregnant woman was not to sit or sleep on a bear's skin and the skin of an animal known as 'zhang zi' (Chinese Water Deer), as it was believed, if a pregnant woman came into contact with a bear's skin and a zhang zi's skin, she would have a miscarriage.

196

There must not be any loud noise in the bedroom because it was feared that the baby would be born deaf. There must not be any repair work done on the door or windows as it was feared that this might cause the baby to be born blind.

Any big furniture such as chests, tables, chairs, wardrobes, and beds were not to be moved, to prevent moving the god of foetus. If furniture were moved about, it might cause the mother to have a miscarriage or give birth to a deformed baby.

If something were burned in the bedroom, it was believed that the baby would be born with moles, birth marks or badly burned.

These taboos in the bedroom were obviously meant to create a quiet and peaceful environment for the pregnant woman to have her baby. Sometimes it was impossible not to break any rules so when this happened a red paper was used to write down the characters 'tai shen is here' and it was stuck in one area. This way, the god of foetus was invited to a safe place so that people could do whatever they liked in other areas of the bedroom. Some people hired Taoist priests or Buddhist monks to chant some prayers, stick a strip of fu on an area so that people could do their work. If the god of foetus was accidentally moved then a kind of rite was performed by using a broom facing the area and moved horizontally three times and the words 'god of foetus, please move to another place and bless the mother and baby' were said. It was believed that the broom possessed a power. In the past, women were placed in a low status and that they were meant to do the sweeping and cleaning of the house. That was why the characters of 'woman' and 'broom' were very similar to each other. As women were also seen as broom witches a broom was therefore used to deal with the god of foetus.

TABOOS OUTSIDE THE BEDROOM

If the bedroom were the place the god of foetus usually hung around then when the pregnant woman left the bedroom she would be moving away from the protection of the god of foetus. Although sometimes the god of foetus stayed in the stomach of the pregnant woman but not all the time. When the pregnant woman went out of the bedroom there were certain taboos that she must observe.

Crossing over the bottom of the door frame with a pinch of salt in her hand was a taboo. If she did, she would have a miscarriage during the birth. If she did that, she would offend the god of the door frame and when she was giving birth the baby's hand would come out first, so it was said.

Standing at the front door to look at people outside the house sticking her head in and out of the door was a taboo. If she did, during the birth, the baby would not be able to come out easily. In Honan, it was a taboo for a pregnant woman to sit under the eaves, it was afraid that the foetus would have a stroke.

Staying up all night outside the bedroom was also a taboo because at night-time there were too many ghosts outside the bedroom. It was afraid that the 'evil air' might harm the baby. As it was said, the 'black tiger god' and the 'white tiger god' were active at night and if the pregnant woman saw them it would be bad for the foetus. Another worry was, she might be attacked by evil demons and as a result gave birth to a 'guai tai' meaning a 'non-human baby'.

In Yunnan, among the Yi people in the Wei Shan area, it was a taboo for the pregnant woman to climb fruit trees. Climbing trees was of course dangerous because she might fall and hurt herself and the foetus. Also, the fruit of the trees were like the foetus in the womb, if the fruit were picked then the baby would be born prematurely.

198

Among the Manchurian people, a woman who was more than five months pregnant was to keep away from the animals, not to enter the stable and not to pull the horses. An Ewenke pregnant woman must not sit on a mule cart, fearing that she might be kicked by the animal which would hurt the foetus. Among the Han-Chinese and the She people, it was a taboo for the pregnant woman to step over the ropes used for tying the cows as it was believed, a cow carried her calf for twelve months and if she did step over the ropes it was feared that she would be pregnant for twelve months and that was a sign of a difficult birth.

In the past, it was a taboo for a pregnant woman to step over a scale because there were sixteen liang in a jin, (one jin is equivalent to 1 1/3lb, one liang is equivalent to 2 1/2 ozs). If she did, it was feared that her pregnancy might be extended to sixteen months. When a She woman was pregnant, she must not step over a bearer's pole if she did, she would have a miscarriage.

In Honan, it was a taboo for a pregnant woman to sit under the vine. According to legend, deities and ghosts liked to hide under the vine, so it was feared that the pregnant woman might be struck by 'evil air'. Also, they worried that she would give birth to a 'pu tau quai tai', meaning, a non-human foetus which looked like a bunch of grapes. In Hunan, it was a taboo for a pregnant woman to step on fallen flowers otherwise during the birth the legs of the baby would come out first. Among the Yi people in Wei Shan in Yunnan, a pregnant woman was not allowed to hang her clothes to dry next to a beehive, it was a taboo. In the old days, the moon was regarded as the symbol of a woman. Due to this belief, it was a taboo for a pregnant woman to look at the eclipse of the moon or anything unusual as it would lead to her becoming anaemic and having a miscarriage or having a deformed baby.

In Taiwan, the seventh month was said to be full of hungry ghosts. During this month, it was a taboo for the pregnant woman to take the bathtub to the courtyard just in case she forgot to bring it back before dark and offend the black tiger god, lonely spirits or hungry ghosts and it would be bad for the foetus.

It was a taboo for a pregnant woman to watch opera shows and puppet shows and there were many reasons. One reason was, after watching puppet shows a pregnant woman would give birth to a baby without liver and lungs, boneless or weak bones. Another reason was, after watching opera shows a pregnant woman would give birth to a baby with marks on the face. All these reasons had to do with the concept of huan tai. In Hupei, it was a taboo for a pregnant woman to look at an ugly character in the opera show because it was afraid that the foetus would be huan tai and the baby would look like the ugly character with a raised bump on the head and two lumps of flesh hanging from each side of the ears.

During the Manchu period, in the capital Beijing, when a Manchurian woman was pregnant, she had to stay at home because going out meant that she had to wear the Manchurian headdress and Manchurian high heel clogs, risking herself and her baby to a fall. Also, as most carriages had large wheels, so a journey out was not a pleasant one, a bumpy ride was bad for a pregnant woman because it might hurt her foetus. If someone said a woman was 'taboo about the carriage' they meant that she was pregnant. This huan tai concept left a deep impact in many people of the old society and many believed without doubt. Even if there were people who did not believe they did not dare to risk not to observe the taboo. However, it was one way to restrict a pregnant woman from going to a crowded place so that she would not be pushed about or fall and hurt herself and the foetus. Also, if she watched the show, she might be too emotional laughing or crying and all these emotions were bad for the foetus.

ZHOONG FAN TABOOS

Some taboos connected with pregnant women evolved from the concept of 'zhoong fan' which originated from the concept that women were dirty or unclean and that their 'uncleanness' would offend the gods and deities. Of the various unclean concepts of women, pregnant women were considered the worst. Perhaps Zhoong Fan could be translated as a powerful offensive force.

Due to the unclean concept about pregnant women and the 'si zhoong si' taboo, (mentioned in Marriage Customs), it was a taboo for pregnant women to have anything to do with weddings. Not only pregnant women were not allowed to attend weddings but also not allowed to even look, especially not to go near a bride and not to touch the bride's sedan chair or her marriage ornaments, not to go to the new room and certainly not to sit on the bride's bed and not allowed to attend the wedding banquet. These taboos were observed by the Han-Chinese, Manchurians, Bai, Yi and many other groups of minorities in China.

Generally, these types of taboos had to do with the concept of si zhoong si that they might affect the foetus but more to do with the other party the bride and groom, it was afraid that they might be affected. It was thought that if a pregnant woman had touched anything in a wedding it would bring bad luck to the bride because a pregnant woman was seen as 'unclean'. In those days, a pregnant woman was called 'swang ren te', meaning, 'double human bodies' because of her unusual shape and the danger she had to face in childbirth. These reasons were enough for others to see her body as a taboo body.

It was a taboo for a pregnant woman to have any contact with another pregnant woman or a woman who had given birth. This had to do with the concept of 'si zhoong si', also the concept of unclean against the unclean and it was believed that whenever two tigers fight each other one is bound to get hurt. In the face of these worries, many people would prefer pregnant women not to have any contacts with each other just in case bad luck befall the women or one of them.

Besides the contact taboo, a pregnant woman sitting on the same bench or sleeping in the same bed with another pregnant woman was also a taboo. Apart from the usual worry about the contact, there was the worry of 'huan tai'. One woman might think that she was carrying a male baby and the other woman a female baby and by sitting next to the other pregnant woman, her male baby might be 'huan tai' by the other woman and she would end up giving birth to a baby girl. This kind of thinking was of course absurd but in the days of 'jung nan qing nu', meaning, 'sons are more important than daughters', (sadly, even today, to a very large extent, many Chinese still prefer to have sons than daughters), one could understand why people were so calculative.

Among the Elunchun people, it was a taboo for a pregnant woman to go into the maternity room. It was said, in the past, a pregnant woman said to another pregnant woman who was about to give birth, 'Wait a little longer, we will have our babies together'. Later, the other pregnant woman developed a complication, and the baby could not come out. Since then, pregnant women were not allowed to enter any maternity room. In the Lin district in Honan, a pregnant woman was also forbidden to go into a maternity room. It was feared that she would develop complications when she was having her baby. In the North-East, people there observed the same taboo. It was thought that if a pregnant woman saw another pregnant woman in her labour, she might develop psychological pressure and tension that might lead to a miscarriage.

Similar taboo was observed by the Bai people. After the birth of a baby, a bamboo item, (used for steaming food), was hung on the front door. When a pregnant woman saw this sign, she must not go into the house. Otherwise, it was believed the milk of the other woman would cease and there would be no milk to feed the newborn baby. According to the belief, the foetus of the pregnant woman would suck all the milk from the woman who had just given birth. According to the rule of the Bai people, if a pregnant woman did not know beforehand entered the house of a woman who had just given birth, she had to go to this family to splash water as a way to say that she was sorry and to put things right again.

In the North-East, this taboo was also observed. If a pregnant woman happened to enter the house of a woman who had just given birth, this family would insist that the pregnant woman brought the 'milk' back. The pregnant woman was required to prepare a large bowl of soup noodles for the woman of that house. When she was entering the courtyard of the house she had to shout, 'So and so, I am returning your milk back to you.' At this moment, the woman of the house inside her bedroom had to answer, 'Oh, the milk has come back!' When she received the bowl of soup noodles from the pregnant woman, she had to face the wall and eat and drink all the soup noodles. This practice was the same as splashing water of the Bai people, a way of saying sorry and to mend things. This way, it was believed, the water and soup noodles would turn into milk and go back to the mother's breasts for her to feed her newborn baby.

Among the Han-Chinese, Elunchun and She people, it was a taboo for a pregnant woman to have anything to do with death. She was not allowed to see any of the rites during a funeral. For the She people, their ancestors' tablets or pictures were very colourful, it was believed if it were seen by a pregnant woman, her baby would be born mentally ill. She was not to touch a coffin, watch the corpse being placed in the coffin, watch the funeral, eat any sacrificial food, or touch any funeral equipment otherwise it would bring bad luck. It was a taboo for her to go to a cemetery or walk the same route after a funeral procession had walked past. It was 'xiong zhoong si', meaning, 'inauspicious against happiness' and it would do the foetus much harm. These taboos were designed to protect the pregnant woman and her foetus because the continuity of the lineage was important to the Chinese.

As women were portrayed as unclean, they were not allowed to touch anything on the altar or take part in the worship of the ancestors and deities. For the Han-Chinese, it was a taboo for pregnant women to take part in the worship of the ancestors and deities. If a pregnant woman went near the altar and the ancestral hall her uncleanness would contaminate the place of the deities and offend them. As for the Manchurians, a pregnant woman was not allowed to serve the ancestors. In Taiwan, temples were among those places which were taboo to pregnant women.

In Hubei, it was a taboo for a pregnant woman to look at the portrait of the Mila Buddha. According to a text, whenever there was a monk begging for food in the villages carrying the pictures of the Mila Buddha on his shoulders it was a taboo for a pregnant woman to see him. According to the people of Hubei, if a pregnant woman saw the picture of the Mila Buddha her baby would look like him. Due to this belief, monks who carried the Mila Buddha's pictures or statues were not welcomed by most villagers. If a pregnant woman was unable to avoid the monk the only thing to do was to sit down on the ground, take her sandals off, then put her left sandal on her right foot and the right sandal on her left foot. As for the monk, he had to exchange the poles on his shoulders as well. After this little drama, the pregnant woman would be all right, and the rest of the villagers would chase the monk out of the village.

Watching the construction of a temple and the carving of statues of deities were also taboo. If a pregnant woman were around with this building or carving, it was said, the temple would be 'starved' of joss sticks and candles and the deities would have no power. This meant that the temple would have very few visitors because the power of the deities was contaminated by the pregnant woman. In the old patriarchal society, all decisions were decided by men. Women were unclean or dirty through the eyes of men. Since men looked down on women therefore, they thought that the deities did not like the women either. While performing the rites, if women were around especially if there was a pregnant woman, it would be a lack of respect for the deities. All activities concerning the worship of the ancestors and deities were carried out in a sacred manner which involved prostration which was not easy for women to do, let alone a pregnant woman, (Han-Chinese women had bound feet in the past).

However, according to the author Ren Cheng, this may not be the reason why women were excluded from taking part in the worship of ancestors and deities, (See Zhong Guo Min Jian Jin Ji). In the past, due to the sexual discrimination of women they were excluded from places where important activities were held. There was the belief that women were useless and hopeless in doing things, that they had long hair and that was why they did not know anything, that women 'could not accomplish great things', worst still, they were blamed for any failures. Anything that went wrong or was not done properly was blamed on the women, especially a pregnant woman. It was believed, whatever business, if in contact with a pregnant woman it would be finished, nine out of ten would be ruined. Due to this taboo, pregnant women were forbidden to go to places where important activities were held.

In the past pregnant women were excluded from watching important events in villages such as digging a well, erecting the beams of a building and building a stove. When digging a well, if a pregnant woman went near the place, it was said, it was a waste of time because either there would not be any water, or the water would be bitter or salty unfit for drinking. Building a stove and erecting the frame of a house were important events of rural areas as the stove had a stove god and the beams had a beam god. If the deities were offended by the bad air of a pregnant woman, people would be very angry and might ask for compensation.

In a house, the three most important areas were the stove, the windowsill, and the large stone mortar. It was a taboo for a pregnant woman to sit on these three areas. Perhaps it was all right for a pregnant woman to do her chores besides these areas but if she was tired, she was not allowed to sit on them because the bad air of her body would contaminate these three areas and would ruin the prosperity of the family.

In the North-East, the Han-Chinese there did not allow a pregnant woman to go near the large earthen wares for storing soya sauce. In the past, making soya sauce was an important thing for the rural people and so there were many taboos to be avoided. When the soya sauce was made it was stored in large earthen wares for fermentation. Stripes of red cloth were tied round the earthen wares. It was a taboo to move the earthen wares. For those poor peasants with very low living standards, to them soya sauce was an important ingredient which was used to enhance their simple diet. Due to the belief that pregnant women were unclean they were forbidden to go near the soya sauce earthen wares.

COOKING TABOOS

Although women's lives revolved round the stoves but during their pregnancies there were taboos to be avoided in cooking. In Taiwan, it was a taboo for a pregnant woman to use grass ropes to light a fire because it resembled the saliva of a baby. If a pregnant woman used it to light a fire her baby might have the problem of excessive saliva. In Zhejiang, when a pregnant woman was cooking it was a taboo for her to cut meat and fish otherwise her baby might suffer from broken skins or deformed limbs or a deformed face. When a pregnant woman was frying fish, meat or eggs she must make sure that they were not burned otherwise her baby would have a burned scar or a black mole on his or her body. It was also a taboo for her to roast meat it was believed that she would give birth to a baby with burned limbs.

FOOD TABOOS

In the past, many people believed that the development of a foetus, its features and temperament had to do with the food that a pregnant woman consumed. Due to this belief, a pregnant woman had to be careful what to eat, she must not eat any food that would either affect the normal development of the foetus or later caused the baby to be deformed. There were quite a few taboos in these areas.

When a pregnant woman wanted to eat something, it was believed that it was the foetus who was craving for the certain kind of food. At this time, the cravings of the pregnant woman must be satisfied to the full otherwise it was afraid that the foetus might suffer from 'hong yen pin', meaning, 'red eyes' disease' due to frustration.

Rabbits or hares were taboo food for a pregnant woman. This taboo food was said to be one of the oldest taboos, widely observed by many people. Rabbits and hares have hare lips and so it was feared if a pregnant woman ate the meat of a rabbit or hare, her baby would be born with lips like those of a rabbit. There was a reference in a text of the Han period which said after eating rabbit's meat her baby would be born with the lips of a rabbit. From this it shows that as early as the Han period this taboo was observed by people. However, Xiong Por Loong, a writer, in a text questioned this belief, 'Are we to believe that all the mothers of the world who gave birth to hare lips babies, were due to eating the meat of rabbits?' Xiong Por Loong was right to question because there is no connection between eating rabbit's meat and hare lips. However, eating rabbit's meat was not the only reason for having hare lips babies. In the Honan area, people believed that if a pregnant woman jumped or climbed over a cracked wall or chopped firewood at the bottom of the door frame, she would have a hare lip baby.

According to an ancient custom, if a pregnant woman ate the liver of a goat, her baby would have many dangers. If she ate the meat of a mountain goat, she would give birth to an unhealthy baby who would suffer from many illnesses.

According to another ancient custom, if a pregnant woman included glutinous rice and chicken in her diet her baby would have many worms. Duck was another ancient taboo food for pregnant women. If a pregnant woman ate duck, during the birth her baby would be coming out upside down, that is, the legs would be coming out first instead of the head.

Donkey and horse meat were also taboo food and widely observed. If a pregnant woman ate the meat of a donkey or horse, it would extend the duration of her pregnancy like a donkey or horse. This means that the duration of her pregnancy would be between ten to twelve months. This of course, was enough to worry anybody. This belief was even mentioned by the famous Tang physician Soon Si Miew in his text. From this one could see that this taboo was being observed by the people during the Tang period.

In some areas in Honan, fish was a taboo food for pregnant women. It was said, the baby would have scales over its skin. In ancient times, a pregnant woman was not allowed to eat dried carp, it was believed that if she did her baby would have lots of boils.

According to another ancient custom, if a pregnant woman ate eels and dried shrimps, she would give birth to a dumb baby. Also, it was believed, dog's meat, other domestic animals and wild animals would cause a pregnant woman to give birth to a voiceless baby. In Taiwan and Zhejiang, it was a taboo for a pregnant woman to eat crabs. If a woman had eaten crabs during her pregnancy, her baby would come out sideways causing a miscarriage. This taboo was recorded in the Sung period.

In some areas in Heilongjiang, it was a taboo for a pregnant woman to eat dogs' meat otherwise her baby would acquire the habit of biting people, for example, would bite the mother's nipples when sucking her milk. This taboo was also observed in Honan. In one area here, it was a taboo for a pregnant woman to eat the meat of a black dog. If she did, she would have a miscarriage.

Beef and snails were taboo food for a She pregnant woman. Among the Elunchun people, the meat of bears, wild boars and water deer were taboo food for a pregnant woman, otherwise she would have a miscarriage. Also, for a pregnant Ewenke woman, it was a taboo for her to eat boar's meat probably for the same reason.

According to another ancient custom, if a pregnant woman ate the meat of birds and preserved soya beans, her baby would have lots of freckles and black spots on the face. Also drinking wine would make her baby develop a character of drunkenness.

Eating turtle meat was another taboo for a pregnant woman since ancient times. If a pregnant woman had eaten turtle her baby would have a short neck. This belief probably has to do with the fact that a turtle hides its neck in its shell.

In Honan, in Zhengzhou, it was a taboo for a pregnant woman to eat unusual eggs such as eggs with soft shells or premature eggs with a chicken still inside. According to the people of the area, a pregnant woman would have a miscarriage if she ate these eggs.

According to an ancient custom, a pregnant woman was not allowed to eat shang shun, (like a raspberry), as her baby would come out the wrong way with the legs first. If a pregnant woman ate prunes and plums, she would give birth to a blind baby, also an ancient custom. As for pears, they were said to be 'cool' food, not good for a pregnant woman.

In Honan, it was also a taboo to eat hot chillies. According to one reason, the child would suffer from inflammation of the eyes, red eyes and sores around the eyes. According to another reason, the child might have a violent nature and a bad temper. A pregnant woman was not allowed to eat preserved soya beans and hui xiang, (probably a kind of spice), it would cause a miscarriage. This custom was also ancient.

Ginger was also a taboo food for a pregnant woman. With its finger like appearance, it was not surprising that it was a taboo food because people were afraid that the baby would be born with extra fingers. In the Eastern Han period, it was said, a man named Zhang Zhoong Jing recorded this in a text, proving this custom originated from ancient times. As ginger was considered as hot stuff, it was feared that a pregnant woman would have eye inflammation after eating it. Also, ginger might cause a miscarriage.

Cold and raw food were also forbidden food for a pregnant woman such as cold water otherwise she would have an upset stomach that would affect the development of the foetus. This custom also originated from ancient times.

This food was considered as taboo food for pregnant women because of its appearance and also sometimes due to the groups of food they belonged to, 'cool' or 'hot' food, that might affect the development of the foetus. Some Chinese physicians approved some of the taboo food because according to the author Ren Cheng, China since ancient times, has a history where there was no boundary between witchcraft formulas and medicine, (See Zhong Guo Min Jian Jin Ji).

Besides this taboo food, due to the zhoong fan concept, it was a taboo for a pregnant woman to eat wedding biscuits, wedding fruit, winter melons coated with sugar, crystal sugar, wine, and food from a wedding. This was to avoid 'si zhoong si' that might bring bad luck to oneself or the other party. Also, she was not to eat the sacrificial food and wine that had been offered to the ancestors and deities. The Wa people were especially strict about this taboo. Not only the pregnant woman was not allowed to eat sacrificial food and wine but also the husband.

FOETUS EDUCATION

'Tai chiao', meaning, 'foetus education' was developed as early as the Han period or before. Tai chiao was the responsibility of the pregnant mother who was expected to educate the foetus in her womb throughout her pregnancy. The development of tai chiao came from the belief that mothers were able to influence their foetuses in their wombs by their words and deeds because most mothers and sons had so much in common.

According to a text of the Han period about tai chiao, it said, when a woman had conceived, she should stand up straight, sit up straight, laugh but not, too loud, live in a quiet environment, should not get angry or quarrel and this is called tai chiao. Looking at these, one could see that the foetus education of that time already required the pregnant mother to follow rules and to behave in a certain manner that would influence and so educate the foetus.

According to Liu Xiang, (Han writer, 77-6 B.C.), in his Biographies of Eminent Women, Lieh Nu Chuan, he wrote this:

'After a woman has conceived, she should sleep properly, sit properly, stand straight and not with a hunch back, she should not eat raw, cold, sour or hot food, she should not look at sexual scenes and should not listen to sexual conversation. In the night, she should listen to the classical teachings and engage in good works. Then she will give birth to a clever, wise, and loyal child which will be above other children'.

By the time of the Northern Qi period, tai chiao had developed even further as more rules were added. According to one text:

'First month, must not eat wheat, fishy smelling food and hot food, not to do strenuous work, must sleep in a quiet environment, must avoid being frightened. Second month, must not eat hot food and food with strong smell, need to be in a peaceful environment. Third month, if want to have a son play with an arrow and a bow, if want to have a daughter play with a string of beads, avoid being depressed, worried and frightened. Fourth month be at peace physically and spiritually not to eat too much. Fifth month, rise up early daily, take a bath and change into clean clothes, live quietly, wear thicker clothing, do not eat too fast, do not overeat, avoid food that is too drying, do not expose to heat and avoid being tired. Sixth month, avoid being tired physically, live quietly, eat delicious food but not to overeat. Seventh month, do not bathe and do not wear thin clothes, avoid cold food, not to speak loudly or cry, make sure that the environment is warm, live quietly. Eighth month, meditate quietly, avoid being angry, avoid spicy food, avoid losing temper. Ninth month, not to get wet and cold, not to wear summer clothes'. (see Zhong Guo Min Jian Jin Ji)

212

From looking at what was said about the third month, 'If want a son, play with an arrow and a bow, if want a daughter, play with a string of beads', this shows that the ancient Chinese actually believed that the sex of the foetus was not yet formed in the third month and with some help from certain objects they might be able to get the son or daughter they desired.

It is said, some people still believe in this concept today. For example, in Zhengzhou, in Honan, the people there believe that when a woman has conceived, she must first eat a cockerel and she will give birth to a son. Also, the people there believe that if a pregnant woman eats peaches, she will have a son, if she eats eggs, she will have a daughter. Even Soon Si Miew, the Tang physician, recorded in one of his texts, that the ancient Chinese believed that the sex of a foetus was not yet formed during the third month of pregnancy. According to the author Ren Cheng, tai chiao was a form of witchcraft religion, (see Zhong Guo Min Jian Jin Ji). Like the rest of the taboos of the pregnant woman, he said, all had to do with foetus education, and most were included in the ceremony and medical texts.

Although the pregnancy taboos of pregnant women were meant to protect them, they really protected the welfare of the men as they were designed to ensure the continuity of the lineage of a man. Women in those days were treated as baby machines by men. Women did not enjoy special treatment during their pregnancies, in fact, they were robbed of their liberty and spirit throughout their pregnancies. In their diet, they were deprived of lots of different food. All in all, these pregnancy taboos were a form of pressure against the women. By looking at all these taboos, one could see that in the past, Chinese women had no say in their own lives and the hardships they faced. Today, the position of Chinese women no doubt has been raised especially those living in the cities, having access to modern medicine and who do not have to suffer like the women of the old days.

TABOOS IN THE PLACE OF BIRTH

During a birth, blood and water follows the baby out of the mother's womb. In the old days, it was considered as dirty blood, (to a large extent many Chinese still think that way today) and would offend the deities and would bring disasters to the family. This dirty blood was called 'sher kwang ze jai' which literally means 'blood light disaster'. Due to this, there were many taboos to be avoided at the place of birth.

As giving birth was an unpredictable event therefore usually a place was set up for this purpose. It was a taboo to give birth in the house. In the past, it was a taboo for an Elunchun pregnant woman to give birth in the place where she lived, a temporary shack was built away from the house for her to give birth. After the communists took over China, as a respect for this practice of the Elunchun people, a special maternity building was built in every village of the Elunchun people. Women had their babies in this building and stayed there for a full month. Later some people moved away from this practice and allowed their women to have their babies at homes. Ewenke and Herjer people also practised this practice in the past. Women who were giving birth had to stay in temporary shacks and were only allowed to go back to their homes after one month.

This practice was also practised by the Tibetan people, a woman was not allowed to have her baby in the tent where she lived, she had to give birth away from the tent. The Dulong people practised the same thing, it was a taboo for a pregnant woman to give birth in the house. It was believed that the 'unclean' air of the pregnant woman would zhoong fan the arrows, bows and other hunting equipment and hunting would not be successful anymore. When a woman was about to give birth, she had to give birth outside the house. She was only allowed back to the house after she had given birth and after the newborn baby was thoroughly washed. Today, this practice is still being practised

214

by the Dulong people. As for the Qiang people, they too had a similar practice. According to their practice, it was a taboo for a pregnant woman to have her baby in the house, she had to give birth in the animals' quarters among the cattle and goats.

Among the Han-Chinese, they too had a history of similar practice. As early as the Han period, there were records of such a practice. According to a text of the period, a nursing mother and her baby were 'unclean'. People did not like to socialise with a family who just had a baby, especially those people who were preparing for a wedding or a birthday celebration or those who were going into the mountains or those going for long journeys, they would avoid going near a mother and a baby as though they were avoiding a plague. Here is an account about this taboo which was still observed by people in China not so long ago before the second World War:

'Many rickshaw or wheelbarrow men would not carry a woman that had given birth to a child only a week or ten days before. They would only take a mother if the baby was a full month old, thirty days, when all evil was reckoned purged away. Often Miss Hsu would send out the servant to call a rickshaw, only to find the man pick up his shafts and go away when he realised that he was to carry a woman with a week-old baby. Then Miss Hsu would get angry and cry out, 'And where did you come from? Did not a woman bear you? Have you no mother? to the back of the departing man.' (See Birdless Summer)

The text also mentioned two contradictory views on this practice, it said that in Anhui and Jiangsu it was a taboo for a woman to give birth in the house but in the Jiangbei area a woman had her baby in the bedroom and they were not seen as unclean. From this it shows that different areas had different views about this practice and after a few millenniums of changes in the history of China this practice has virtually died out among the Han-Chinese.

215

For many people, including the Han-Chinese, Hani, Zhuang, Miao, and many other minorities, it was a taboo to let a pregnant woman give birth in her natal home. Once a girl was married, she belonged to her husband's family and so it was not right for her to have her baby in her parents' home. If something went wrong with her or the baby, her parents might be blamed for it. It was said, the 'dirty blood' of the birth and the 'bad air' would bring 'blood light disaster' to her natal home.

Once a Hani woman became pregnant, she would stop living in her natal home and would live with her husband. According to Hani traditional custom, all pregnant women were not allowed to give birth at their natal homes otherwise it was unlucky. If disaster befell the villagers of her parents' village the woman would be blamed and would be punished by her natal family and the community.

When a Miao woman was pregnant for eight months, she was not allowed to visit her natal home just in case the baby might be born prematurely at her parents' home. According to the custom, if a married out daughter gave birth to a baby in her natal home the prosperity of the family would be taken by her baby and herself to her husband's family because the baby did not share the same family name as her natal family. Also, they might bring disasters to her natal family.

If the woman could not wait to get back to her husband's home quick enough to have her baby then her sister would have to erect a straw shack for her to give birth. If there was no time to erect a straw shack and the baby was born in her parents' house, then a rite was performed later to get rid of the bad luck. After the woman and her baby had stayed the duration of a full month, they were then sent home. The husband of the woman would hire a witch to perform a rite in her natal family home known as 'cleaning the house.' Everything in the house was 'cleansed' and evil spirits chased away. Only then, the natal family was rid of disasters. By looking at all these one could see the importance of this practice.

This taboo was also observed by the Han-Chinese as early as the Han period. A text of the Han period mentioned that a woman should not give birth in her natal home because it was afraid that something might happen to her physically. Also, just in case, if it was a boy someone might exchange a girl in its place. During the Han period, people were very strict about this. In Shandong, in a place called Tai-an, if a woman had her baby in her natal home then her natal family would be poor forever. In another area the baby born in his or her mother's natal home would not live to adulthood. If this happened, the husband of the woman had to use an ox to plough round the courtyard of his house, to break the curse. This practice was widely practised in China. In contrast, according to the Uighurs custom, a married-out daughter has her baby in her natal home, especially the first born.

After the Sui and Tang dynasties, the Han-Chinese no longer observed the taboo that a woman should not give birth in the house. However, the unclean concept about the birth of a baby still lingered on therefore it was still a taboo for a woman of another family to give birth in one's house and also a taboo for one's wife to give birth in someone else's house. It was said, if a family let a woman of another family give birth in their house, their prosperity would be taken by the newborn baby. It was also said, the family who let a woman of another family give birth might not be able to have any more children or children with prosperity. Due to these worries, usually people were reluctant to let a woman of another family give birth in their homes.

If a baby happened to come early and a woman had to give birth in someone else's house, then according to the practice of the North-East, the family of the woman had to buy a new red cloth for the other family to cover the kank and the lids of the cooking pots. This would get rid of the 'bad air' and so ensure good luck for the family. In Taiwan, when this sort of thing happened, the family of the woman was required to give the other family a red cloth to hang in the doorway and sacrificial things such as cakes, biscuits, joss sticks, firecrackers and paper money to worship the other family's ancestors and deities. This was to redress the loss of the other family and to guarantee that the prosperity of the family was not taken by the woman's family. These practices reflected one of the proverbs which said, 'Rather lend someone to die but not lend someone to give birth.'

Even if a woman was giving birth at home there were still unclean taboos to be avoided. Due to these taboos, the location of the birth was carefully chosen. Among the Manchurians it was a taboo to use the west side of the house for giving birth. However, for some Manchurians, the central room was a no-go area for giving birth. To the Manchurian people, the west room was the place reserved for their dead ancestors, nothing must be hung on the walls of this room. The west room was a sacred place, and no one could simply sit or sleep in it. If the room were used for giving birth it would offend the spirits of the ancestors and anger the deities therefore it was a taboo to use the west room as a maternity room.

In Yunnan, a Hani woman usually gave birth in her husband's little hut, it was a taboo to use her parents-in-law's big house for giving birth. In Yunnan, in Xi Shuang Ban Na, the Jino people used to live in a long house made from bamboo. Within this long house were several small family units. Every family unit had their own 'huo tang' literally meaning, 'fire pond'. This was an area where cooking was done. Women were not allowed to give birth in the long bamboo house, they could only use the kitchen areas which were underneath the long house, to have their babies. After a woman had given birth she had to wait until her baby's umbilical cord came off before she could go back upstairs to the long house. Among the Hani people in Yuanjiang, a woman had to give birth in front of the huo tang. The practice required her body to face the back of the house not the sides otherwise it would be unlucky.

As I have mentioned before in Marriage Customs, the people of the North-East slept on 'kanks', heated beds made from bricks. There was such a saying among the Han-Chinese, 'The bottom of the door frame is the neck of the head of a family and the mattress of the kank is the face of the head of a family.' In the old society, it was a taboo for a woman to give birth on the kank's mattress. When a woman was about to give birth, the mattress was rolled up and put it aside. Some straws were placed on the kank for her to lie down on it so that the baby would be born on the straws and not on the mattress. If the baby was born on the mattress, it would be seen as though the woman had soiled the face of the head of the family so life would be difficult for both of them and hard to get on with each other. In the past, in Taiwan, there was also a similar practice of giving birth on a bed of straws. The only difference between the two places was that in Taiwan the people there placed the straws on the floor next to the bed but not on the bed. It was feared that the dirty blood would zhoong fan the 'zhuang mu' meaning 'bed mother' (a deity).

In the North-East, it was also a taboo for the bed to face the chimney when a woman was giving birth. People were afraid that they might offend the tai sway god. It was said, if the tai sway god was zhoong fan, the womb of the woman would cease to have children. According to the people of the area, it was believed that this tai sway god moved about on earth, moving in parallel with the sway xing in heaven, (xing means star). This sway xing, also known as ta tai sway, (ta means big), was above the siao tai sway, (siao means small), because heaven was considered above the earth. If the siao tai sway was zhoong fan, a woman would not be able to have children for six years and if the ta tai sway was zhoong fan then she would not be able to have children for twelve years. In those days, people embraced the idea of having many sons and grandsons, so it was only natural that they felt threatened.

In Taiwan today, some people still believe in 'zhan tu', meaning, 'birth picture' which is also known as 'an zhan tu', meaning, 'peace birth picture'. The birth picture lays down the right position where the bed should be placed for the birth. These birth pictures existed since the Tang dynasty where they were stuck in the bedrooms and it was a popular practice. According to the practice, if the birth picture was not followed the expecting mother and her baby were at risks from dangers or a miscarriage.

The place where a birth was taking place was a forbidden place and some people were not allowed to go in and out of this place. Among the Han-Chinese, Manchurian, Miao, Achang, Ta Khan Er and Elunchun people this included the husband of the woman giving birth. When a woman was in labour, if there was no other woman around in the house to help with the cooking then the husband would do the cooking. When the food was cooked, he would give the rice pot to his wife using a long pole standing outside the door. For the Yi people, during a birth, the husband also was not allowed to stay in the room to look after the wife, he had to leave the house with the rest of the men of the family.

If the woman who had given birth wanted to go out of the house an auspicious day had to be picked, her face washed, and floor swept. If not, she would be taking 'dirty things' out of the house. Ta Khan Er men were also not allowed to enter a room when a woman was having a baby because they were thought to be careless and might step on the baby. If a man accidentally went into the birth room he would be blamed if there was something wrong with the baby afterwards, for example, the baby had a cold later then people would say that it was because he had 'stepped' on the baby. One way to remedy this was for him to cut some of his toenails and give them to the family with the baby. These toenails were then burned with mugwort. When it was burning, the baby was carried over the smoke and someone would spit and say, 'Evil air, go away quickly.' Only this way, was the family able to evade harm and disasters. For the Achang people, after a woman had given birth, it was a taboo for men from other families to enter the courtyard of her house for seven days.

There were many reasons why it was a taboo to let a husband to enter the birth room. One reason was, it was afraid that the uncleanness of the woman would be a threat to men. Another reason was, as men belonged to 'yang' and women to 'yin', during the birth, the 'yin' of the woman was said to be weakened and so it was not able to stand against the 'yang' of a man. Letting a husband into the birthplace might expose the woman and her baby to great harm. Besides these reasons, there was a strict rule concerning the sexual life of a husband and wife, they must abstain from sexual intercourse after the birth of a baby.

Not only the birth room was a taboo for men to enter but even women were also not allowed to simply walk in and out. There must not be too many people in the birthplace or room. In Heilongjiang, the people there believed that if there were too many people in the birth room the woman would have a miscarriage. If there was one extra person in the room it would affect the birth, extending the labour by one extra hour. Due to this belief, the less women in the birthplace the better.

If someone was suffering from an eye infection, they were not allowed to enter the birth room otherwise the infection would be worse. Among the Han-Chinese, it was a taboo to bring any

221

metal objects such as copper and iron into the room. It was especially a taboo for someone carrying a key or keys. Things must not be taken out of the room or borrowed out. These taboos had to do with the belief that the woman's milk might be 'taken' away from her. To prevent this from happening, in the North-East, the people there used a lock to secure the mattress on the kank. It was said, this way, the milk was locked safely, and it would be all right if someone came into the room with keys. Among the Ewenke people, not only it was a taboo for someone to carry keys into the birth room but also a taboo to carry a shot gun or a horse whip. Maybe these things related to men and that was why these things were not allowed in the birth room.

Among the Manchurian people, it was a taboo to have jade in the place where a woman was giving birth. It was also a taboo for a woman who was about to give birth to look at jade. Before the birth, anything made of jade such as jade vases and ornaments had to be taken out of the room and wrapped with red materials.

According to the custom of the North and in Hangzhou, a month before the birth, the maternal grandparents sent gifts such as silver plates filled with rice straws covered with brocade or paper, flowers, food stuff, jujubes, chestnuts and embroidered clothes for the baby were placed on them. This was to hasten the birth.

The idea of burning paper money was to communicate with the deities, to wish for their protection. However, it was not recommended in the birth room or area, it was thought that when the deities descended the area, they would be zhoong fan by the dirty blood of the woman. This encounter might harm her and would not be lucky for both sides. There was another belief that if paper money were burned in the birth room the baby would get red marks or black marks on its body.

In Wuzhou, if a pregnant woman were in labour for a long time there were two things the husband could do to help. One thing was to break an oil container and the other thing was to bring a little lamb into the room where the pregnant woman was having a baby to 'ba' a few times. If these were carried out the woman would soon have the baby.

In Guizhou, if a woman was having a difficult birth, yellow fu, (strips of yellow papers taken from Taoist or Buddhist temples), were burned or worshipped so the 'chui sen niang niang', a female deity was supposed to help bring about a smooth delivery of the baby. Another method was to make a lot of noise by breaking a large bowl or an urn. Other methods included scattering some plants or classical texts in the bedroom so that the evil spirit that was preventing the birth would go away and the baby would be born safely.

If a Yi woman was having difficulty with the birth, her family would worship the stove god. If there was a sorcerer in the village, he would be invited to the house to chant some scripts to the stove god. After chanting, he would take some stones from a river or just round stones weighing from two to three ounces and put them in a burning fire to be burned. After this, he would put a small cypress branch in a gourd ladle half filled with water. Then he would put five hot stones on top of the cypress. At this moment, the aroma of the cypress would fill the air and he would take the gourd ladle and go round the head of the woman three times for her to inhale the cypress aroma. Finally, he would take some ash from the stove, mixed it with the water and let the woman drink it. It was said, this method was very effective and after drinking the ash and water the woman would give birth after half an hour.

Any woman who is giving birth for the first time is bound to be a little apprehensive if not terrified especially of the countless stories about women who have suffered complications or died in childbirth. According to one old Chinese saying, 'The more frightened a person is the more the wolf will frighten the person', it was said, it was all in the mind. In the past, when a woman was about to give birth, she was encouraged to feel relaxed and not to think about anything that might upset her as it was a taboo to think about anything that was not right, for example, anything that would worry her. Only this way would she have a smooth delivery.

Normally, as soon as a baby leaves the mother's body, he or she will make the first cry into the world. However, if a baby did not cry, according to the people of Chongqing, if someone walked to the door frame of the bedroom and called the name of the baby's father then the baby would be able to cry. Usually, people picked the baby up and gently slapped the back a few times to make the baby cry. In ancient times, the umbilical cord or a spring onion with warm water was used to beat the baby's back gently to make the baby cry.

BIRTH TABOOS

According to an old belief, it was possible to predict whether a baby was able to survive after birth by the month it was born. Usually, it was. believed, if a woman carried the baby up to the tenth month then she would have a smooth delivery. If it were a premature birth, it was said, a baby born after seven months would live but a baby born after eight months or nine months would not survive. This kind of prediction was said to be quite accurate because people had so much experience after seeing many cases.

In the past, when a baby was born after seven months a vetting was performed to decide whether to keep or abandon it. According to a text with a reference about the Miao people, when a woman had given birth to a baby after seven months, it was placed in some water, if it could float, the family would keep it, if it sunk to the bottom of the water then it would be abandoned. Also, it was afraid that if a baby boy was born prematurely or a baby girl was overdue, they would not be able to survive, according to the belief.

In the past, in the North-East area, if a woman already had a few babies that died shortly after birth, it was believed that she had 'fan', (offended), the White Tiger and that most likely the child she was carrying would not live long either. There was, however, a way to break this. After the birth, the naked baby was put in a wok, then from the wok slowly put in the stove and then pulled out from the opening or mouth of the stove. This way, it was said, the baby was not snatched by the White Tiger instead it was 'pulled' back to safety. This means that a disaster was averted. Some children in the area are given baby names such as 'la wor zi', meaning, 'pull wok child' which originated from this practice.

The Eight Characters was a practice that had dominated the lives of the Chinese people throughout the centuries or even millenniums. As soon as a baby was born its Eight Characters were decided at that moment. Most Chinese were superstitious, and they believed that the fate of a person was decided at the moment of birth.

Among the Han-Chinese, it was important to remember the Eight Characters otherwise one was unable to consult a fortune teller to find out about one's life, unable to know the 'good luck' and 'bad luck' of the future and even to find a future spouse would be a problem. In those days, people believed in the Eight Characters, for someone who did not know his or her Eight Characters it was like a stranger a 'black person' and there would be no prospect of marriage.

In the past, the Han-Chinese used to believe in an old taboo originated from ancient times. People were afraid if a baby was born in the same month as the father. There was a reference in a text which mentioned that a child that was born in the same month as the father would harm the father. This taboo was also believed by some of the minorities like the Bai people. As soon as a baby was born a fortune teller was consulted to write down the Eight Characters. If there were any similarities with the father's Eight Characters then the baby would be 'adopted', (not a real adoption), by someone or a deity. Another alternative was to erect a signpost on the road to avert this bad luck.

Within the Eight Characters, it was a taboo to be born in the year of the goat, as it was said, a person born in the year of the goat would encounter all sorts of disasters in life. There was even a saying to echo this belief, 'Ten goats, nine are not complete' which means nine out of ten people born in the year of the goat would not live their lives to the full. However, someone did some research on many people who were born in the year of the goat, the result was, their lives were not any different from those people born in the years of the other animals, their parents were alive, they had sons and daughters and they themselves were healthy and did not suffer from any physical disabilities. From this, one could see that people were blinded by this superstition.

Concerning the birth of babies, in the past, there were a few days that were considered as taboo, for example, the first day, (Chinese New Year), and the fifteenth day, (Lantern Festival), of the first lunar month, the fifth day of the fifth month and the fifteenth day of the seventh month. The first month was the New Year holidays. A baby born during this time would be seen as wicked not allowing the parents to rest during this time. Most people looked forward to the New Year annual holidays to enjoy themselves but if the baby came during this time not only would it be hectic but also the parents would be worried, anxious and tired about the birth. It was said, a baby born during this time would harm the parents when he or she grew up. In Honan, there was such a proverb which says, 'Male afraid first day, female afraid fifteenth.' If a baby boy was born on the New Year day, his life was considered as 'big'. As people were not allowed to hit their children during New Year day the parents therefore might find it difficult to discipline the child and the child would harm the parents. The fifteenth day of the first month was the Lantern Festival a time to admire the beautiful lanterns. If a baby girl was born on this day the parents would not be able to watch the lantern display but this was not a big thing, the case for concern was that when the baby girl grew up she would be difficult for the parents to control, only interested in leisure activities. There were cases that baby girls born on this day were being abandoned by their parents after birth.

Babies born on the fifth day of the fifth month were taboo babies. (I have mentioned this in the Duan Wu Festival). In fact, the whole of the fifth month was considered an evil month. Also, the fifth day of the fifth month was called the 'five poison day' and was considered an unlucky day. Any baby born on this day was believed to be the reincarnation of the 'five poison animals' and there were cases where babies were being abandoned or drowned by their parents. This shows how superstitions destroyed people's lives.

In ancient times, this taboo was challenged by Meng Zhang Jun, a scholar, (his real name was Dien Wen mentioned in Duan Wu Festival, Meng Zhang Jun was a title), who himself was also born on this day. Today, not many people believe in this anymore. The fifteenth day of the seventh month was called the 'ghosts' festival' in the past. On this day, people used to place lanterns on rivers. This day was believed to be the day when wild ghosts were reborn. Most of the babies born on this day were said to be reborn from the wild ghosts which were in the lotus lanterns and reborn again. Any baby born on this day would grow up to be a difficult child giving the parents a problem with discipline.

Any child born on this day would harm the parents. This was believed by the people in the North.

If a baby was born with its legs coming out first it was called 'ni sen'. In the past, usually the baby would not be able to survive in this kind of cases. According to a saying, 'The descendants of someone born in a ni sen condition would die in a tragic way but the descendants of a person born in a normal way would die in a normal way'. If a baby were born in a 'hern sen' condition it was just as dangerous as a ni sen because the hand of the baby would come out first and both the mother and baby would die. These two conditions were most feared by people during a birth.

In ancient times, if a baby was born with its eyes opened, it was considered as abnormal known as 'xing sen', as recorded in the historical text Zuo Zhuan. It is said, today some people still believe this. However, on the contrary, during the Han period, a Han scholar named Inn Sau had a different interpretation, he said, 'If a baby is born with its eyes still closed then it is called xing sen and this baby will harm its parents.' These two arguments contradicted each other but both focused on one area, that is the eyes, the 'opening' and 'closing' of the eyes.

If a baby were born with hairs on its face, for example, hairs on its upper lip, it was said, it would harm its parents. According to a text, 'A man should grow a beard, (Chinese men do not have beards but some old men grow a goatee beard) when he has reached the age of forty five but if a baby is born with a beard then it will harm its parents'. Also, it was a taboo if a baby was born with hairs on its forehead. This was a sign that prosperity came too early for the baby and it was not good because it would harm the parents. If a baby were born with teeth it would worry the parents because it was a sign of bad luck and it was believed the baby born would hurt the parents.

If a baby was born with an extra finger on each hand or had a hare lip it was a sign of bad luck. According to the Hani people,

228

it was believed that if a couple married on the day when there was an eclipse of the sun or moon they would have a baby with six fingers on each hand or with a hare lip. In the past, if someone gave birth to a baby with six fingers on each hand it was unlucky. According to Hani practice, the baby would be killed, and the parents would be kicked out of the camp. Their house would be burned to the ground and their possessions would be divided among the people of the community. Some people suffered greatly under this superstition with their families divided and homes ruined. Today, this superstition is eradicated. According to the people of Guizhou, if a baby was born with six fingers then the mother must have stolen somebody's ginger when she was pregnant. According to the people of Chongqing, if a baby was born with a hare lip then the mother must have chopped the door frame with a chopper during her pregnancy.

Deformed babies such as Siamese twins, those with two heads or those with extra hands were considered as unlucky and they were usually abandoned by their parents. In ancient times, it was thought the birth of a deformed baby was a sign to tell people that something was going wrong in the nation or in the world. There was such a reference in a text of the Han period.

It was seen as abnormal if the genital of a newborn baby was a pale colour. If the scrotum of a baby boy had a pale colour, it was said, he would not live long but if it were a dark colour then he would live a long life.

If a baby urinated and opened its bowel as soon as it was born it was a taboo. This means that the baby's life was hard and would harm the parents. Different areas had their own ways of breaking the taboo. In Honan in the Lin district, the newborn baby was picked up and his head was knocked on the wall gently three times and the taboo would be broken. In Taiwan, a bowl of water was placed in the birth room, if the baby had made a mess, then it was placed in the bowl of water and given a quick wash, and everything would be all right. However, if a baby had trouble with his or her bowels the solution was to pull the nails out of the bedroom and clear the rats' holes. This way, it was believed the baby would have his or her bowels opened.

Among the Han-Chinese and many minorities, having twin babies was not a taboo, in fact, having twins was regarded as a lucky thing. However, in ancient times, it was a taboo among the Han-Chinese to give birth to triplets. According to one text of the Han period, having three babies at the same time was like the animals and they would harm the parents. Nowadays, people are not worried about having twins or triplets anymore.

In the past, among the Hani people in Xi Shuang Ban Na, it was a taboo to give birth to twins it was considered as an abnormal birth and unlucky. At the order of the village chief and the religious leader the twin babies would be killed and the parents would have to leave the village, their house would be burned and their belongings would be divided among the people. If the couple concerned were well off, they could ask the religious leader to perform rites for nine days and slaughter many animals for sacrificial offerings. Then they could go back and live in the community, but they were not allowed to socialise with anyone for a year and never allowed to be involved in any of the religious gatherings. As for those who were poor, unable to afford to pay for the rites, for them, the only way was to move to other communities or find somewhere to live in the forest. This cruel practice is now eradicated.

As mentioned before, it was a taboo if a baby was born with the umbilical cord hanging over its neck. This condition was known as 'suang gua zhoo', literally meaning, 'double hang pearl', and was considered as an unlucky thing. If this happened, the baby was not expected to live even if it did live to adulthood. It was believed, in future, the person would be murdered or die as a result from hanging themselves. In the North-East, there was a practice known as 'por swor' meaning 'break lock'. If this kind of thing happened, a lock was used to lock the umbilical cord, the key was given to the midwife and she then unlocked the lock. This way, a tragedy was averted. After the baby was born safely the family had to go round to seven neighbours to beg for ancient coins and seven different colours of threads. The ancient coins were tied with the threads in a string and worn by the baby round the neck. It was called 'zhang min swor' meaning 'long life lock'. This lock was to be worn until the child was six or seven years old. In Taiwan, if a baby was born with the umbilical cord hanging over the neck it was also a taboo. When the baby grew up, a wizard was hired to perform rites several times to rid disasters.

Sons were greatly valued among the Han-Chinese but not daughters. If someone had given birth to a son, it was called 'ta si', meaning, 'big happiness', having a daughter was called 'siao si', meaning, 'small happiness'. There was a proverb which goes something like this, 'When a son is born there will be fortune. When a daughter is born every year will be poor. When a daughter is born the stove god will be angry for three days.'

In the past, among the Han-Chinese, there was a practice of drowning baby girls. This was also practised by some minorities. When a Tadjik baby boy was born, three shots were fired or someone shouted three times, to wish him a life of courage when he grew up. When a girl was born, a broom was placed near her head to wish her a life that was good in doing house chores. Looking at these two different wishes, it is not difficult to see that it had to do with the concept that sons were more valued than daughters. Perhaps one should not be surprised why a baby girl was not valued after one has read about the different treatment given to a baby girl and a baby boy since ancient times.

Here is a passage from the poem szu-kan recorded in the
Book of Odes:

'When a son is born,
He is cradled on the bed,
He is clothed in robes,
Given a jade sceptre as toy,
His lusty cries portend his vigour,
He shall wear bright, red knee-caps,
Shall be the lord of a hereditary house.'
'When a daughter is born,
She is cradled on the floor,
She is clothed in swaddling-bands,
Given a loom-whorl as toy,
She shall wear no badges of honour,
Shall only take care of food and drink,
And not cause trouble to her parents.'
(See Sexual Life in Ancient China)

Unfortunately, it is still the case today among many Chinese.
Due to the fact that sons were more valued than daughters
therefore when a woman had given birth it was a taboo to ask
whether it was a boy or a girl, just in case it was a boy and it died
later and if it was a girl the mother would feel sad and it would
affect her physical and mental state.

In the past, in China, due to the government's one child policy,
a couple was only allowed to have one child and old mentality
died hard so having a son is still better than having a daughter.
However, the Gaoshan people in Taiwan today still prefer to
have daughters than sons.

AFTER BIRTH TABOOS

To the Chinese, the placenta was also called 'tai yi', meaning,
'foetus clothing'. The storage of the placenta was very important.

Usually, 1t was put in a large tile pot and then buried under the bed, (this could only be done if the floor were not laid with cement) as it was a taboo to throw it away.

During the Ming dynasty, rules of burying a placenta was recorded. Here is the account of how a placenta should be treated:

'Er yi', (meaning baby clothing), needs to be washed with clean water, make sure that there are no sand, soil and grass in it, then wash with pure wine, place a coin in it, put it in a new jar, cover the mouth of the jar with green cotton material and store it in a safe place. After three days, pick an auspicious site in an area with plenty of sunshine and bury it three feet deep in the ground. If the jar is buried deep enough, the baby will enjoy longevity; if not, pigs and dogs will eat it and the baby will go mad; if it is eaten by worms and ants the baby will suffer from boils; if it is eaten by birds the baby will die; if it is buried near temples the baby will see ghosts; if it is buried near deep water and ponds the baby will drown; if it is buried near an old stove the baby will be frightened; if it is buried near a well the baby will become deaf and blind; if it is left in the road the family's lineage will cease; if it is thrown into a river the baby will become blind; if it is thrown into a fire the baby will develop very bad bleeding boils; if it is buried near old wood in a forest when the baby grows up it will hang itself.

In the past, in Honan, in the Lin district, the people there used to bury the placenta in the ground at the foot of the kank or at the corner of the wall or in a quiet spot in the courtyard. Some people buried a baby boy's placenta under the front door, it was said, to 'support the door'. The placenta of a baby girl would be buried under a fruit tree because a fruit tree would bring forth blossoms and fruit.

In Heilongjiang, some people thought, in order for their sons and daughters to obtain high official positions, (more for the sons than for the daughters really), they would bury their placentas in hills and high areas, as the saying said, 'Stand high could see far away'. Some people buried them under the front door so that, 'Their eyes could see six roads and their ears could hear from eight directions.' Some people buried the placentas of their babies underneath the door frame inside the house, it was said, to support the door frame. These had to do with the belief that the placenta could affect the future of the baby. This was the belief of fate reflecting in the practice, according to the author Ren Cheng. (See Zhong Guo Min Jian Jin Ji).

In Heilongjiang, there was even a belief that the way the placenta was buried could affect the appetite of the newborn baby. The placenta should not be simply buried, the opening of the placenta must be buried upward. This way the milk was in place and the baby would have no problem in sucking the mother's milk. If the placenta was buried with the opening facing downward then it would spill the milk and the baby would have problems, vomiting the milk most of the time. Also, if a placenta was buried inside out then the next baby would be a different sex, say, if the baby was a girl, then the next baby would be a boy. If the placenta was buried without turning inside out, the second baby would be the same sex as the first. For those families who were desperate for baby boys this was something people would not forget to do, to make sure that the placenta was turned inside out before burying it. When burying the placenta, it was a taboo to attract a crowd, so this was usually done at night when it was dark and quiet. After it was buried it was not to be moved again.

In Yunnan, the Hani people had a different way of disposing their placentas. Some people there covered it with hot ash and let it disappear into the ash. Some people dug a small hole near the huo tang, buried the placenta in it and then covered the hole with a mixture of ash and soil. If the baby was born with the umbilical cord curling round the neck, then the placenta must be wrapped with palm leaves and taken to the-back of the village or to the two sides of the village. It was then left on a tree to wither away. Later if maggots were found eating the placenta, then hot boiling water was poured over them to kill them off. From this, one could see that the Hani people took care in disposing their placentas and that they also believed that the placentas were mysteriously linked with newborn babies.

Besides the Hani people, many other people also believed that the placenta was mysteriously connected with the baby and so if it was not buried properly the baby would not suck milk properly and would die as a result. Also, if there was a fire at the area where the placenta was buried then the baby would be burned to death later. The placenta was seen as a second 'self'.

After the umbilical cord was cut, it was a taboo to throw it away. According to the belief, the umbilical cord was the same as the placenta, also linked mysteriously with the fate of the baby. It was said, if it was kept safely it would bring luck to the baby when he grew up and if he was being sued he would win the case if he wore the umbilical cord on his body because it would give him confidence and he would not be afraid when he was facing the judge. Also, the umbilical cord was considered as a 'bao', meaning, 'treasure' and was worn on the body for gambling, it would help the person to win money. Anyway, it was believed that one's umbilical cord possessed some kind of power that would protect oneself therefore it must be kept safely and it was a taboo to simply throw it away and it was a taboo if it was stolen.

After the birth, all bed linen was disposed of either by burying it or throwing it into a river, letting the current wash it away. It was a taboo to burn the linen. If the linen were burned the baby would have red marks on its body like being burnt. It was believed because the baby had contact with the linen so if they were burned, the baby would suffer too or even not live long.

After birth, the dirty water had to be disposed of properly. If the water was thrown away all over the place it would 'dirty' the 'sung sen niang niang', meaning, 'give birth goddess' (a deity who was believed to be responsible for delivering the baby) or 'dirty' the other deities and ghosts because it would attract criticism or even revenge from them. This taboo was observed by many people.

After the birth, a woman had to make sure that she kept herself warm. As it was believed, when a woman was giving birth all her bones 'would open', if at this time she caught the chill, then it would lay down the roots for a lifetime of illnesses. Due to this belief, a woman after birth had to cocoon herself in her bedroom, any gaps in the door and windows were sealed tightly against draughts. In Honan, after giving birth a woman must not expose herself to cold wind for a hundred days, otherwise she would develop 'zhan hou foong', meaning, 'after birth wind' which is a kind of rheumatism.

Among the Han-Chinese, Miao, She, Buyi and Yao people, it was a taboo for a woman after giving birth to bathe in cold water. Within the first three days, it was a taboo for a Miao woman to wash clothes. Among the Yao and She people, a woman must not have contact with cold water within forty days after birth. In Honan, Anhui and Shandong, it was a taboo for the woman to bathe, wash clothes or even wash her face and hands with cold water during the month after birth. Due to the concern that women must not wash in cold water, in the Honan areas, within the month after birth a woman was not allowed to draw water from the well. Similar taboos were observed by the Buyi people, but it was also due to the concept that women were unclean after childbirth. In one district in Honan, it was said, if a woman who had given birth went to draw water from a well, this well would be infested with 'siao hong zhoong zi', meaning, 'little red insects.'

Noise must be kept to a minimum at the area of birth because the woman who had just given birth must have some peace and quiet. Cleaning the wok and chopping firewood near the birth area were taboo because the noise would frighten the newborn baby.

After a Bai woman had given birth, other women were not allowed to enter her house as it was believed that they would 'step away her milk'. This had to do with the belief that women possessed the power to 'transfer' the milk from the woman to their own bodies to feed their own babies. To prevent this, many people set up their own rules. In Hubei, if a woman accidentally stepped into the room of a woman who had just given birth then they both had to exchange their belts. After a Han-Chinese woman had given birth, strangers were not allowed to go to her bedroom for a month, especially pregnant women, widows, those who belonged to the tiger horoscope, new brides and those in mourning. Usually, only family members or servants were given access to the room but if they happened to fall into one of these categories they too would not be allowed into the room because it was afraid that they would bring disasters to the mother and baby. In Qinghai, after a Tibetan woman had given birth, she was not to receive guest for a while.

In ancient times, after a baby boy was born, a wooden bow was hung on the left side of the front door of the house, it symbolised the strength of a man. If a girl was born, a scarf was hung on the right side of the front door it symbolised the femininity of a woman. Nowadays, among the Han-Chinese, a red material is hung over the front door to let people know that a baby is born.

Among the Zhuang and Miao people, they hung a straw hat on the front door to stop outsiders from going into the house after a baby was born. Among the Miao people, if someone went into the birth room accidentally, to avoid stepping dry the milk then that person had to wash his or her feet when coming out of the house. Another way to remedy this was to drink a bowl of cold water.

In Yunnan, among the Mongolian people, they hung a hat outside the front door. If the baby were a boy, it would be hung on the left panel and if it were a girl it would be hung on the right panel. This practice was to prevent outsiders from stepping dry the milk. As for the Yao people, fresh grass was knotted into a little figure and hung outside the front door to let people know that a new baby was born. According to the Yao people, it was a taboo for an outsider to wear straw sandals into the birth room.

In the past, in an area in Shanxi, a bunch of maize and wheat was tied with a piece of red material and was hung outside the front door. It was called 'kua hong zhi', meaning, 'hang red characters.' If the baby was a boy, a bow and garlics were added besides the red material. If the baby was a girl only garlics were added. This way, according to the practice, that it would stop people from entering the house and it would prevent the newborn baby from being ill and die.

Like the Yao people, the Hani people also practised a similar practice. Thorns, wild ginger leaves and another kind of leaf was cut into figures and hung with a wooden knife on the front door. These things were said to possess similar power as the ancient tao fu was able to deter any evil spirits coming into the house and to let people know that they must not enter. If someone who had no knowledge of the culture happened to enter the house then a member of the family would quickly pick up a hot charcoal and put it into a small bowl filled with water and gently flick some of the water at the baby. By doing that it would get rid of evil.

After a baby was born, the Qiang people hung a red banner outside the door to stop strangers entering the room of the birth, as it was believed that strangers would bring ghosts to the room and the mother and baby would be harmed. The Dong people used soft grass and chicken feathers, tying these with a cloth and hanging it outside the door of the birth room to stop outsiders from going in. If it was a boy, a red cloth was used if it was a girl a green and blue cloth was used. Some Dong people in other areas hung eggshells and green leaves taken from trees. Other minorities like the She and Lahu people also observed this practice.

Bed linen must not be moved until after a month, it was a taboo, otherwise the baby would not live long. This taboo actually let the woman rest peacefully for a month. In the areas where majority of Han-Chinese lived this taboo was observed.

During this period, the woman must not hit her baby as it was believed there was poison in her fingers. If she hit her baby or touch her baby's eyes, the baby would develop 'hong yen pin', meaning, 'red eye illness' or grow up not afraid of corporal punishment or become a difficult child. This taboo was observed in the South.

Before a woman gave birth and after birth, she must not have any contact with weddings and funerals, to avoid 'happiness against happiness' and 'inauspicious against happiness'. It was believed that it would not do any good to both sides.

After birth, it was a taboo for a woman to visit other people before the full month was over. During this period, it was known as 'chor yueh' literally meaning 'sit month'. When a woman was still in the chor yueh period, she was still bleeding 'unclean blood'. During this period, she was called 'blood smell ghost'. If she visited other people, she would zhoong fan their houses and her 'hot blood' would be all over their doors, being dirty and unlucky. If a woman visited someone shortly after giving birth it was believed after her death, she would have to wash the door frame of that family as a ghost. However, there was a way to avert this if she covered her head with a red strip of material, burned joss sticks and paper money and placed some cypress branches on the altar of the ancestors and deities of that family. Only by doing all that, she was able to break the unluckiness and to be released from the zhoong fan. This taboo was said to be observed by many people all over the country, especially among the Han-Chinese, She and Wa people.

During this period, a woman was not to visit a temple or be involved in any sacrificial worship of ancestors and deities. No doubt, these taboos originated from the concept that a woman was unclean after birth. It was afraid that she might zhoong fan the ancestors and deities.

During this period, a woman was not to congratulate another woman in the same situation as her. This taboo was to avoid 'happiness against happiness'.

After giving birth, a Tujia woman had to observe many taboos. When she was going out, she was not to wear a coat made of straw or grass, (it was a raincoat), not to carry empty buckets into the house, not to step her foot into a fireplace nor on a three-legged stool. After birth, if a Bai woman wanted to go out, she had to put on a bamboo hat because it was a taboo to let the sun shine on her head. If not, it would be an offence against the sun. In fact, it was to protect the woman from strong sunlight.

During the month of the confinement, it was a taboo for the woman to go out especially at night. Even if she was sitting in her own courtyard, it was a taboo to sit until the stars came out as it was believed, night time was the time when ghosts and deities began their activities. If they were zhoong fan it would bring bad luck to the woman and her baby. If it was absolutely necessary for her to go out of the house, then she had to use an umbrella. In the areas where Han-Chinese lived and in Taiwan this taboo was observed.

The droppings of geese were said to be poisonous and so it was considered a sensible thing not to raise geese if someone had given birth in the family. If the woman stepped on the droppings of the geese, it was said, her baby would get chicken pox. In the South, people believed this.

In Honan, in the, Lin district, after a woman had given birth, during her one month confinement, it was a taboo to shallow fry and deep fry any food and when boiling or cooking anything in the wok, the liquid must not dry up otherwise the baby would have blisters in its body. These cooking taboos were meant to discourage an oily diet after childbirth. However, if any cooking dried up, to remedy this or as the Chinese said, 'to break it', a bowl of cold water was placed in the wok.

Women who had given birth were deprived of certain food and this was widely practised by many minorities in many areas as it was believed that health and food were related and that food could affect their health and the health of their babies. Also, after birth a baby depended on a mother's milk. Due to these reasons, a special diet was planned for the mother which included food that were supposed to help her to produce plenty of milk to feed her baby. Different areas had their own different diets due to geographical reason and religious beliefs. Usually, the first few days after birth, the Han-Chinese, She people and some other minorities did not allow a woman to eat raw and cold rice, buns, hard food and food that was difficult to digest such as meat and oily food. Food such as eggs, brown sugar, chicken soup, noodle soup and porridge were encouraged. According to the people of Honan, raw food, hard food, and cold food were bad for a woman after given birth because they would not help her to produce enough milk to feed her baby.

241

In Hubei, it was a taboo for a woman after birth to eat pork and beef. According to the people of the area, pork was bad for the blood and beef would cause the baby to have difficulty in swallowing the milk. In Honan, it was said, if a woman after birth ate pork, she would be weak in her old age. However, in Honan, it was also said, pigs' hocks would help a woman to produce plenty of milk. Not sure why this part of the pig's body was any different from the rest of the body. Perhaps the poor peasants could not afford to buy pork for their women after giving birth, so they made up a story that pigs' hocks produced plenty of milk for a nursing mother. In this area, it was also a taboo to eat celery and chillies these were considered as bad because it would not help the mother to produce milk. For the She people, before a hundred days was over, it was a taboo for a woman after birth to eat ducks and geese. Also, a taboo to eat green vegetables and salt before forty days. Among the Hani people, a woman was not to eat sour, peppery, fishy smelling, cold and deep-fried food, beef, geese, ducks, rooster, ducks' eggs and ginger for the first two weeks after given birth.

After giving birth, an Elunchun woman was not to eat anything from inside a deer, pau, (Capreolus) and han, (Alcesalces) such as the hearts and livers. Also, she was not to eat the heads of these animals either. At the birth area, she was not to fry and eat the fresh meat of any animal. If it were eaten, the husband would not be able to aim at the animals properly during hunting. In Taiwan, it was a taboo to eat ducks and cold food such as pak choi, (Chinese vegetables), Chinese radish and salt. It was afraid that the woman might develop rheumatism after eating this type of food. According to the people of Taiwan, salt would cause rheumatism, and ducks' meat was considered as 'cold' food and poisonous. Plus, the word 'duck' sounds like 'capture' and 'dumb'. With so many unlucky reasons the duck was not to be eaten by a woman after childbirth.

There was a difference in the diet for a woman after giving birth between the North and South of China. As the Northern climate is cold and dry, rice porridge was usually eaten as the staple food and it was a taboo to eat boiled rice simply because there was more water content in rice porridge which was good for the cold and dry weather in the North. In the South, where the weather is humid and wet, boiled rice was the usual staple food for a woman after childbirth.

In Guangdong, in a place called Dongyuen, after a woman had given birth, a woman was hired to cook, wash clothes and look after her for a month, it was called 'pei yueh' which literally means 'accompany month'. If the family could not afford to hire a woman to help the woman then the mother-in-law had to help. The job of the pei yueh woman was to look after the mother and baby. Her chores included cooking all the meals for the mother, feeding, and washing the baby and washing the clothes for the mother and baby.

Nowadays, in Malaysia, most Chinese women after giving birth still follow some old practices and customs. After giving birth, in the first month, a woman must have ginger in everything she eats. Usually, a woman in her confinement must stay in the bedroom for a whole month, have pigs' hocks cooked in sweet vinegar almost every day and chicken, white wine and ginger soup eaten with rice the staple food. However, if the family could not afford pigs' hocks and chicken every day then dishes such as eggs fried with ginger and pigs' kidneys fried with ginger and rice wine are eaten with rice. According to the Chinese, ginger eaten in large quantities by a woman after childbirth is very beneficial to her health because she will not suffer from rheumatism in later life. I still remember very vividly, one of my aunts saying to me, 'When you get married one day and when you have a baby, you must eat lots of ginger so that it will get rid of all the wind and you will not get rheumatism when you are old'.

Currently in Malaysia, among the Cantonese speakers, those who can afford it, still hire a pei yueh woman to take care of a woman after giving birth. As the position of women has raised due to equality of the sexes, the old concept that childbirth is dirty is close to losing its market. Old taboos are dying out as people have access to birth education and birth rooms and birth places are now public areas open to all pregnant women and visitors. These areas are not taboo areas anymore. Although some taboo practices including some superstitious taboos are not easy to eradicate but only in very remote areas, they still have their values, some people are still observing some of these taboos to give them a peace of mind. Since it is still impossible to eradicate the danger in childbirth therefore the mystery remains and so any old taboos associated with childbirth will linger on for a long time.

NURTURE TABOOS

In Zhejiang and the coastal areas there was a practice called 'beg for milk'. In some of the areas, people only fed their babies with liquorice water or honey water but not milk in the first three days. Milk was fed to the baby only after the third day. Before feeding the baby with milk, the family had to go to one of their neighbours to beg for milk. If the baby was a boy then they must go to a neighbour who had given birth to a baby girl to ask for a little milk and vice versa. It was a taboo to beg from a family who shared the same family name. The whole idea about this practice was one's desire to wish that one's daughter or son was able to find a good future spouse but in Sichuan it was believed that it would bring more children later. However, a woman who had just given birth would not give her milk to other people, but it would be all right after she had given birth four months ago, otherwise, there would be the problem of 'happiness against happiness'.

244

When the mother was breast feeding the baby, she was to make sure that she was not suffering from hypothermia, hyperthermia, in a rage, or drunk so that the baby would not be harmed. In Chongqing, if the milk of the mother had dried up, then the solution was to boil a chicken in a wok. When the water was boiling some water was taken out and put in a bowl then splashed under the bed of the nursing mother. It was believed, this way, the mother's milk would flow again. Alternatively, the family could go round to seven neighbours and asked them each to give the family a little rice, cooked the rice into a porridge for the mother to eat.

In the past, it was not uncommon for a woman to hire a 'nai ma' or 'nai niang', meaning, 'milk mother' to breast feed her newborn baby. The reasons were usually, if the woman herself did not have enough milk or in the case of the wealthy they did not want to be bothered with the feeding. Only a healthy woman would be hired. Those with a body odour, skin problems such as eczema or with infectious diseases would not be considered just in case the baby was infected. In Wuzhou, a wet nurse, before setting off to her boss's house would first wash her nipples with salt water. By so doing, it was said, the baby and her would have 'yuan'. I am not sure there is an equivalent to this character, but it roughly means that they would get on well. A milk mother also hoped that after tasting the salty taste from her nipples the baby would not refuse her milk.

In Guizhou, after a baby was born his or her hands would be wrapped tightly with no freedom of movement. This way, it was said, it could prevent the baby from becoming a person with 'three hands' which means a 'thief'. Newborn babies were wrapped with materials, usually old materials were much preferred than new ones as it was afraid that new materials would rub against the skin of the baby. Some people used old clothes as nappies which belonged to the grandmother or great grandmother, for example, old skirts. Wearing these old clothes, the baby would live a long life.

Nappies must not be too thick otherwise the baby would be prone to develop boils or it would cause the body to become weak, and it would not be able to stand the cold weather. After they were washed the nappies must not be hung up high to dry. Also, they must be fetched indoors before dark and must not be left outside all night otherwise it would attract the evil spirits and harm the baby. After a baby was born, on the third day it was given a bath. This bath was called 'si san', meaning, 'wash three'. In Sichuan, red dyed eggs, silver and gold jewellery were put into the bathtub. After the bath, the baby's head was rubbed all over with an egg so that he would not develop boils.

After the bath, the baby was given a little 'siao gua zi' to wear, a little Chinese top but no trousers because it was a taboo to wear trousers at this time. According to the superstitious belief, it was said, a baby was not allowed to wear trousers until after a hundred days. Wearing trousers would restrict the movement of the baby's legs and if it died, it would not be reborn because its legs would not be able to move fast when it reached the underworld, so it would not be able to return to be reborn again. In fact, not wearing trousers would help the baby to develop freely. Twin babies had to be dressed the same as it was believed that it was the wish of heaven that the two babies were born in the same likeness. Parents were also proud of their twins and they were dressed the same to show off.

In Puning, in Guangdong, on the third day after birth a baby was bathed in water scented by twelve types of herbs and flowers. In Chongqing, on the day of the si san, a cooked cockerel was offered as a sacrifice to the 'zhu sen niang niang', meaning, 'bless birth goddess'. If the beak of the cockerel were closed, then the mother would give birth to a baby boy next time but if it were opened then the next baby would be a girl.

On this day, eggs were boiled together with mugwort and the hard-boiled eggs were used for rubbing the baby's head. Women without children would give birth later after eating these eggs, so it was believed.

Among the Lisu people, they are still practising an old practice. As soon as a baby is born, he or she will be given a bath in warm water. After the bath, a little honey or sugar is put on the lips of the baby so that he or she will grow up to be a good singer and that the songs are as sweet as honey.

Among the upper class in Hangzhou in the past, the baby was given a bathing ceremony at the end of the first month. The baby was put into a silver bowl which was filled with scented warm water. The elders of the family started the ceremony by stirring the water with gold or silver hair pins. Jujubes were thrown into the water and the young women present at the ceremony fought over them and ate them. After the bath, the mother held her baby in her arms went round and thanked everyone separately. After this, she handed her baby to her sisters-in-law, this was called 'changing the nest'.

Bathing the baby too much was a taboo as it was believed that it would develop boils and other skin diseases. The temperature of the bath water must be lukewarm not too hot and not too cold, and the washing time must not be too long. After the bath, a kind of talcum powder was put on the baby's body, to get rid of evil spirits. In the past, bathing a baby had to be done on an auspicious day. After bathing the baby, it was a taboo to splash the water everywhere otherwise it would offend the deities. As it was believed, during the first four months the god of foetus was still staying close to the baby therefore people had to be careful in what they did. If the god of foetus was offended, harm would come to the baby and that would mean death.

In many areas, a long-life lock was used as a gift for newborn babies. Some babies were given 'bai jia swor', meaning, 'hundred families lock' to wear. This means that the baby was able to borrow the prosperity and longevity of a hundred families and that the baby would live long. In Beijing, a family with a new baby boy would send someone to every street in the neighbourhood to beg for money. Each family was asked to contribute one coin. These coins were then tied with a string to make it into a chain and a lock was added. In Jiangnan, the people there had a different way of getting the coins. Seven grains of rice and seven Chinese tea leaves were wrapped in a piece of red paper. Usually, the family would have to wrap about two to three hundred pouches to give to relatives and friends. Those people who received the pouches usually gave one coin to the family. This money would be used to buy a silver lock with the inscriptions 'bai jia pao swor', meaning, 'hundred families treasure lock' on one side and 'zhang min fu gui', meaning, 'longevity and prosperity' on the other side. These coins were then tied up into a chain together with the silver lock. According to the custom, any baby wearing this chain would live a long life.

Babies must not be given any food that was raw or hard and any food that was difficult to digest. In the North, 'you bing', meaning, 'oil biscuit', (like a pizza), and vegetables must not be given to babies. In the first month, the baby was only breast fed, other food was not allowed. After the first month, it was given rice porridge, soup noodles, vegetable soup and meat stock but meat and soya products were not allowed otherwise the baby might become ill. When the baby was one year old it could eat rice and meat like the grown-ups.

In the South, after the first month, babies could eat rice and meat. In Zhejiang, in a place called Wenzhou, the people there practised a practice known as 'lik kuang' which means 'bring light'. Before the baby was about to start eating rice and meat the family must go to their neighbours to beg for chicken, duck, fish and pork for their baby but only when there was a wedding going on in the neighbourhood. According to the custom, it was to take some of the 'blissful light' from another family into one's house therefore it was called 'bring light'. If, however, there was no wedding at that time then the baby might have to wait several months before it was given normal food, just to get some luck.

Usually, the hair of a baby was shaved after a month or after a hundred days. As the hair of the baby was said to have been contaminated with the mother's dirty blood, therefore, it had to be shaved on the day of the full month before the mother and baby came out of the bedroom, to avoid offending the deities. In some areas, the times of shaving the baby's hair were not limited to the full month or the hundredth day. Male and female babies were shaved on different days, for example, a baby girl was shaved on the twentieth day and a baby boy was shaved on the twenty fourth day after birth. However, in some areas, a baby boy was given a head shave two months after birth and a baby girl one month after birth. In Puning, in Guangdong, one week after birth, the baby was given a first haircut. Shaving the baby's head was the same as a man shaving his hair. It was a taboo to have it done on the first month of the year which means the month of the Chinese New Year.

In the Zhejiang area, shaving the hair of a baby was known as 'ta kuang kuang', meaning, 'beat light light'. After the haircut, the hair was wrapped in a piece of red paper together with some dog hair and cat hair, (cut from the dog and cat's bodies), and tied with red and green strings. These hairs were to be kept in a safe place and not to be destroyed. In Hangzhou, shaving the baby's head on the hundredth day was called 'bai le', meaning, 'hundred joy'.

When shaving the baby's hair, it was important not to shave the whole head but to leave a tuft of hair at the top of the head unshaved. This tuft of hair was called 'xiao soon farr', meaning,

249

'filial hair'. In Honan and Shandong, it was also practised. After the hair was shaved it was wrapped in a red material and later taken to a temple to beg the deities to bless for longevity for the baby. In some areas, after shaving the baby's head, it was rubbed with almond as a precaution against rheumatism and boils. In Puning, the people there had a different practice. The rest of the baby's hair was shaved off all except a tuft of hair in front and at the back of the head. After that the baby's scalp was rubbed with some ointment. On that day, children of the neighbourhood were invited to eat soft boiled eggs and brown sugar so that they would be nice to the baby when he or she grew up. In Sichuan, a newborn baby had the first hair cut when he or she was forty days old. During the cut hair ceremony, the parents must not be present. The cut hair was rubbed into a little ball shape, tied with red and green flowers, and hung somewhere high up in the ceiling in the living room.

In Suzhou, the first haircut of a baby was considered a first happy event especially if the baby was a boy. Wealthy people used to invite musicians to play some music. Even those who were not rich would also invite people to a full month meal with wine and noodles known as 'te tou jio', meaning, 'cut hair wine' and 'te tou mien', meaning, 'cut hair noodles'. Every person who was invited to the meal was also given five red dyed eggs to take home. This custom is perpetuated till this day among the people in Suzhou.

In the past, a baby girl had her hair cut after one month, but a boy had his hair cut after two months. Before the hair cut day, relatives and friends would bring gifts to the baby. Gold and silver chains, gold and silver bracelets, ankle bracelets inscribed with the characters 'longevity and prosperity', expensive clothes, and materials. It was the custom of this area that a baby boy kept a tuft of hair at the top of his head while the rest was shaved off. As for a baby girl, a tuft of hair was left unshaved at the back of the head. Some baby boys had the top of their head shaved. This hair style was associated with Buddhism in that the baby would grow into adulthood. All the cut hair was rolled into a ball shape, tied with red silk threads, wrapped with a red and green silk or cotton material, and hung on the baby's bed to keep the evil spirits away. After the haircut, the baby boy was given a new hat and was carried by the wife of his maternal uncle for a walk around the neighbourhood. The aunt would carry a red open umbrella and a book with a string of coins tied with red and green silk.

Among the Yi people, some babies had their hair cut after one month, but some kept their hair and did not have their first hair cut until they were three years old. On the day of the hair cutting, the parents had to give a feast and guests had to bring gifts to the child. Before the haircut, the religious leader first read a script which had something to do with educating the child about manners, to respect the parents, to grow up to be a useful person. After this, one of the elders of the family would cut the hair of the child.

In Malaysia, most new born babies have their heads shaved on the day of the full month and I have not seen a baby with a tuft of hair on top of the head but I have seen a baby with a tuft of hair at the back of his head. Rather curious, I decided to investigate about the hair style because I had never seen anything like that before. I asked my neighbour, who happened to be the great aunt of the baby, why a tuft of hair was left unshaved on the baby's head and she said, 'Ah, this is called 'liu hou', meaning, 'leave behind' so that whatever he does, he will always leave something for other members of the family.' This is a legacy from traditional China and only the very traditional families still practiced it.

It was said, the top of the head was the area where the soul moved in and out therefore nothing must be done to hurt this area. This area must not be touched or beaten, if this area was hurt the baby would become dumb or become mentally retarded. Whenever the baby was given a haircut the hair on this area was left untouched and was tied into a ponytail and a red thread was tied over it. This was practised among the Han-Chinese. The baby boy would keep his ponytail till he was twelve or thirteen years old. Some ponytails were plaited into plaits, it was called 'eighty plaits'. In the South of Honan, it was called 'wei wei yi', its meaning was to wish the little fellow longevity because sons were especially favoured by the Han-Chinese but it also included the belief that the soul was moving beneath the hair.

Everything must be made sure not to frighten the newborn baby and so there were many taboos to be observed. No one was to shout or talk in a loud voice in the bedroom. Objects had to be made sure that they were not being knocked about in the bedroom. Strangers were not allowed in the bedroom. The light in the bedroom must not be too bright. The baby must not have any contact with things that were too cold or too hot. At this stage, the baby must be given a quiet and secure environment and when it has grown a little older its horizon and contacts would be widened. If the baby had a fright, the adults must not shout or raise their voices, just touch the baby's ears lightly to calm the baby. In Honan, in the Lin district area, there was a practice known as 'kua shen swor' which literally means 'hang god lock'. This lock was said to be able to prevent the soul of the baby being frightened or the soul being led away by strangers or wild ghosts. When a baby was born, a lock was locked on the door until after one month. Another alternative was to tie four copper coins with red thread in a string which was then worn round the baby's neck. As it was believed that the soul of the baby was like the things in one's house and could be secured in such a way.

Touching the sole of the baby's feet was a taboo as it was believed that it would grow up to be a timid person, afraid to walk over a bridge. Although, not touching the sole of the feet of the baby was to avoid frightening the baby.

After a baby was born, many people of different minorities practised the practice of hanging an object on the front door. One of the reasons was to prevent the baby from seeing strangers. In Wenzhou, in Zhejiang, a baby was housebound for a hundred days after birth and it was a taboo for outsiders to look at the baby, otherwise, this would zhoong fan the baby and would lead to the death of the baby. The She people also observed this practice, and it was a taboo for a baby to see any strangers during the first month after birth, afraid of zhoong fan.

According to the Yao people, if someone was wearing white clothing and straw sandals entering the bedroom of a baby, it would cry day and night, refuse milk and would not sleep leading to serious consequences. Among the Bai people, it was a taboo for someone who was carrying a bow and arrow to enter the bedroom to see a baby girl, but it was all right to see a baby boy. In Taiwan, a person with the horoscope of the tiger was not allowed to look at a baby, it was afraid that the ferocious nature of the tiger would zhoong fan and frighten the newborn baby. In Chongqing, two babies under one month old must not meet otherwise either one of them would die or the two of them would become mute.

Not only it was a taboo for a baby to see a stranger but also animals. In Yunnan, among the Wa people, it was a taboo for a baby to look at rats and ants because it would develop pimples. Before a baby was one month old it was a taboo to bring any hunted game or animals or vegetables into the birth room. This was observed by the Jino people. However, after the sun had gone down it was all right to take these things into the birth room, other times would be unlucky for the baby.

Hunting equipment such as a horse lamp, hunting knives, a hunting axe or similar things were not allowed to place inside a baby's cradle, it was a taboo otherwise, harm would come to the baby. This was observed by the Elunchun people. Among the Han-Chinese, it was a taboo to rock an empty cradle otherwise the family would have a baby that cried all the time. Rocking an empty cradle was as though the family had lost the baby therefore it was considered unlucky to rock an empty cradle.

Watching puppet shows was a taboo for a baby, it was feared that it would be harmed by zhoong fan or thought that it would become physically handicapped, as a result of watching these types of shows. Perhaps people were afraid that the baby would have problem with its limbs like the dangling limbs of a puppet.

In the Lin district in Honan, after a baby boy was born, it was a taboo to mention the word 'boy' within the first month, it was afraid that the evil spirits heard the word and snatched away the baby boy. No doubt, the idea was to deceive the evil spirits and to pretend that the baby was a girl. This shows that how much people valued their sons and the people who had a son were afraid to lose him. When people treasured something, they were afraid to mention it, fearing it would be lost.

In Hangzhou, it was a taboo to mention 'bai ri', meaning, 'hundred days'. When the baby was a hundred days old, the words 'bai le', meaning, 'hundred joy' were used instead. The mention of 'bai ri' was taboo because it was associated with funerals, the rite which was performed on the 'hundredth day' after death. On the day of the baby's full month it was a taboo to speak throughout the whole day, it was to ensure that the day of the full month went by smoothly. This was observed by the Jino people. This taboo was certainly a little extreme because it must be difficult for a family all under one roof not to speak to each other for one whole day!

Among the Han-Chinese themselves, it was a taboo to mention whether the baby was ill or not. If someone asked whether the baby was ill or not this was a taboo because the baby might be ill later, and the illness become worse. Also, if someone replied that the baby's 'health was good, never been ill before', this was also a taboo because if the evil spirits of illness heard this, it would inflict an illness on the baby. Also, it was a taboo to mention the weight of the baby whether it was fat or thin. If someone said that the baby was thin, it was afraid that it might lose weight and vice versa. This reflected the belief that 'If you say bad luck you will get bad luck, if you say good luck you will get good luck', so, the best thing was to bridle one's tongue not to say anything about the baby.

BABY ZHOONG FAN TABOOS

In the past, the concept of zhoong fan was seriously believed by many people in society. People had to be careful in what they were doing so that they did not zhoong fan the deities. People had to be extra careful especially when a baby was born during the first few days. During the first three days, people did not dare to be happy and celebrate the birth of the baby, over elation might take away some of the baby's prosperity and lead to its death. This kind of zhoong fan concept reflected people's belief in deities and evil spirits.

In those days, people believed that the eyes of a newborn baby were 'clean' and were able to see very clearly what was going on, including ghosts and evil spirits. If the baby started to have a fit, was frightened or looked at a straight direction with its eyes unable to move its pupils, this was a sign that the baby had seen something that the adults were not able to see. Due to this belief, for the protection of the baby it was not allowed to take part in any worship of the deities just in case it was frightened by the evil spirits and deities. Whenever there were any temple festivals, Buddhist rites or worshipping, it was a taboo to involve the baby or let it go near these events. Weddings and funerals were also the same. If unfortunately, it was unable to avoid a wedding or a funeral then a Taoist priest was hired to do something about this. Once it was dark, the baby was not allowed to be taken out of the house as it was afraid that it would be frightened by wild ghosts.

In the South, the people there believed that there was a 'zhuang mu shen' meaning, 'bed mother god', although some people called 'bed father god' but usually it was known as 'zhuang mu shen'. According to the belief, the baby was protected by the bed mother god the moment he or she was born. This bed mother god taught the baby during its sleep. When a baby was smiling, twitching its eyebrows, and twitching its mouth in its sleep these were signs that the bed mother god was teaching the baby. At this time, it was a taboo to wake the baby, if its learning were curtailed then it was afraid that it would become mentally retarded. As there was the belief about the bed god mother, people were afraid of any zhoong fan that might anger her therefore people had to keep her happy by worshipping her regularly. During the worship, clothes, food, joss sticks and candles were offered to her but wine was taboo, just in case the bed mother god became drunk and could not do her job properly, causing the baby to fall off the bed. Also, it was believed, when the baby was asleep the bed mother god would take the soul of the baby for a stroll. Due to this belief, it was a taboo to put any colours on the baby's face just in case the soul returned and would not recognise the baby. (In China, people put yellow sulphur powder on their children's faces during Duan Wu Festival, to keep away evil spirits). If the belief was true, then the baby would lose its life.

If someone had prayed in a monastery or a temple for a baby, then after giving birth the family had to return to the place to offer sacrifices. If not, they would anger some of the deities such as the 'sung zi guan yin', 'sung zi lao nai' and the 'sung zi niang niang'. 'Sung zi' means ' give son', 'guan yin' was the name of the female deity and 'lao nai' means 'old nanny' or 'old grandmother'. If they were not worshipped, out of anger they might 'take' the baby back. When the baby was three days old, a cooked cockerel was sacrificed to the sung zi niang niang. If the beak of the cockerel was closed, then it was believed that the next baby would be a boy. If the beak of the cockerel was open, then the next baby would be a girl.

At the temple, apart from presenting the agreed sum of money to the deities, a brick wrapped in yellow golden paper was placed in the temple, on it was written the name of the person who had prayed for the baby. This was a form of giving thanks to the deities. This superstitious legacy is still with the Chinese people in China today.

In Taiwan, if the family was offering sacrifices to the deities after the birth of a baby, unlike ordinary sacrifices, the chicken was prepared in a different way. Usually, the legs of the chicken were pushed inside the chicken but for this sacrifice they were not so that the legs of the baby would be long and he or she would have prosperity to eat well. Also, unlike the ordinary way of pouring the wine into the wine cups a little at a time taking three times to fill the cups, for this sacrifice, the wine must be poured and filled in the cups in one go. This way, it was said, hopefully the baby would urinate in one go in a large quantity instead of urinating many times with the mother having to wash lots of nappies.

According to a text, some people even linked the life of a baby with the picture of the stove god they worshipped. According to the custom, a picture of the stove god together with a horse and a dog was stuck on the wall next to the stove or hearth. There was a particular thing that people had to watch out for when they were buying the picture because they must not choose one with the mouth of the dog wide open as it was believed the new baby would not be able to live long. If the mouth of the dog was tightly closed, then the baby would be strong.

In the past in Jiangsu, the people there used to practise the custom of giving 'hai er teng', meaning, 'child lantern' to childless couples. These child lanterns were made of mud, it was believed that those families who received these lanterns would have children later. If a family received one of these child lanterns, they had to offer wine and food to the person who gave them the lantern. This child lantern was to be placed on the family altar in the living room. After the baby was born the family had to treat this lantern with care as if it was the 'life' of the baby. If the limbs of this mud lantern were damaged it was believed that the family had zhoong fan the deities, then the baby would be physically handicapped in the future.

In one area in Hunan, the people there used to practise a similar custom to child lantern known as 'sung zi', meaning, 'give son'. This tradition had a long history of several hundred years. Usually, on the night of the Mid-Autumn Festival, the fifteenth day of the eighth lunar month, the people with children would go into someone's vegetable plot and steal a big winter melon. People would not steal from good neighbours but only from someone with a bad reputation. With a writing brush, the face of a baby boy was painted on the melon, a thin bamboo stick was pushed into it and filled it with water. When this was done, the people would go into the bedroom of a childless couple secretly and put the melon with the bamboo stick facing upwards in the bed and cover it with blankets. At this moment, people were usually celebrating the festival in the courtyard. When the childless couple decided to retire for the night, as soon as they pulled over the blankets the water inside the 'melon baby' would flow out of it through the bamboo stick and wet the bed like a baby. Although the couple would have to change the wet linen, they were usually very pleased to receive a 'melon baby' from well-meaning neighbours. The following morning, the person who lost the melon would stand in his vegetable plot and scold his neighbours for stealing his melon!

HAPPY CEREMONY TABOOS

In the areas where the Han-Chinese lived, having a new baby whether a boy or a girl was considered a happy thing, hence there were many rites to celebrate the birth of a new baby. 'Si Li' means 'happy ceremony'. According to one old text, in an area known as Xinxiang district, the birth of a baby boy or girl was reported to the maternal grandparents on the third day. Food such as rice, noodles, a chicken, and wine were packed into special food boxes for the maternal grandparents. If the baby was a boy a cockerel was given, if it was a baby girl a hen was given. As a rule, the maternal grandparents would accept all the wine and only some of the food but not all of it. If a cockerel was brought to them, they had to pair the cockerel with a hen to be taken back and vice versa. If a goat was included in the gifts, they had to pair the goat with another goat, if not, they had to pay some money to pay for a goat. On the fifth day after the birth, the maternal grandparents had to bring presents such as jewellery and clothes to the new grandchild. Relatives and friends would give chickens and wine to the family. An auspicious day was picked to celebrate the birth of the new baby, known as 'zhe mein', meaning 'eat noodles'. After the full month, the maternal grandmother would send someone to fetch her daughter and grandchild to stay with her for a while. This record reflected the practice and superstitions of the areas where Han-Chinese lived and the ways they celebrated the birth of a child.

There were variations in some other areas. In the Lin district in Honan, the first baby whether a boy or a girl, 'pao si', meaning,

259

'report happiness', was celebrated with the biggest fuss. In traditional China, a rich family could afford several food boxes, wine and two mountain goats with bells hanging round their necks, to attract attention making a ding dong sound, all the way to the maternal grandparents' house. After 1949, among the peasants, during pao si, the 'si ter', meaning 'happy card' was placed in a small wooden box and then placed in a money bag to be carried by a young boy all the way to the maternal grandparents' house to report the good news. If the baby was a boy, the lad had to hang the money bag on his left shoulder, if it was a girl, he had to hang it on his right shoulder. On the way he was not allowed to change from left to right or from right to left because when he arrived there the people would know whether the baby was a girl or a boy. After he had arrived at the maternal grandparents' house he was treated with hospitality, given food such as 'low you bing', (like a pizza), egg noodles and a kind of soup. It was a taboo to give rice to the person who came to pao si otherwise it was said, the baby would always have a runny nose.

In an area called Shangchai, pao si was commonly called 'zhe si jio', meaning, 'eat happy wine'. However, besides this common term, it was also called 'zhe si mein del', meaning, 'eat happy noodles' by the paternal grandparents' family and was called 'sung zho mi', meaning, 'give bless rice' by the maternal grandparent's family. After the birth of the first baby, the elders of the paternal grandparents had to make a trip to the maternal grandparents' house to report the good news. During this visit, apart from giving the usual gifts there was one extra thing to bring. If the baby was a boy, they had to bring a cockerel; this was known as 'ta si', meaning, 'big happiness'. If the baby was a girl, they had to bring a hen; this was known as 'siao si', meaning, 'small happiness'. If there were twins, then there would be two cockerels or two hens or one of each. Once the maternal grandparents saw the cockerel or the hen, they would know whether the baby was a boy or a girl. Both families would then decide the date of the 'eat happy noodles', which is the full month feast. This full month feast must not be celebrated during 'zhong shi', meaning, 'midsummer'. It was a taboo because 'shi' sounds like 'die'.

Bamboo baskets were not used to transport the food boxes. It was a taboo because there was a saying which goes something like this, 'Use bamboo baskets to fetch water they will always be empty'. Among the presents given to the new baby by the maternal grandparents a chicken must be included. If the baby was a boy, they had to give a hen if it was a girl then a cockerel was given. This custom was to wish that the baby would find a good spouse when he or she grew up. During this feast, the paternal grandparents showed their hospitality to their in-laws. Garlic noodles was one of the dishes of this feast that was why this feast was called 'eat happy noodles'.

According to the custom of the Yi people in Yunnan, after a woman had given birth, her husband had to make a trip to her parents' house to report to them the happy news. Besides bringing wine and food with him he had to bring a chicken, but the custom was different from the Han-Chinese areas, a cockerel was brought if the baby was a girl and a hen if the baby was a boy. When the parents-in-law saw a cockerel immediately they would know that the baby was a girl and if they saw a hen, they would know it was a boy. After the parents-in-law received a cockerel they had to give a hen to the son-in-law to take home with him and vice versa. This cockerel or hen was to be allowed to live out its natural life, not to be slaughtered for food. The chicken that the son-in-law brought to his parents-in-law's house was to report the good news but the chicken that was given to him by his parents-in -law was considered as the "life" of the baby therefore it was not to be slaughtered. Later the maternal grandmother would send an urn of rice wine, a baby blanket, some cotton nappies, a baby suit and several hundred fresh eggs to the in-laws. If it was a first baby, the safety belt was embroidered with five different colours.

In Kaifeng, when reporting the good news, eggs were given as a symbol of birth. On the day of the birth of the baby, the son-in-law paid a visit to his parents-in-law's house to report the good news carrying some eggs with him. If the baby was a boy, six to eight hard boiled eggs were given. The number of eggs had to be in even numbers because single numbers were taboo. These eggs were dyed in red colours and each was dotted with a little black ink or ash taken from under a wok. If the baby was a girl, five to seven eggs were given, because even numbers were taboo. Red colour was also used to dye all over the eggs but not black ink or ash. After reporting the good news, the mother-in-law would give the son-in-law a piece of 'low mein bing', (a dough like a pizza) to take home with him. On the way home, he would tear the dough and feed the dogs until it was finished. According to the custom, this way, it would guarantee the baby to grow up into adulthood, saved from infant mortality because the low mein bing which represented his or her 'life' was already fed to the dogs therefore the baby had nothing to fear anymore, it would not face any more tragic crises.

During the Manchu period, the Manchurian elites in Beijing practised a custom called 'si guo er', meaning, 'happy fruit'. Si guo er consisted of chestnuts, eggs dyed with red additives, groundnuts dyed with green additives and apricot kernels dyed with yellow additives, packed in a small tray with four compartments, painted in red and gold and sent to relatives by servants after the birth of the first baby whether a boy or a girl. After this, whenever there was a baby boy happy fruit would be sent to the relatives. Relatives who received the tray of happy fruit would come to the house to attend the full month feast. Elderly people usually tell their newly married sons and daughters-in-law to eat some of this happy fruit, as they believed, after eating it, the daughters-in-law would have babies very soon.

In Puning, in Guangdong, after the birth of a baby, an announcement was made to the relatives and friends which was usually accompanied by a sweet rice pudding. After this, those who could afford it, would shower the baby with presents such as bolts of material, gold and silver jewellery, toys, pigs' hocks, or eggs but poor people would only give pork or eggs. Gifts from the maternal grandparents usually consisted of baby clothes, pig's hocks, red rice dumplings, eggs and pork boiled in wine. However, if the baby was a girl there would be no announcement and she would only receive noodles and white sugar as presents.

In Hangzhou, after the birth of a baby, relatives and friends came to the house to present the mother with rice, coal, and vinegar. The month preceding the full month was the month of confinement where the mother was confined to the bedroom for one whole month. Some people brought their gifts on the first day of confinement or on the seventh day, the fourteenth day or the twenty-first day.

On the third day of the birth, among the Dong people in Guangxi, relatives brought gifts of fresh eggs, chickens, glutinous rice, shoes, socks and three to five feet of home-made yellow fabrics used to make a little yellow outfit for the baby. The maternal grandparents were responsible for giving baby clothes and a square thing with four long strips which was used by the mother to carry the baby on her back, (a safety belt). Among the Dong people in Hunan, on the third day of the birth of a baby, relatives and friends were invited to a meal called 'eat third morning'. Those who were invited usually brought eggs or a couple of bowls of rice for the baby. During the meal, the host family would ask the fellow villagers for their support to keep an eye on the baby.

According to Tibetan custom, after a baby girl was two days old and a baby boy was three days old, relatives came to the house to present her or him with hada. Giving hada has a symbolic meaning of blessings and this custom is still practised by the Tibetans today. Everyone would use the hada to wrap round the baby's head. In the cities and towns, relatives usually brought a kind of Tibetan wine, oil tea, (tea brewed with oil) and baby clothes and hats for the baby's family. Hadas were offered to the mother and baby. In the rural areas, wine and oil tea and some food stuff were given to the baby's family.

Among the Bai people in Yunnan, after a woman has given birth, her parents will bring her gifts such as eggs and different clothes for the baby. All the clothes, shoes and hats and the eggs must have six each because the number 'six' means respect.

In Sichuan, after the maternal grandparents had received the red dyed eggs or chicken, they would give the baby clothes, shoes, hats, brown sugar, eggs and glutinous rice to the baby. In Hunan, among the Tujia people, when a baby was ten days old, the maternal grandmother would visit the baby bringing rice, chickens, ducks, eggs, baby clothes, socks, shoes, bed linen and a rocking cradle. This visit was known as 'huang yueh li' which literally means 'visit month ceremony'.

According to the custom of the Naxi people in Lijiang, in Yunnan, when a baby was one month old, the first thing the family would do was not to prepare for a full month feast but to go to the stationery shop. On this day, the mother and the elders gave the baby a bath, rubbed a perfumed oil and 'shui fen', meaning, 'water powder', (a kind of powder made of rice flour and water) and dressed the baby in green clothes. A pretty, good-looking girl was asked to carry the baby on her back to the streets using a brand-new safety belt beautifully made with cord or embroidered or knitted yarns. A gloriously patterned rug was used to cover the baby. As the girl walked along the streets, she sang till she reached the shop. In the shop she would buy a Chinese writing brush, an ink box, some Chinese black ink, and an exercise book. In the past, a book known as the 'san zi jing' was added to the list. These were the presents or treasures from the parents and elders to the baby. These were kept safely in a trunk or box until the baby was old enough and was ready to be educated. This custom was said to be originated from ancient times and it is still observed today among the Naxi people, it reflected the people's hope in their children to be well educated and cultured people. According to a survey, the Naxi people top the list of degree holders among the minorities in China.

In Anhui, on the day of the full month, after the baby was given a head shave, he or she was carried out to the streets for a stroll. When they met a man, the uncle would say to the baby, 'Do you recognise this 'shu shu' meaning, 'younger uncle'? Do not be afraid'. The idea behind this was to make sure that the baby grew up to be a confident person not afraid of strangers.

On the morning of the full month, according to Zhuang custom, the baby is taken out for a walk around the neighbourhood. Early in the morning, the maternal grandmother and relatives visit the new baby bringing gifts such as a special Zhuang safety belt, clothes, socks, shoes, cotton nappies and towels. At the paternal grandparent's house, food like flour balls in water, and different kinds of cakes and biscuits are offered to the guests. Every guest present must eat a little of the flour balls because it symbolises family harmony and the sweetness of life. After this, the baby wearing new clothes is carried by a young girl of thirteen or fourteen using the new safety belt to walk around the neighbourhood. Before stepping out of the door, the girl will be given an umbrella, it has the symbolical meaning that the baby will grow up with courage, able to go for long journeys, and be unhindered by the physical elements. At the same time, a few papers or a few pages from a book are placed on the chest of the baby so that he or she will grow up to be literate and know the rites well. Also, a few spring onions are thrown in as well, which has the symbolical meaning that the baby will grow up to be an intelligent person because 'zhoong', (spring onion) sounds like 'zhoong min', (intelligent). Afterwards, a feast is laid out for all the guests to celebrate the full month of the new baby.

On the day of the full month, like some of the other people, a Lisu baby is also taken out to the neighbourhood for a stroll. If the baby is a boy, an abacus, a Chinese writing brush and a few papers are carried by the person who is carrying the baby, it is to wish that the baby will grow up to be literate. If the baby is a girl then the person will carry a piece of new fabric and a pair of new scissors so that she will grow up to be good in dressmaking.

In Dongyuan, in Guangdong, after a baby was born the family would offer sacrificial food such as fruit, duck eggs, a type of very fine noodles and fried bean curds to the ancestors and various deities in the house. All these were cooked together like a broth. After the worship, the broth was given to neighbours and clans in the village. On the tenth day, the maternal grandparents would bring chickens, ducks, wine and ginger for the mother and baby clothes for the baby. In return, the family had to cook some food and send it to the maternal grandparents and to the neighbours. This custom was known as 'do ten days'.

When the baby was one month old, the maternal grandparents had to bring more presents for the baby. On this day, red dyed eggs were sent to relatives and friends by the paternal grandparents. This was called 'zhe te tou ya tan', meaning, 'eat shave head ducks eggs'. This custom of eating red eggs is still observed by many Chinese today. In this area, only the birth of the baby boy was valued, whether rich or poor, a family would always give a full month feast for a boy but for a girl the family would just simply cook some duck eggs and send some to the maternal grandparents, relatives and friends.

In Malaysia, among the Cantonese speakers, on the day of the full month, chicken, eggs dyed in red additives and preserved ginger, (preserved in sugar and vinegar), are sent to relatives, friends, and neighbours. In addition to the red eggs and preserved ginger, relatives and friends will also receive roast pork. These red eggs are sent irrespective of the sex of the baby. Usually, a feast is given at home, cooked by the family for the relatives and friends. Alternatively, for those who could afford it, a banquet is held in a restaurant known as the Full Month Feast. Relatives and friends are expected to give a present to the baby. Usually, jewellery such as gold bangles are given to the baby, (worn on the leg), but neighbours are not expected to give presents as they receive less eggs than relatives and friends and no roast pork.

In the west of Shanxi, on the day of the full month, the maternal grandmother will bring some tinned food, some food stuff and a couple of bread loops for the baby. Usually two bread loops are given, one small one fits inside a large one, but the family must return the small one to the maternal grandmother when she leaves. These bread loops are made with salt, pepper and sesame seeds decorated with edible red flowers and green leaves. Those who are invited to the full month feast usually bring baby clothes, fabrics, shoes, toys, and a bank note tied with red threads according to the financial situation of the individual. This is a legacy of the long-life chain of the past. On this day, in front of all the guests, the mother puts the baby through the large bread loop. This ceremony has two symbolical meanings: first, the round shape of the bread loop is like the full month; second, the baby is protected by the loop from sickness and infant mortality and will grow up into adulthood. After this rite, the bread loop is broken up and everyone is given a piece to eat. Noodles are a must on this occasion because the length of the noodles means that the baby will have a long life. This is the reason why noodles are eaten on the birthdays of the Chinese.

Among the Yi people in Yunnan and Guizhou, after a woman has given birth, during the first month, relatives and friends will come to the house to give her eggs. On the day of the baby's full month all those who brought eggs earlier are invited for a meal, known as 'eat happy wine'. Outside the front door of the house, a long red cloth is hung over the door touching the ground. When hanging the cloth singers are invited to sing songs of blessing.

When a Uighur baby is forty days old, female guests and children are invited to the maternal grandparents' house to celebrate a ceremony. There will be at least forty children under seven years old, boys and girls, amongst the guests or maybe more. More than forty biscuits are prepared for the children. (According to history, these biscuits were brought to China by the Turkish people. Not surprising that the Uighur people consume this kind of biscuits because their ancestors were Turkish). Jam and a kind of spread made with flour, oil and sugar are spread on each biscuit. Each child will hold a biscuit, together with their mothers they will say a blessing, praising the little baby that he or she will grow up into a good looking boy or girl, respect the elders, respect the parents and to be an able person. After this ceremony, all the guests, old and young are entertained with a feast. After this is over the paternal grandparents will send someone to fetch the mother and baby back to their house to live. This will be the first time the paternal grandparents see the new baby.

In Hunan, in the Qingyang area, before a baby was one month old, it was called 'tai mao gwei', meaning, 'foetus hair ghost' and it was a taboo to take the baby to visit relatives or neighbours. After a month had passed, the maternal grandparents would come to fetch the mother and baby to their house to stay for a while. This custom was known as 'jo man yueh', meaning, 'walk full month'. Before the journey, the baby was to be shaved for the first time, and the barber was given a red pouch with money. Before leaving the front door, the mother had to wrap a strip of red material round her head with a twig of peach or cypress. The baby's head was also wrapped with a red material. Wrapping the heads with red materials and wearing a twig of peach or cypress were necessary as it was afraid that the 'bad air' was still circulating around the mother and baby. This was to avoid any zhoong fan. When they were about to leave, the baby's paternal aunt, the sister of the baby's father had to put a black mark on the baby's nose. When they arrived at the maternal grandparents' house the maternal aunt, the sister of the baby's mother would wipe away the mark. According to the practice, the baby would live a long life. Mother and baby had to stay there for at least ten days, if not, as it was feared that the baby might not live to adulthood. At the latest, mother and baby would stay for a month. When they were leaving for home, the maternal aunt had to put a white mark on the nose of the baby, it would be wiped away by the paternal aunt later. There was a saying which goes like this, 'Black come white go, the baby can live to ninety nine'.

In Kaifeng, when a woman was paying a visit to her natal home with her baby, her brother had to welcome her baby to his house but if she did not have a brother then her mother had to do it. After staying for a month, on returning home, the paternal grandfather had to come to the maternal grandparents' house to welcome the baby back to his house, as it was a taboo for the paternal grandmother and paternal aunt, (the wife of the baby's paternal uncle), to welcome the baby. According to the custom, it was said, women were full of 'yin' and it was afraid that it might be unlucky for the baby's first trip going out therefore it was a taboo to let women welcome the baby.

From the time when the baby was born till it paid a visit to the maternal grandparents' house it was a happy occasion for both families during this period. However, at the same time people had to be extra careful so that it would not lead to anything going wrong that would spoil the happy occasion.

NAME TABOOS

As soon as a baby was born or before it was born, the elders had to think of a name for the baby. Usually the Han-Chinese used the surname of the father and two characters or one character are added to form the name. A Chinese who wants to invent a name for his or her baby has the entire vocabulary at his or her disposal. Quite often the given name he or she finds is a masterpiece of imagination. In the past, due to various superstitious beliefs, some people in some areas, before naming a baby had to consult a fortune teller. If something was lacking in the baby's life then people would try to do something about it by finding a good name for the baby to 'compensate' this 'lack', for example, if the baby's life lacked 'water' then a character with 'water' would be chosen, if 'fire' was lacking then a character with 'fire' was added.

In Kaifeng and in Zhengzhou in Honan, after a baby was born, on the first morning, according to a practice, the father had to go out and 'poong xing', meaning something like 'meet surname'. When he met the first person, it did not matter whether the person was a man or a woman, whether old or young, he had to kneel down and knock his head on the ground say to the person he had a new baby at home and ask the person to name his baby. In the past, people who woke early in rural villages were usually old men doing their work collecting human waste from door to door! These human waste collectors were mostly unprepared when they were being approached to name a baby but they could not refuse because it was the practice of their areas and so they simply gave a name such as 'kou liu', meaning, 'dog girl', 'zhu wa', meaning, 'pig girlie', 'shi kuang', meaning, 'dung basket' and 'lou tou', meaning, 'square basket'. 'These were

270

only baby names to be called by the family, so it did not matter. Some people even believed that these kinds of names were good because they would not attract any trouble.

If a family had no children or no sons, they would pray to their deities. If a son were born later, they would see that as a blessing from their deities. Hence some baby boys were named after their deities such as 'Guan Pau', meaning, 'protected by Guan Di'. (Guan Di was the General Guan Yu who lived during the Three Kingdoms. After his death he was made a deity, the god of war). In the north, some baby boys were given girls' names as it was thought their parents would have no trouble bringing them up. Some baby boys were given names such as 'little dog', 'black pig' or 'beg for food' for the same reason.

In Puning, among the wealthy, a male member of the family would ask someone of the gentry class or a well-educated man to name the baby. Special care must be taken when choosing the characters because they must not be the same as the father or an uncle. If the baby was often sick or had an unfavourable horoscope then the proper name was put aside temporarily and a name such as 'pig', 'dog' or 'stupid' was given to the child to prevent calamity. In some extreme cases, the child even had to address his or her own parents as 'foster father' and 'foster mother'.

Whether born as a female or a male, a Lisu is named twice in his or her lifetime. When a baby boy is seven days old and a baby girl is nine days old, they will be given their names for the first time. On the day of their weddings, they will be given another name for the second time. Usually, a baby's name is chosen by the father, grandfather, or great grandfather. Some names are chosen because of their symbolic meanings of peace and longevity. If the person who is choosing the name happens to see a bird flying, a dog barking or a pig squeaking, then very likely the baby will be named 'bird fly', 'dog bark' or 'pig squeak'. To many people, these names are hilarious but to the Lisu people, a bird is a symbol of freedom, a pig is the symbol of prosperity and a dog is the symbol of security. Some babies are named after people who are either wealthy or literate. This first name is called 'hoon min' translating as 'soul name'. This soul name is never used again after marriage except after death when the wizard calls the soul name of the deceased.

According to Hani custom, after a baby is born, the oldest person in the family will pick up the baby and use his index finger to touch the top of his or her head and give them a baby name. 'When the baby is three days old, a naming ceremony is held. On this day, the family will cook some glutinous rice, beans, and a hen. At the start of the ceremony, a bamboo table is placed in front of the house. Glutinous rice is rolled into round balls as big as a fist and laid out in neat rows on the table. Some chicken and beans are put on the top of each rice ball. When this is done, someone from the family will invite all the people of the camp to come and eat these rice balls. No one will come empty handed; each person will bring an egg for the family. Everyone will put the egg on the table and then pick up a rice ball. Usually, people bring several eggs and take several rice balls for other members of their households. After everyone has taken their share of the rice balls the family will perform another rite which has to do with education. If the baby is a boy, someone will use a hoe and dig the ground three times in front of the front door. If the baby is a girl, a chopping knife is used instead. They have symbolical meanings that the child will grow up to be a good farmer and to be domesticated. After this rite, all the villagers will be invited for a meal. If the baby is a boy, he will be given a name which is linked to the father's name. However, if the baby is a girl then she will not be given a name that is linked to the father's name.

According to Loba tradition, the name of a baby boy is linked to the father's name. Usually, there are two syllables in a Loba's name and there is no surname. If the father's name is Xing Yew then the son will be called Yew Pu, a name is added to the back of the father's name. The father's name is linked to the grandfather's name. For a baby girl, she will also be given a name that is linked to the father's name but her children's names will not be linked to her father's name because Loba women are married out of their families.

Among the Yi people, if a baby cries a lot the parents will take the baby out to 'meet name' like the Han-Chinese custom in Kaifeng and Zhengzhou but with some differences. The parents must prepare some food such as cooked chicken, a pot of rice and a bottle of wine and to make a small wooden bridge which is light enough for a man to carry it alone. These things are placed in a place near a brook and the small bridge is put over the brook. The parents with their baby will then hide nearby and wait. If a young man over twenty years old walks over the bridge they will quickly come out and ask him to give them one of the buttons from his shirt. The parents will ask the man to give their baby a name. When naming the baby, the man will hold the baby and bow three times in each direction of north, south, east, and west. After this rite, the man is officially the godfather of the baby. This will be followed by warming the chicken and rice at the spot. Afterwards, they will have a toast of wine and consume the food before going their separate ways, they will exchange their names and addresses and will promise to keep in touch.

In some areas, the ones who named the babies were asked to be the godfather or the godmother. Those with the surnames Liu and Zhen were the favourites because Liu sounds like 'keep' and Zhen sounds like 'success', these were considered as lucky characters. There were surnames which were considered as taboo such as Wang and Shi because Wang sounds like 'death' and Shi sounds like 'die'. Unlucky words, it was said, would cause the baby to die. However, if the godfather happened to have one of these unlucky surnames there was nothing the family could do about it as the practice did not permit them to poong xing again. The only thing the family could do was to pray to their deities hoping for the best. From looking at this, one could see that the practice of poong xing had something to do with 'poong yuen', meaning, 'meet fate'.

Among the Bai people, after a baby was born, if the eight characters were against the eight characters of the parents then the family would need to find a godparent, either a person or a deity. If the baby had adopted the emperor as the godfather, (of course, the emperor himself did not know about this. This emperor was the last emperor of the Manchu period. Aisin-Gioro Pu Yi), then his or her name would have the character 'Ai'. If the baby had adopted the deity Guan Di then the character 'Guan' was added to form the name.

In one district in Honan, it was a taboo for a man who was still single or a married man with no children of his own or a married man with a young baby to be a godfather. According to the practice, if a man became a godfather of a baby boy then he himself would not have any more sons. In China, a godson was called 'gan er zi', meaning, 'dry son' and a goddaughter was called 'gan nu er', meaning, 'dry daughter'. There was a saying 'get a dry son will lose a wet son'. From this saying, it is not surprising why some people were reluctant to be godparents because they had to protect their own lineages first.

In the Beijing area, usually only relatives and close friends were asked to be the godparents. An auspicious date was picked for the ceremony. On this day, the parents gave a banquet and had to give some gifts to the godparents. For the godfather, the most important gift was the hat. For the godmother, the most important gift for her were the shoes. Apart from these, gifts of fabrics were also given. A rice bowl, a pair of chopsticks, a long-life chain, a suit, shoes, socks, and a hat were the things given to the baby by the godparents. However, some people preferred the godparents to be poor and had many children as the Chinese believed that the children of the poor people were hardy.

In some areas in Shanxi, on the day of the baby's full month either the paternal grandmother or the grandfather would take the baby out of the house for a walk. The first woman they met would be asked to be the baby's godmother and the first man would be the godfather. Usually, people did not leave the meeting to chance, it was arranged beforehand to meet the right people, friends of the family or those with position in society.

In some areas, the godmother had to put on an extra-large pair of trousers on the day of the ceremony and sit on the kank. Someone would then put the baby into her trousers and the baby was taken out from her trouser legs. This means that she would treat the baby as her own son. After this, the godmother would put the long-life chain round the neck of the baby and gave him a baby name. During every meal, the baby would use the bowl and chopsticks given by the godparents. It was believed that the baby would be able to borrow the prosperity from the godparents and live a long life.

BURIAL CUSTOMS

INTRODUCTION

As early as the Shang dynasty, the Chinese had developed a strong sense of looking at their past, hence, the development of ancestors' worship. From the discovery of inscribed bones at Anyang in Honan in 1899, it uncovered that ancestors' worship has been practised by the Chinese since the earliest recorded times. From looking at these inscribed bones used for taking oracles it shows that a thousand years before Christ was born, the kings of the Shang dynasty, (1766-1112 BC), were making sacrifices to their ancestors and worshipping them as powerful gods. During the Shang dynasty, it was believed that the souls of the ancestors had to be fed by the living. If the living descendants neglected the offerings and sacrifices, the ancestors would suffer and might take revenge. They were believed to share exactly the same needs as the living and it was for this reason that the first Shang kings were buried with their wives, (buried alive similarly to the Egyptians), servants, their horses, dogs and possessions such as chariots, weapons, jewellery, working tools and utensils.

However, it is not known whether the common people of Shang practised ancestors' worship as their kings because so far there is no archaeological evidence from the common people of Shang engaging in ancestors' worship. However, it is assumed that the common people of Shang also practised ancestors' worship as their kings. During the Zhou dynasty, burials of this kind were still practised though on a smaller scale and less often. Passages in the Zuo Zhuan, the historical chronicles which cover the years from 722 - 453 BC recorded that this practice of collective burial aroused disapproval as it was considered barbarous.

From looking at burial things such as working tools, weapons and utensils of the Shang period uncovered at excavations, one could see that people of that time had already developed the concept of after life, that human beings continued to live in the other world after death. It was thought, the area where humans lived was the yang area, an area of 'light'. Yin, being the 'dark' area was the place where dead souls dwelled. After the death of a human being, he or she became a ghost and his or her life in the yang area came to an end. In the other world, the dead continued to live like before, their bodies still needed clothes to keep them warm, they knew their relatives and whether people were treating them well or not. Death meant that the soul of a human being had left his or her body, becoming an invisible, unpredictable spirit who possessed mysterious power therefore was able to harm or protect those who were still living in the yang world.

This concept was enough to make people not to simply get rid of their dead, instead they must be buried with a ceremony in order to show reverence and respect for them. If people wished the souls of their dead to be well in the yin world and to continue to protect the descendants in the yang world then after the burial many more rites were performed and the dead were offered tea and incense every day. Even today, people still regard burials as very important. Among the different groups of people in China in different areas there are different burial customs. These burial customs showed how people treated their dead and how they believed the souls of the dead were able to rest in peace only after performing the rites to them. Otherwise not only were the spirits of the dead not able to rest in peace but the living descendants were also unable to have peace.

DEATH TABOOS

No one can escape death, but everyone wants to prevent it from coming near. To the ancient Chinese, death was a much-feared subject therefore most people were afraid to talk about it unless the old or the sick themselves talked about the subject. Otherwise, people would try to avoid it. In the past, due to the fear of death, in Honan, the face of an elderly person suddenly becoming dark was a sign of death. There was even a saying, 'If a face has become black the person will not last for half a month'. When a person's temples and face became dark these were the warning signs of death. It was a taboo to say someone's face had become darker in colour because the comment was unlucky. When an elderly person was trying to hold a child and if the child was afraid and trying to get away it was an unlucky sign because it was believed that the child had seen the 'ghost' of the elderly person. People believed that the eyes of a child were 'pure' and so could see ghosts. There was even a proverb which said, 'A man is afraid of wearing boots a woman is afraid of wearing a hat'. It means that if a man had swollen legs and a woman had a swollen head these were the warning signs of death.

There were many taboos about the place and time of death. According to the Bai people, if they let an elderly parent die in their arms it was a chance to thank him or her for the kindness they gave, looking after them when they were young. To the Bai people, this was called 'receive the breath' and it was a sad thing if there were no children around to 'receive the breath' of an elderly parent. The Han-Chinese and a few other minorities believed it was a taboo if someone died without even a relative around or died without seeing the person he or she wanted to see. According to the custom, if someone died with a wish unfulfilled the soul would not rest in peace.

In Beijing, before a person was about to die, he or she was moved to another bed, it was an ancient practice. During the Chun Qiu period, Zeng Zi, a disciple of Confucius, was ill in bed and dying. Seeing that his master was lying on a beautiful bamboo mat, the little servant boy said, 'The bamboo mat is so gorgeous and glossy. Do you want me to remove it?' Zeng Zi replied, 'Yes' and then ordered the boy to help him out of his bed to remove the mat. As soon as Zeng Zi lay down again, he breathed his last. The mat was granted to Zeng Zi by a nobleman. This kind of beautiful mat was made for the official class. Zeng Zi was not an official therefore he was not allowed to die on it. Since then, it became a practice. However, not many people knew the real reason for changing the bed. It was said, if the deceased died on the kank it would increase his or her sins. It was also said, changing the bed was a way to zhoong si, that the sick person might recover and escape death. People were also afraid that the spirit of the deceased might linger on the bed. Changing the bed was for the benefit of the living descendants so that the one who was to use that bed would not be afraid of the ghost of the deceased.

Usually, people hired a bed from the caretakers, it was called 'lucky bed'. Those who could not afford to hire a bed would just take down one of the doors from the house and use two benches to support it to make it into a temporary bed. When moving the sick person, the eldest son had to support the head and the second son had to carry the waist and the third son carried the legs. If the sick person had only one son then grandsons and nephews could help to carry. When moving the sick person, sons and daughters would say 'father, (or mother), we help you to zhoong si'. When putting the sick person on the temporary bed, the head had to face the west and the legs had to face the east. Facing the west had something to do with the belief that the west heaven was the resting place for the dead.

In some areas in Sichuan, when a person was about to give up his or her last breath, he or she was moved from the bed on to a chair with the legs resting on a tray for measuring grains. According to the belief, if a person died on the bed, he or she would have to carry the bed on the back in the other world.

If the dying person died on the bed, he or she who slept on it was unlucky. In Honan, when a person was about to die, he or she was taken to another room and laid on a straw mat to breathe his or her last. If the person had died in the bedroom, it was considered unlucky. If this happened during the funeral, the coffin was accompanied by a live chicken so that the bad luck would be broken.

The best place to breathe one's last was the front living room, it was considered as the sacred place of one's house and to be able to breathe one's last here was a joy to most people. It was believed, if someone died in the bedroom before being moved to another room then the soul would remain in the bed in the bedroom. If this happened the dead person would not be reborn immediately and would be a bother to the family later. Under these circumstances, some people of some areas burned the bed including the beddings so that the dead soul could go to heaven. Another alternative was to hire Taoist priests to chant some Taoist scripts for the deceased.

If the dying person had living parents, then he was not allowed to move into the front living room to die but was taken to another smaller living room to wait for death to call upon him. However, for the eldest son who had benefited the family, say, looking after the fortunes of the family and uncles, he was allowed to die in the front living room even if their elders were still alive. For those who had not reached adulthood they had to die in other living-rooms on the floor and the beddings were laid on top of some straws. In Taiwan, when the dying person was being moved to another room, pictures of deities and urns were removed and hid in another place so that the dying person would not zhoong fan the deities. Among the Manchurians, it was a taboo to die in the west and north kanks because the north kank was the most important place in the house and the west kank was special and it would be unlucky if someone died in these two places. Usually, a dying person was moved to the south kank to die. In some areas, the dying person was moved to a special bed for this purpose.

In Yunnan, among the Yi people, if the parents were living upstairs and were critically ill, they had to be taken downstairs to the front living room to die. It was said, there were two reasons: the first was, it was feared that if a person died upstairs the dead soul was not able to come downstairs; secondly, it was afraid there might be movement upstairs. In truth, people were afraid that the ghost of the parent would come back to linger in the place where he or she died. As people believed in the concept that if a person died upstairs the area would be unclean and full of ghosts, hence, the practice of moving a dying person downstairs to die. However, since the beddings of the deceased were burned afterwards anyway there was no need for this practice as it caused much distress to the dying person. From this practice one could see that these people were trying to give themselves peace of mind. Burning the beddings was a hygienic practice.

When a person was about to die, the blanket was removed quickly. In Honan, it was believed that if a person died still covered with the blanket then the person would not be reborn as a human being again. It was feared that a person who died with the blanket on, might be reborn as an animal such as a pig, horse, ox, or goat. This probably had to do with the reason that if a person died with the blanket on then it had to be thrown away later therefore it was removed before the person died. Perhaps the people were being practical and made up the superstition as a cover up for their stinginess as an excuse so that others would not say that they were being unfilial. According to the author Ren Cheng, there are reasons to be sceptical about these superstitions because many of these superstitions had to do with practicality and they were in fact invented to cover people's stinginess since ancient times. (see Zhong Guo Min Jian Jin Ji).

The time of death was also a matter to be concerned by people. In the north and central China, people did not like a person to die between the first day of the first month, (Chinese New Year), and the seventeenth day because it was the New Year period. Dying in the twelfth month or the sixth month was just as bad. It was said, the people must have done something bad to die during these months. Although it was because the twelfth month and the New Year period were times of leisure and the sixth month was a busy month in agriculture so if someone died during these times the relatives would not be able to enjoy the festive season in the twelfth month and the first month and as they had so much agricultural work to do in the sixth month, the last thing they needed was a funeral to add to their busy months.

In Taiwan people did not like a person to die after the evening meal. The best time to die was in the morning before the morning meal. Dying at this time was as though the deceased had left 'three meals' for the sons and grandsons for the day. It was called 'liu san tun', meaning, 'left three meals', this means that the living descendants were not in want of three meals a day for the rest of their lives. If the person died after the morning meal it was afraid that the descendants have less food to eat later. If the person died after the evening meal, it was the worst thing, as if the deceased had taken all the three meals of the day away and the descendants would become beggars later. This was a very unlucky thing and the descendants had to call the Taoist priests to chant some prayers to avert the disaster.

It was thought that there was a link between 'death' and 'age'. In Anhui, those who died young during certain days in Spring and Summer were thought to be unlucky. It was said, they might turn into 'jiang shi', the living dead. One way to prevent this from happening was to go to a Taoist priest to write some characters on a strip of yellow paper then stick them on the coffin.

Those who had reached the ages of eighteen, twenty seven, thirty six, nine, nineteen, twenty nine and so on; could die any minute because they were at the 'gates' of death. All the ages containing the number nine, were called 'ming jiu' which literally means 'bright nine', meaning that the 'nine' was visible. Eighteen, twenty seven and thirty six were called 'un jiu', meaning, 'shade nine' which means that the 'nine' in these ages was hidden for example, there are two 'nines' in eighteen. It was said, death would call upon anyone approaching these ages, even if they were lucky to escape death, they would not be able to escape illness. Those that belonged to the group of 'shade nine' were said to be worse off than those in 'bright nine' because they were the most likely to be ill or dead.

Twenty three was also a danger age, another 'guan', meaning, 'gate', (presumably if anyone would pass through the guan would be all right) because a man named Law Cheng died at this age. According to a legend, a man had to compare his height with a snake, if he was shorter than the snake then he would not live longer than twenty three. To measure whether a man was longer than a snake, a bamboo stick was used as a substitute. If the man was longer than the stick, then he would be all right. There was a saying, 'Thirty six is a human being's natural life'. People were afraid to die before the age of thirty six because it was said, as long as a person lived over the age of thirty six the next life would be longer otherwise it would be shorter. Usually, the average age of life expectancy was fifty five, for those who died after the age of sixty it was considered as having lived to a great old age.

At the age of sixty six, it was considered as another danger age as there was a saying, 'At the age of sixty six, Yan Huang wants to eat meat'. Yan Huang, sometimes was called Yan Law Huang who was the ruler of the underworld. In the north-east of China, when a sixty six year old man was celebrating his birthday he was given sixty six jiao zi, (dumplings stuffed with meat and vegetables), to eat. These dumplings were made smaller than usual so that they were eaten in one go so that the old man was able to pass over this danger otherwise he would not. In Honan, when a man had reached the age of sixty six, he was given a piece of meat by his married daughter. Perhaps it was to return the debt to Yan Huang so that he would leave the man alone for a while. In some areas, this piece of meat was cooked and cut into sixty six pieces for the sixty six year old to eat. This way, it was said, the old man would be able to pass through the guan successfully.

Seventy three and eighty four were also two guans that the elderly had to pass through. There was a saying which goes like this 'Seventy three and eighty four, Yan Huang calls you to discuss business seventy three and eighty four, even if Yan Huang did not invite you, you will go and see him yourself". This was because Confucius had died at the age of seventy three and Mencius died at the ripe old age of eighty four. In Honan, an elderly person who had reached these two guans was given a live carp to eat, already cooked of course. According to the custom, it had a symbolical meaning, after eating the carp it was hoped that the elderly person would be as lively as the live carp, would be able to jump over this guan. In some areas, on the morning of the first day of Spring of that year, the daughter of the elderly person had to cook two boiled eggs, go down to the wheat field, roll the eggs on the field, bring them back to the house and let her father eat them outside the front door. It had a symbolical meaning that the elderly person had rolled over like the eggs and thus he had passed through this guan.

In Zhejiang, if someone died at the age of eighty one it was also a worry because nine times nine is eighty one. It had something to do with counting money and nine times nine was said to be the last count. It was a sign that the family's fortune would decrease. One way to break this bad luck was to break an abacus when the dying man was about to breathe his last breath and then throw it out of the window. Only this way, it was said, that the family was able to avert themselves from this bad luck.

Many people did believe in the concept that a good person died peacefully, and a bad person died a violent death. Those who died far away from their ancestral homes, those who died young, women who died in childbirth, those who died without intact bodies, for example, a leg or a hand missing or the head and the body in different places, those that were murdered, those that were drowned, those that were burned and those died under the wheel, (killed by horse carriage), were all in the category of violent death. According to the belief, not only the person suffered before death but had to suffer again when he or she reached the underworld and the descendants in the yang world might not be able to have peace. There is a Chinese curse which goes like this 'Rung nin pu tek how si', meaning, 'You are not going to have a good death'. If there was a violent death in the family, people would hire a Taoist priest to do some chanting so that the dead soul would have peace in the other world.

PREPARATION FOR BURIAL

Since ancient times, the Han-Chinese and many minorities practised the funeral rite of bathing the corpse. In ancient times, among the Han-Chinese, during the rite, the body of the deceased was washed from top to bottom. If the deceased was a female the men must not be present and vice versa. Among the Miao, Yao and Zhuang people there was a practice called 'buy water to wash the corpse'. Before placing the corpse in the coffin, a member of the family had to sacrifice paper money next to a river or stream and then fetch some water from it known as 'mai shui', meaning, 'buy water'. The water was used to wash the corpse as it was believed that after washing the corpse with this 'water' the dead soul was able to join the rest of the ancestors otherwise it would not be accepted and would become a ghost. Similar routines are practised by the Han-Chinese today by those who still engage in Ancestors' Worship. Usually, the eldest son of the deceased or a nephew if there is no son in the family, must fetch water, preferably from a natural source, to wash the face of the deceased. It is said, so that he or she may be properly presented to the ruler of the other world.

According to the custom of the Mo Swor people, the corpse was washed by the older men of the family and women were excluded from this funeral rite. Nine bowls of water were used if the deceased was a male and seven for a female. From head to toe the corpse was washed in a symbolic manner. As for the Yi people a male corpse had to be washed by men and a female corpse by women. The corpse must be washed thoroughly clean, if not, there would be disasters among the living descendants. White cloths were used to wash the corpse, after use they were kept safely. The water used to wash the corpse must be thrown away carefully so that people would not step in it, as it was believed if anyone stepped in it, the feet would split open. The wooden tub was thrown away in a place far away from the house where no one should pick it up or bring it back to the house otherwise it would be unlucky.

When Muslim people are preparing the corpse for burial, nails and toenails are cut, and any gold or false teeth are removed. After this the clothes are removed from the corpse and the body is washed thoroughly. The top half of the body and the bottom half are washed separately. Two kettles of water and two pairs of gloves are used. According to Uighurs' practice, the paternal male cousins will wash the deceased's body. If the deceased is a female it will be washed by women of the same generation. Before bathing the corpse, the living spouse can see the deceased but not after the bath, otherwise, the living spouse might zhoong fan the deceased causing his body to be uncleaned. During the wash, the imam will pray at the door for the deceased's sins to be forgiven.

After a person had died, he or she was dressed in a 'shou yi', the clothes for a dead person, literally meaning, 'longevity clothes'. Putting on the shou yi was a serious thing, it had to be worn before the person died. In the North-East, Beijing and Tianjin, it was a taboo for the deceased to meet Yan Huang,

286

(the ruler of the other world), with no clothes on so people tried to make sure that the shou yi was put on before the person died. However, in some areas, the shou yi did not have to be put on before death but still it had to be put on shortly after death before the corpse became stiff. When putting on the shou yi, which was actually a few layers of clothing, the son of the dead person could put it on himself then take the whole lot off together and then put all of the clothing on the dead person. At this moment, it was a taboo to have a pregnant woman around because people were afraid that the spirit of the dead person might snatch the unborn baby.

There were certain rules about the shou yi, the Han-Chinese preferred odd numbers, five, seven or nine layers of clothing for the dead. Even numbers were a taboo as it was feared that death would call upon the dead man's family again. In some areas, people did not want to use 'nine' layers of clothing because 'nine' sounds like 'dog', also it was thought to be unlucky and un-respectful. The sleeves had to be made longer than the arms because if hands were seen then in the next life the deceased would be a beggar.

Usually, the colour of the shou yi was blue or white or even red. Black was a taboo colour as it was believed that wearing black in death would result in being reborn as a donkey. In some areas, red was used so that the deceased would not be harmed. It was thought after death, the deceased had to go to a place where a messenger of the underworld would tear his or her clothes with a knife. Wearing red would deceive the messenger that the deceased was bleeding, that he had already done his job so he would leave the deceased alone. If the deceased was wearing black he or she would be hurt by the knife of the messenger.

Satins known as 'tuan zi' were not used for making shou yi because it sounds like 'broken sons' therefore people were afraid that they might not have any future generations. Silk was a favourable material for shou yi because 'chow zi', (silk), sounds like 'plenty of sons' and people hoped for many sons and grandsons. Using animals' fur for making shou yi was also a taboo. According to one text, it was said that a dead person must not be buried with animal's fur because it was a precious thing and it would not benefit the dead but it would benefit the living. It also said, if a dead person was buried with fur he or she might come back as an animal in the next life. It was afraid that the human corpse and the animal fur might be mixed up together and would be difficult to identify the bones later.

Different kinds of wood were used for making coffins but for the Han Chinese they preferred wood of the cypress tree because the cypress symbolised longevity. Using wood of the willow tree was a taboo because willow did not bear seeds or cones and it was thought that it might cut off the lineage. Another wood known as 'yu', (Siberian elm), was also taboo because it was hard, and it was feared there would be no clever children in the next generation. In some areas, some China fir wood was added to the cypress wood because it was said, a coffin made from cypress wood alone would be hit by thunder. In Shandong, the people there also used wood of the poplar tree. Among the Buyi people, they preferred catalpa wood, china fir and hong zhuang wood rather than cypress because they thought that once a cypress tree was chopped down it would not grow again. Using cypress wood might cut off the lineage. Another wood known as zhi bao wood was never used for making coffins, it was believed, the children of the deceased would suffer from leprosy because the bark of the tree was full of little things that looked like scabs. Usually the coffin of the Hani people is made from wood cut from a single tree taken from the nearby forest. All the inside of the tree is taken out and made hollow and there is a top half and a bottom half. The bottom half is supported on two stands.

After the coffin was made it should not be moved around, it should be left in one place otherwise it was not good for the person who made it. The coffin had to be placed in a dry place the drier the better, it was said, the person who made the coffin would have less pain and illness in his next life. The coffin had to be painted as soon as possible if waited until after the corpse was placed in it, it was said, the deceased would not be able to see in the dark.

In central Shanxi, before placing the deceased in the coffin, some straws were laid first and some of the belongings of the deceased were placed inside the coffin. The deceased's face was covered with a special paper because the deceased had already gone to the yin world so should not see daylight anymore. The deceased must not wear any metal things because it was considered unlucky.

Among the Yao minority, there is a group of Yao people known as the Qing Yao living in Guizhou. Fond of wearing black clothes earned them the name of Qing Yao. Unlike the Han-Chinese who bought their ready- made coffins from a coffin shop the Qing Yao only started to make the coffin after someone had died. The shape of their coffin is simple like a long box with no elaborate design. One unusual thing is that the top and bottom of the coffin are movable. After the deceased is placed in the coffin, a cotton bag stuffed with rice is placed underneath the head. Apart from the bag of rice nothing else is placed inside the coffin with the deceased. On top of the coffin lid, a large bamboo or straw hat and a bunch of tobacco leaves are placed. These provisions are provided for the deceased to enjoy on the journey to the ancestor's resting place.

Among the Russians, after the corpse was cleaned, the head was wrapped with a red cloth and a hat was worn over it, and new clothes and straw sandals were put on. If the deceased was an unmarried young woman or man, then a ring of flowers was worn on the head.

According to the custom of the Tadjik people, if the deceased was a male his head would be shaved and if a female the hair would be plaited, and white materials were used to wrap the whole body except the head and legs. This meant that everything was peaceful.

According to Ta Khan Er practice, if the deceased was an old man, his rice bowl, chopsticks, pipe, pot, knife, some rice and noodles were wrapped with a thread net and placed in the coffin on his left side. Some watermelon seeds were placed on one of his hands.

Among the Bulang people, those who died from tragic deaths and young children were not placed in coffins but wrapped with bamboo hedges. Before placing the deceased in the coffin his or her clothes were placed in it first. Like the Qing Yao people, a small bag of rice and some money was placed inside the coffin so that the deceased would not be hungry in the other world. If the deceased was a female her jewellery was also buried with her.

Among the Han-Chinese, the legacy of burying personal belongings with the deceased was practised but metals such as gold and silver were not used in burial. This perhaps had something to do with the ban in all the dynasties by the ruling emperors. It was the same for the Achang people, it was a taboo to bury gold and silver with the dead person. Even gold and silver teeth fillings were extracted, and gold buttons were removed from clothing before burial. It was said, these things would affect the rebirth of the deceased.

Among the Herjer people, using skins in burial was a taboo because the people believed the soul of the deceased would not ascend to heaven and would not be reborn as a human being again. When an Elunchun man had died, his horse was killed to bury with him. It was thought this way he would be able to use his horse in the other world. Before burying the deceased's bowl, a small piece had to be chipped off the bowl, if not, it would be unlucky for the living descendants. In south-east Asia, some Chinese are still burying a complete set of utensils with the deceased.

Certain things were also buried such as a stick and some dog biscuits. It was believed, the deceased had to pass through a village full of fierce dogs in the yin world. If the deceased was faced with fierce dogs the stick would be used to beat them but if the dogs were good dogs, then the biscuits would be fed to them. In some areas, a stick, a rope, a bag of cement and a bag of rice were placed either inside the sleeves of the deceased or on the side of the coffin.

In Honan, before placing the deceased in the coffin, a copper coin was placed in the mouth, believing if not, the dead person would be mute in the next life. After the corpse was placed in the coffin, the coin was then taken out, if not, it was thought that the deceased would take the family's fortune to the other world. Placing a coin in the mouth of the deceased was a legacy of ancient times. According to a text of the Han period, after an emperor had died, a pearl was place in his mouth. In ancient times, some people wrapped uncooked rice in a piece of red paper and placed inside the mouth of the deceased. In recent times, tea leaves had replaced the rice. However, according to the Hani people, placing a coin and some rice in the mouth of the deceased will enable the deceased to have rice to eat and money to spend in the other world.

Before putting the corpse in the coffin, both legs had to be tied with ropes, it was to prevent the soul of the deceased running all over the place, like running into people's houses in the yang world. In some areas, some people used white papers to tie the legs and they were untied when the corpse was in the coffin, otherwise, the deceased would not be able to walk in the other world. In ancient times, a jade cup was placed on the chest, but the custom did not perpetuate in later periods. Instead, a book, a mirror and weighing scales were placed, one on top of the other. This practice was known as 'fill the chest'. When all the relatives had arrived the face of the deceased was covered with a special paper but only after everyone expected was present because it was believed once it was put on, it must not be removed again until later. When the corpse was placed in the coffin the special paper was removed, not by hand but a fan was used because removing it by hand was an insult to the deceased. When all the relatives had arrived the deceased's face must be covered with the paper quickly, if not, the deceased would secretly count the acorns and it would be unlucky for the family.

At the place where the borders of Guangxi, Yunnan and Guizhou met, the practice there was after a person had passed away, the corpse must not be left outside the house but the last office, (cleaning the corpse) must be done inside the house. If a person died outside the ancestral village the corpse was not allowed to be brought back into the house nor the village, town, or city. This practice was also observed in the areas where the majority of the Han-Chinese lived. When placing the corpse in the coffin, people had to make sure that the feet were facing the inward towards the house and the head facing outwards. If the deceased still had a living spouse, a low pillow was placed inside the coffin so that the deceased would not be able to see his or her feet, if not, he or she would 'call' the other spouse to go along to the other world. It was said, if the deceased could see his or her feet then he or she could also see their spouse. This practice probably had something to do with the way some people used to sleep, the wife with her head at one end of the bed and the husband at the other.

In Zhejiang, the date for placing the corpse in the coffin had to be in odd numbers, even numbers were taboo. In Anhui, when a married daughter had died, her husband's family must wait until all her natal family's relatives had arrived before they placed the lid on the coffin. In Yunnan, it was the same for the Yi people. After a person had died, all the relatives were invited to arrange the funeral together. Usually the coffin was not covered until all the relatives had seen the deceased's clothes and the things to be buried otherwise the villagers would cause trouble for the family. In Honan, in the Kaifeng area, it was a little different here, after putting the shou yi on the deceased, the family had to wait for all the relatives to be present before placing the deceased in the coffin.

When placing the deceased in the coffin it was a taboo if someone present had a horoscope that clashed with the deceased's horoscope it would be bad for the deceased. It was a taboo for people who did not belong to the family to be near the coffin. Before placing the coffin's lid on, only those close relatives could stand near the coffin the rest had to watch at a distance or moved to another room. According to the belief, it was not wise for a person to stand too close to the coffin just in case the shadow was shut in the coffin and the person's health would be damaged, also his or her soul would be sealed in the coffin.

In Honan, when putting the coffin's lid on, children and grandchildren of the deceased had to wait outside the room as it was a taboo for them to be near the coffin at that moment. All the mourners had to leave the room except the caretakers. Every time they heard the sound of a nail going in the coffin they shouted loudly 'dor ding' meaning, 'hide nail'. In Shandong, when a married-out daughter had died in her husband's house, according to the custom of the area, her parents and brothers were the ones who nailed her coffin. If the deceased's natal family had not arrived, her husband's family would not dare to take the responsibility of nailing the coffin. There was a case where a deceased woman's husband and his family were being blackmailed by her natal family because the coffin was nailed before they arrived.

According to the practice of the Bai people, the last nail was reserved for a close relative to tap it in. If the deceased was a woman or a married-in son-in-law, (chow nu shi), then the last nail was reserved for the woman's natal family or the son-in-law's family to hammer in. In Yunnan, the Yi people there were rather different, the nail in the middle of the coffin was not really hammered in at all. This nail was called 'zi suan ding', meaning, 'sons and grandsons' nail'. On the nail a red string was tied. The son of the deceased pulled the string and the caretaker hammered at the nail lightly. This means that the deceased had left something for the living descendants. It was a taboo to nail the middle nail in the coffin completely as it was believed that it would be bad for the living descendants. According to the Sanis, the maternal uncle had the highest position in the world and because of this concept the coffin would not be covered until the maternal uncle's family had arrived.

In the past, the Han-Chinese believed that once a person had passed away on a certain day the soul departed from the deceased body in the form of 'air'. To prevent an encounter, the family had to get out of the way. It was believed that when the soul departed from the deceased 's body, if it hit a person he or she would die, if it hit a tree it would wither away. Usually, people consulted the opinion of someone who was the expert in everything to do with yin yang concepts. Usually, the soul departed from the dead body on the third day. On this day, at the exact time given by the yin yang expert, all the doors of the house were opened wide and the whole family had to leave the house for cover outside including the domestic animals, chickens and dogs. On the front door, a sign was put up indicating the date and time of the dead soul leaving the house, to prevent people from coming into the house.

294

It was said, after a person had died the soul would not want to leave the house but had to leave on the third day because the ghost guards of the underworld were waiting to take the dead soul to the underworld. An hour later, someone from the family then threw a pole into the courtyard, this was intended to chase away the rest of the little ghosts that might still be lurking around. Afterwards, a member of the family carried a round thing made of copper and made a 'bang bang' noise as he went into the house. This way, the whole family had passed over this 'bad day'.

However, it was a different story in the south of China. The people there not only never ran for cover but received the soul of the deceased. In Shaoxing, Zhejiang, it was said, after a person had died the soul would return to the house on a certain day, accompanied by a messenger of the other world. This messenger was known as 'sha shen', with an ugly face and hands like the claws of a chicken. On the night before the visit, a dummy dressed in the clothes of the deceased was placed in the deceased's bed. With a round ceramic pot as the head it looked as if a real person was lying in bed. On a table, favourite food of the deceased was laid. When everything was done the door of the bedroom was shut and no one could go in. If some of the food was found to be missing later, it would be an indication that the soul had eaten some of the food. Food was also laid on the stove for the sha shen, if not, he would torture the soul of the deceased. If there were any claw's prints found on the ash it would be an indication that the sha shen had been. Food was also laid in front of the coffin. If it was after the burial, then it was laid in front of the ancestor's tablet on the altar.

Everyone who had attended the funeral had to be present. If someone was unable to attend, then the clothes of the person would be hung on the wall to represent that person to make up the number. During the receiving of the soul, joss sticks, and candles were lit in the bedroom and the stove and the Taoist priest would chant some scripts and the whole family and relatives would take turns to worship. At this time, it was believed that the soul had already returned home. Between 23.00 and 01.00 hours the priest would do another round of chanting in the bedroom and the stove and then step out of the front door. At this moment, the whole family and the relatives had to cry loudly. This was known as 'sung sha', meaning, 'send away the sha'. Someone had to hold a basket with a cockerel inside and beating the basket with a wooden stick while walking behind the Taoist priest. Beating the basket was to make the cockerel crow. It was afraid that the soul would not leave until dawn and because the sha shen was a much-feared character people did not want him to be around too long therefore the cockerel was made to crow to deceive them that dawn had arrived.

In another area of Zhejiang, Xiao Shan, on the day of receiving the soul, a Taoist priest led the living descendants round the room where the coffin was and then into the kitchen and out of the house towards a temple. Every six steps everyone turned round and looked back, this means that the deceased did not want to leave those who were still living. In the living room, the deceased's clothes were put up in an upright position and were offered joss sticks and sacrificial food. Nowadays, ancestors' worshippers still believe that the dead soul returns to the house on the seventh day after death.

After the corpse was placed in the coffin there should not be any red colour in the room. In Honan, it was a taboo to use a red colour for writing characters. Among the Yi people, they were rather extreme, the son of the deceased was expected to write characters with blood from his finger. This was a way to express gratitude to one's parent. According to the practice, if a son did not use the blood of his finger to write the characters on the wooden tablet then he had no right to inherit property from his parents.

After the corpse was placed in the coffin it must be protected from the rain as it was believed that if rain fell on it, the living descendants would suffer from poverty later. There was even a saying which says, 'If rain falls on the coffin lid, children and grandchildren will not have blankets to cover themselves, if it falls all over the coffin every generation will be poor', and so it was a taboo to leave the coffin in the courtyard. If it rained during the funeral, it was still considered as unlucky, but it was a different matter if it rained after the coffin was buried because as another saying says, 'Rain falls on the grave every generation will be rich'. This concept was popular among the people in the Yubei area.

Between putting the deceased in the coffin till the time of the funeral, people were extremely careful that no cats went near the corpse or coffin. It was believed that if a cat or any other animals went near the corpse it would give it a shock causing it to jump up and just grab any living person or object and would not let go again. It was also said, cats were animals with the nature of tigers, according to legends, if a cat with white paws jumped over or touched a corpse, the cat would die immediately and the corpse would turn into a living corpse. It was said, this was due to the yang air in the cat that had gone over to the corpse that caused it to rise up like someone who was sleep walking and would grab anybody or anything in the way. When this happened, they knocked it down with a toilet broom or threw a broom or a pillow at the living corpse to stop it, otherwise if it did grab a person, it would mean death. These stories without doubt were not true only used to warn the children of the deceased to care and look after the corpse as part of their filial duty to a parent or elder.

MOURNING TABOOS

Crying is a way to express one's feeling when a close relative has died. However, in the past, there were rules even in mourning, one had to control one's sadness. Exactly when was the time to cry and when was not the time to cry were all written down in the book of Li Chi. It said, 'When guests are arriving or leaving the women should not be in the living room. They must not cry in the living room. Men must not cry in front of people when they come out of their bedrooms'.

In Anhui and Honan, it was a taboo to shed tears on the dead body as it was feared that the corpse might rise and turn into a living corpse. Among the Xibo people, when a parent had died, it was a taboo if someone started to cry out loud before putting the shou yi on the deceased. Crying loudly at this time was thought to be unlucky. Before washing the corpse and putting on the clothes the Hani people forbade anyone to sing wailing songs, but crying was allowed. When a Yi elderly person had breathed his or her last, anyone over the age of ten gathered around the bedside to 'receive the breath' for which they either used their mouths or bamboo sticks to blow air into the deceased's mouth, it was a taboo to cry at this time.

In Anhui, after a person had died it was a taboo to cry on the third day. It was believed that the dead soul had to go to a place called 'wang shiang tai' on the third day. If the living descendants cried at this time, it would cause much grief to the deceased because before going to the 'wang shiang tai' the dead soul did not know that he or she had already died and had already joined the ranks of the dead ancestors.

In Shanxi after putting the shou yi on the deceased, paper money was burnt as it was to send the dead soul away. Ashes were wrapped in a piece of paper and placed on the chest of the deceased. Before burning the paper money, it was a taboo to cry.

Only when the packet of ashes was placed on the chest of the deceased were the living descendants allowed to kneel and cry.

Among the Manchurians, after a person had died, the younger generation could cry out loud but after the burial, crying was not allowed anymore. The saying was, 'There should not be any crying on the day of the funeral'. There were two reasons for this: first, it was afraid that crying might frighten the deceased, second, it was afraid that it might bring another death or might be unlucky for the family.

When someone had died in the family, it was necessary to announce the news to all the relatives, it was called 'pao sung'. During pao sung, the person, usually a son of the deceased must not enter the house of a relative but had to kneel at the front door. In the north and central China, when a 'xiao zi', meaning, 'filial son' was announcing the news to a relative he had to knock his head on the ground even if the relative was a lot younger than him. There was a saying, 'Xiao zi's head, roll all over the street'. In some areas in the south, during pao sung, no matter rain or shine, the filial son had to carry an umbrella. According to the belief, the deceased's soul went along too by hiding in the umbrella. The filial son had to hold the umbrella with the handle forward.

According to the practice of the Yi, Miao and Benlong people, after the death of a person, three shots were fired, to inform relatives and friends. However, among the Yi people, after the death of a mother, the family had to send someone to report the news to the maternal uncle, bringing with him the earrings, bracelets and silver chains and handing them over to the maternal uncle. These were the dowry given to the late mother when she was married. Even if the maternal uncle was stricken with grief about the sad news, he had to slaughter chickens to entertain the person because it was like as though the deceased had come home for the last time. During the meal, a place was reserved for the deceased with a bowl, chopsticks, and a wine cup. Every now and then wine was poured into the wine cup and vegetables and meat were put in the bowl as though the soul of the deceased was present at the table. According to the practice of the Benlong people, relatives and friends will bring pots of tea, rice, and meat to the deceased's house to pay their respect and to offer their help with the funeral.

In the north during mourning, it was a taboo for the children of the deceased or young women to sit on the bed where the deceased was laid. Usually, the conversation was all about the funeral and nothing else. Washing one's face was a taboo. Women were not allowed to put on any make up and men were not allowed to shave or have their hair cut. All metal things from the horse carriage were replaced by wood, coloured silk strings were taken out and replaced by ordinary ropes. In one area, those who had seen the deceased being placed in the coffin, when returning home, they had to walk over a bunch of burning straw in front of the house before entering the front door, if not it was unlucky.

In the past, it was the custom for everyone to attend a funeral to bring a present to the deceased's family. After receiving the present, the deceased's family had to give two presents in return. No doubt, the practice had to do with the concept that 'double' numbers were lucky and 'single' numbers were unlucky.

These days, anyone who attends a funeral does not bring a gift for the deceased's family like in ancient times. Having said that, however, people who attend a funeral are expected to give some money to the deceased's family. One could say that they are contributing to the funeral's expenses. One could say that the Chinese are rather practical.

In high antiquity, music was forbidden in funerals, this was recorded in the Li Chi but in the later periods, music was introduced, and it became part of a funeral. Since then onwards, anybody with the financial means to do so hired musicians to put on a big show in funerals. In Honan, in Shang Shui, according to a text of this district, it criticised the way funerals were held. It said, in the funerals of the wealthy, Buddhist monks were hired to chant prayers to the deceased, musical instruments included drums, banquets were held for relatives and the xiao zi consumed meat as on a normal day. Today, music is still part of a Chinese funeral. As far as the Chinese are concerned, they do not like to bury their dead quietly.

BURIAL TIME TABOOS

Every type of burial had its customary rule. In high antiquity, the Han Chinese had their own rites to follow that a dead person must be put in a coffin on the third day. 'Lien' was the term for putting the dead body in a coffin. According to the Li Chi, it was hoped that the dead person might come back to life during these three days and that was why the corpse was not placed in the coffin until after three days had elapsed. However, in some areas, this rule was not strictly followed. Some people buried their dead after one day, some after the seventh day or even longer. The day of placing the corpse in the coffin had to be in odd numbers, double numbers were a taboo, this was observed by the Han-Chinese, Manchurians, and Koreans. An auspicious day was picked for the funeral after the lien. In the south of China and in Taiwan, it was a taboo to hold a funeral on the seventh month of the year because people believed that it was the month of ghosts. In this month, ghosts came out of the underworld to look for food in the yang world therefore people would avoid having a funeral during this month.

In the past, in Zhejiang, if the deceased was born on the second gong, (between 2100-2300 hours) and happened to die at the same time then the funeral was held in a different way. Usually, the corpse was placed in the coffin between the third and fifth gong and was placed in a place outside the village. Sack cloths were not worn by the family members and they were not allowed to cry either. Only after a lapse of seven days were the family allowed to inform relatives and friends and to hold a belated funeral. This was known as 'jung sung'. Men were employed to beat the gongs at certain times of the night and early hours.

However in Taiwan, if a funeral was held on a certain day of a certain month, for example, the first day of the first month, the second day of the second month, the third day of the third month and so on, there might be another funeral in the family. This was called 'jung sung', meaning, 'another funeral'. There was even a belief that if a funeral was held on a certain day called the 'three sung day' there would be two more deaths in the family. The date of the funeral must not be held on the birthdays of the deceased or any of the living descendants, it was believed that it would bring bad luck. Among the Achang people, the day of the funeral must not be on the days of the tiger, dragon, or monkey, otherwise crops would fail, and the family would not be blessed with many children and grandchildren. Similar practice was observed by the Bai and the Xibo people.

Some minorities and some people in some areas not only had a taboo about the date but also the time of the funeral. In one area in Honan, if a parent had died the funeral date had to be in odd numbers. Usually, the funeral was held in the afternoon, otherwise it was not good for the other parent still living. Among the Yi people, when somebody had died, the body was not left in the house for long. Usually, if someone died in the morning they were buried in the afternoon or if they died in the afternoon, they were buried the next morning. Midday was a taboo because it was believed that a funeral during this time would bring disasters.

DIFFERENT TYPES OF BURIAL

In China, there were many types of burial such as ground burial, cremation, wind burial, sky burial, water burial, tree burial, pagoda burial, wasteland burial, stone burial, cliff cave burial, straw house burial, under the bed burial, attic room burial, under the house burial, sitting burial, bone burial, bedroom burial, hanging burial, mass burial, naked burial, fu burial and even gruesome burial such as decapitated burial.

Besides these burials there were double burials, usually two sites were purchased for husband and wife even if the wife was still alive at the time of her husband's death or even four sites one for the wife and the other two were reserved for the two concubines. This seems to be a common practice among the rich Han-Chinese. When my cousin's maternal grandfather died in Penang in Malaysia, four burial sites were purchased, intended for him, his widow wife and two concubines. When his widow died, she was buried next to him but when the first concubine died, she was buried in another city where her own son lives. Many years ago, I heard a conversation between the second concubine and someone, that the other two redundant sites should be sold because the first concubine was buried in another place and it would be many years before she died. What she was trying to say was, it was no point saving the site for her because the other concubine was already buried in another place, it would not be a foursome burial so they might as well sell off the other two sites.

Generally, two factors determined the development of the different types of burial, one was environmental and the other was religious. The geography of an area often determined the environmental factor, for example, a stone burial could not have developed in an area with no stones and cliff cave burial would not be possible in an area with no natural cliff caves.

However, if the environment had permitted all forms of burial then people would choose according to their religious beliefs. Religious belief often played an important part in people's decision in choosing a certain burial or observing certain taboos during a funeral.

'Tu zhang' means 'earth burial', was the most common form of burial, it was and still is favoured by most Han-Chinese. This preference had very much to do with the saying 'ru tu wei an', meaning that the deceased, 'will have peace in the earth'. Ground burial was often seen as a rite by those groups of people who practised it. Rules were set up and people were expected to follow different levels of burial. In feudal times, an emperor who was at the top of the hierarchy could afford to exploit the country's resources to build him a tumulus. In contrast, a poor peasant often could not even afford a straw mat to cover his dead body. Among the Han-Chinese a rule was laid down, those who were engaged in low class occupations such as actors and actresses and prostitutes and those who died from sudden death with no apparent reason and tragic deaths were not allowed to be buried in the ancestral grave as a punishment. To a Chinese, to be buried among one's ancestors was considered as one of the qualifications to be a human being. Those who were not the real flesh and blood of the family, those who suffered from certain diseases like leprosy, those died before marriage and women who died before their husbands, were all unfortunately not to be buried in the ancestral grave.

Similar rules were also seen among the Muslims. Opium smokers, drunks, gamblers, those who were executed and those who broke Islamic law were excluded from the public cemetery. For these groups of people, their souls could only rest in a place away from the public cemetery to distinguish them from other people. Among the Ewenke and Ta Khan Er people, those who were killed by bears, died from gunshot wounds, struck by lightning and women who died in childbirth were also not allowed to be buried in the ancestral grave.

Among the Herjer and Ewenke people, it was a taboo to bury dead infants. Usually, the Herjer people covered the body of the dead infant with the bark of a tree and then hung it on a tree. The Ewenke people usually put the dead infant in a white case like a pillowcase, then took it to a hill and then threw it in some tall healthy-looking grass with plenty of good sunlight. According to the practice, it was believed that the soul of an infant was small, if it was buried in the ground it would not come out and the parents would not be able to have any more children.

In the past, when a Han-Chinese died in another town or village outside his ancestral village, it was a taboo to bring his body back to his village for burial. Either he was buried in the place where he died or his body was transported back to his ancestral village but usually his body was not allowed in his home and would only be placed outside the village for burial. It was afraid that the person who died outside the ancestral village would bring disasters to the family. There was a saying which said, 'Wild ghosts are not allowed to meet the gods of the family'. It was afraid that the person who died outside the ancestral village would zhoong fan the dead ancestors in the house.

Cremation or 'huo zhang', meaning, 'fire burial' was seen as an unfilial act therefore it was opposed by the Confucian leaders. Throughout history, the Han-Chinese were always against cremation and the practice. This had very much to do with the Xiao Zing, (one of the classics of Confucius), which said, 'The body and hair are given by parents therefore one must not do anything to harm them'. Since one must not harm one's body then one must certainly not harm the body of one's parents either. During the Sung dynasty, the founding emperor Sung Tai Zu was said to have issued an edict to ban the practice.

This practice was also banned among the Han-Chinese in the Mongol, Ming and Manchu dynasties.

However, cremation must have been practised among the Han-Chinese otherwise there would not be a ban at all. It was said, during the Sung period, cremation was practised among the inhabitants in Anhui and Jiangsu.

Crematoriums were seen in many areas. During the Mongol period it was more popular. Even Marco Polo had recorded that in Beijing, Hobei, Shanxi, Jiangsu, Zhejiang and Sichuan, cremation was practised by some people. However, the practice of cremation among the Han-Chinese was only in the minority. Although the Chinese government in China has encouraged cremation, (most probably to save space), many people are still not used to this practice. Many people still prefer ground burial, because the thought of burning a body is enough to give any Chinese fear. As it can be seen now in cities burial is going through reform and cremation has come to stay. Government's pressure no doubt has contributed to this reform but other factors such as the environmental factors, the scarcity of burial land plus the religious factor.

Cremation actually existed in ancient China as there was a reference about a cremation: 'On the west of the Qin kingdom there was a kingdom called Yigu, when a relative had passed away the corpse was placed on top of a pile of wood and then burned'.

According to the Tibetans, cremation is only reserved for living Buddhas, (the first living Buddha was Die Da Lin Ba), senior lamas, chiefs and serfs' owners. The corpse is placed on dried wood and oil is poured all over it. When this is done the lamas will recite their sutras. Afterwards the corpse will be burned till it is turned into ash. The ash is either stored in a funerary pagoda or is buried on top of a hill or mountain. According to the practice of the Menba people in Tibet, the corpse is tied with

306

a rope or the belt of the deceased, in a position like a foetus in a mother's womb. The corpse is carried on the back by someone, back-to-back, to the burial ground. The reason for carrying the corpse back-to- back is to protect the person who is carrying it so that the deceased could not see him and could not haunt him later. At the burial place, the corpse is placed on top of a pile of wood in a sitting position. The lama will decide where the deceased's face is going to face whether north, south, east or west. While the corpse is being burned the lama will recite the sutras for the soul of the deceased. Afterwards, either the ash is left in the area where it is cremated, thrown in a river or mixed with mud and made into the shape of a pagoda and stored in a stone pagoda where other ashes are also stored. Once a corpse is burned into ash the soul will ascend to heaven.

Cremation was a taboo if someone had died during the busy months of agriculture, the growing season or the harvesting season. It was thought there would not be any harvests and both human and farm animals would face disasters if cremation were carried out at this time of the year. Those people who practised cremation believed that the dead soul would go to heaven through a fire burial. Due to this reason, for those unfortunate beggars, mentally ill and those who died of certain incurable diseases, were not allowed to be cremated but the bodies were dumped into rivers so that the water burial would stop the soul from returning. Those who were executed and those who died from tragic death were also not cremated but were dragged to some remote areas and buried so that the soul would never be able to be reborn again.

Cremation was the common type of burial among the Yi people in Siao Liang Shan in Yunnan but those who suffered from skin diseases, lepers and dead infants under three months old were not cremated but buried in the ground. During the cremation, the son-in-law had to attend the burial, but it was a taboo for sons and daughters to be present. If the deceased was a woman, her face must face the north, if it was a man his face must face the east. When burning the corpse, it had to be burned in one go. It was a taboo to add firewood halfway because it was thought to be unlucky and there might be another death in the family.

Ground burial was the normal practice for the Jingpo, Benglong and Dai people but for those who died after a long illness or women who died in childbirth, they had to be cremated because they were not allowed to be buried in the usual way. Among the Miao people, those who died from hanging, struck by lightning, fell over a rock cliff, died by snake poison, killed by a tiger and those who were drowned were not buried in the ground but had to be cremated first and then the ash was buried in the ground. Similar practice was seen among the Herjer people and Manchurians, it was to prevent the dead bodies turning into demons, believing that the cremation would burn the soul as well. This way, it was thought that they would not cause any trouble for their families otherwise they would most likely haunt their families due to dying from tragic deaths.

The Elunchun people had three kinds of burial, ground burial, wind burial and cremation. Cremation was only for women who died when still pregnant and young people who died of illnesses. As it was believed that those who died in such ways would definitely become ghosts to disturb the family, therefore they had to be burned. If a deceased pregnant woman was not burned it was believed that she would continue to nurture the foetus and it would turn into a demon to harm human beings. Before cremation, the deceased pregnant woman's natal family had to be informed. The corpse had to be burned thoroughly especially the heart, if not, whatever that was left would still haunt the family. Sometimes an Elunchun shaman was hired during the cremation to dance to the gods to get rid of the demons.

The Qiang people had four kinds of burial, water burial, sky burial, ground burial and cremation. Cremation was held at night at about eight or nine o' clock. After the corpse was cremated the ash was put in a little wooden box and buried in the ground. If a young man died without a son, he would not be qualified for cremation. If an elderly person had passed away and if his children did not give him a cremation, they would be criticised by other Qiang people.

According to the practice of the Yi people in Lijiang, preparing the dead body for cremation was rather simple. The first thing was to put on clean clothes for the deceased. The corpse was then placed on a stretcher which perhaps looked more like a bench. On the stretcher pieces of wood were placed, nine pieces were used if the deceased was a male and seven were used for a female. The corpse was tied to these pieces of wood. After this the stretcher with the corpse tied to it was taken out of the house and placed under the eaves of the roof on the left-hand side of the house. At this corner of the house, a temporary shelter was set up. Bamboo was used to build a fence for the bottom half and blue and coloured materials were hung as a cover for the top half. An old lady would sing a funeral song for the deceased so that his or her soul would rest in peace. During the funeral, the direction of the cremation, whether to the north, south, east, or west, far or near was decided according to the time and date of birth of the deceased. Nine layers of firewood were used for the cremation if the deceased was a man and seven layers for a woman. At the start of the funeral, a few shots were fired. Four men carried the stretcher and two men carried torches heading the way followed by the rest of the people holding white sticks. These sticks were willow branches with the barks stripped off. Shouting as they walked and firing shots along the way till they reached the cremation area. Later the ash was placed in a bamboo forest or on a cliff.

Sky burial was practised among the Buddhists and in areas where Buddhism was the religion. Many minorities like the Tibetans, Mongolians, Tu, Qiang, Nu, Pumi, Yugu, She and Lahu people practised sky burial. Sky burial however, could be separated into different types such as bird burial, tree burial, wind burial and wasteland burial. Those who practised sky burial believed that this way the dead soul would ascend to heaven. Sky burial was also known as bird burial in Tibet. When a person had died, the corpse was laid in a house for three days. After that it was taken to the sky burial ground transported by a horse or an ox. Every Tibetan village had a sky burial area paved with slabs of stones. Usually, it was carried out early in the morning to attract hungry birds. At the burial ground, the corpse was then mutilated and left there for the eagles, crows and owls to help themselves as it was believed the more flesh eaten by the birds the better because it was considered as lucky. When the birds had finished eating all the flesh, the bones would be pounded into powder mixed with flour and used as a bird feed. If the birds did not finish off all the flesh or if the corpse did not attract any birds it was unlucky. If this happened, it meant that the deceased had sin in his or her life and that was why his or her soul could not ascend to heaven. Several factors contributed to this kind of burial. Ground burial did not become a popular burial because the land in the plateau was hard and dry and difficult to dig. Water burial would contaminate the water sources. Pagoda burial and cremation were only reserved for the elite group. Another factor was the influence of Lamaism, in which the souls of those who were buried this way would ascend to heaven.

Sky burial was also practised by some Qiang people. Shou yi was not put on the corpse. After the family had chanted some curses, the corpse was taken to a mountain or wasteland and left to eagles, birds and wild beasts to devour it. After a few days, the family would go back to the area to see whether there was still any flesh left on the corpse. If all the flesh had not been devoured the corpse would be taken to another mountain for other birds and beasts to finish the rest of the flesh. Only when all the flesh was eaten would the family consider that the deceased was free from all his or her sins.

Influenced by the Tibetans, the Menba people also practised sky burial. During the funeral, the corpse is taken to a hill or mountain and it is mutilated. Someone will blow a spiral shell to attract the eagles and crows. If all the flesh is eaten by the birds it is considered as lucky.

A similar practice was seen among the Mongolians who practised wasteland burial. After a person had died the corpse was placed in a wooden cart and was taken to a wasteland. The cart was pulled by someone running until the corpse fell out of the cart. If later the corpse was eaten by eagles and wolves then it was believed that the soul of the deceased had ascended to heaven. If however the corpse was still intact after seven days, it would be seen as unlucky and a lama would be hired by the family to chant some prayers for the deceased perhaps to help the soul to ascend to heaven.

Wind burial is practised by the Jino, Ewenke and Elunchun people. Wind burial is also known as tree burial and forest burial and is a traditional burial of the Elunchun people in Inner Mongolia. After a person has died relatives will come to offer sacrificial worship and to cry goodbye. Belongings are placed in the coffin for burial. Some Elunchun people wrap the corpse with the barks of the birch tree. During the funeral, a shaman is hired to dance to the deities. Straws are used to make a figure and a few threads are tied to it. The shaman will hold a thread and the rest are held by the children of the deceased. After the rite, the shaman will use four sticks to break all the threads and will then throw the straw figure out of the house. This means that the soul has left. After this rite, the deceased is carried to the nearby forest and is placed between two trees, about one metre apart, two metres high, the coffin is supported by a piece of wood. The coffin is then covered by barks of the birch tree or branches. The coffin is then left to the elements the wind and rain to do their worst upon it until the coffin rots away. Usually, after one or two years the coffin will fall to the ground and this is considered as lucky. However, the longer the coffin remains on the tree the better. According to the practice, it is believed that the more rain and wind battling on the corpse making it to decay faster the better as this is a sign that the soul has ascended to heaven, has turned into a star and will bring hope to the living descendants. If not, it was considered unlucky.

Wind burial is adopted by the Elunchun people perhaps as it has something to do with their primitive productivity and lifestyle which are inseparable. Their lifestyles are rather nomadic with no permanent settlement, hunting and living from place to place. Social contact with other minorities are rare. Lack of contact with other people means that they are missing the chance to learn new skills therefore remaining primitive. In their nomadic life they never had the chance of learning carpentry and so they just use the barks of trees to make coffins for their dead or even put them in hollow trees. Corpses are buried this way because they do not want the bodies of the dead relatives to be devoured by wild animals if they are left on the ground.

There was not much reference about water burials in ancient times, but it was practised by the Tibetans in some areas in Tibet. Those who practised it usually were people who lived near the rivers. Ropes made from wool then used to tie the corpse into the position of a foetus and boulders or stones were tied to it. The corpse was then thrown into the river, allowing the current to wash it away. In the past, there was a ban on water burials around the areas near Lhasa. One reason was to protect the water sources from being contaminated. If a corpse was found in the river and if no one was found responsible, then the landowner would be fined. Corpses were often mutilated before being dumped into the river so that the identity would not be traced.

Water burial is one of the burials of the Menba people in Tibet. In one area, near the east of the Himalayas it is one of the common burials. During the burial, the corpse is mutilated first so that the soul of the deceased will ascend to heaven soon. In another area, water burial is only for lepers and those who die in tragic deaths. Mutilation is not practised here; the whole corpse is thrown into the river. Mutilation is thought to be inhuman.

Bone burial was the main type of burial among the Zhuang people. After a person had died the body was placed in an inexpensive coffin made from cheap wood or in a coffin made of thin wood and buried in shallow ground so that the corpse would decay faster. Later the coffin was dug up, the bones cleaned and placed in a ceramic jar in a sitting position and then reburied again in the family's graveyard. Usually, the coffin was dug up in three or five years time. Double number years such as four and six were taboo. Personal belongings were not buried with the bones in the second burial, gold and fabrics were especially taboo. Bone burial was also practised by some Han-Chinese. Several years after the corpse was buried, the bones were dug up, cleaned, and placed in a jar with a lid. The jar was then put back inside the decaying coffin and was then reburied again. The difference between the Zhuang and the Han-Chinese in this practice is that the latter chose the best wood they could afford for the coffin.

Many years ago, the bones of my late grandmother were dug up and reburied again. Her remains are now in a jar in her old coffin. According to my eldest paternal aunt, (deceased), my late grandmother conveyed to her in a dream that she was lying in a pool of water and was unable to sit upright. The matter

313

was taken seriously by some members of our extended family. Heads were put together and decided that it was time to dig up my grandmother's grave and give her a reburial. One day we children were told to go to the graveyard along with the adults because my grandmother's grave was being dug up and was ready for viewing. Viewing one's dead ancestor was not a pleasant thing and many members of the family declined the offer! As the 'dream' indicated there was water in the coffin. I believe that there is a logical scientific reason for the water to be in the coffin. After the viewing, it was left to the 'shan gou', meaning, 'hill dog', the graveyard's keeper, to clean up the bones and to place them in a jar. On the day of the reburial, all members of the extended family were present, my father's family, my uncle's family, (my father's eldest brother) and two of my paternal aunts, (my father's elder sisters). Sacrificial food, joss sticks, and candles were offered to my grandmother and worship was according to hierarchy. Taoists priests were not hired to perform rites, just a family worship. After the worship, all the sacrificial food, chickens, roast ducks, roast pork, meat dumplings, cakes and fruit were consumed by us.

Bone burial was also practised by the Han-Chinese who lived along the coast in Zhejiang. The corpse was placed in a coffin and was carried to a hill or mountain and left there to let it rot. After three to five years the children and grandchildren would gather all the bones for burial. The bones were cleaned and placed inside a large jar with a lid then buried in the ground. A similar ritual was practised by the Miao people but with differences. During the reburial, the bones were placed in a new coffin and were dug up for reburial several times till it was impossible to find any more bones whereas in Zhejiang, the bones were reburied in a jar and would not be dug up again.

In Taiwan, bone burial was also practised by those who were emotionally attached to mainland China. Due to political reason, it was not possible to transport a corpse back to China for burial. The solution was to bury the corpse in Taiwan first, known as 'ker zhang', meaning, 'guest burial'. Several years later a geomancy expert was hired to pick an auspicious day to dig up the bones. The bones were cleaned and placed in a ceramic pot in a skeleton shape then reburied again. Meanwhile the family would wait for the chance to transport the bones back to the ancestral village in the mainland for a permanent burial. (Those who fled to Taiwan in 1949 obviously were more emotionally attached to the mainland than the ones who had already settled there before).

The Qing Yao people have managed to retain their unique way of burying their dead. Unlike other races in China, they do not bury their dead, but place them in a natural cave in a mountain or hill. Every clan have their own ancestral caves for placing their coffins. If a cliff cave is fairly large, then more than one clan will share the cliff cave but are strictly separated and never mixed. If a cliff cave is small, then it will only be enough for one clan to use it. This kind of burial system is said to have retained the clan burial system of ancient times.

Cliff cave burial is also a form of burial practised by some Menba people. The corpse is placed in a wooden box and is taken to the mountain and is placed in a natural cliff cave. Burying the corpse this way actually helps to preserve it longer because of the cooler climate in the high mountains. This form of burial is favoured by some high lamas. Some parents also preferred to bury their young children this way.

Suan Guan Zhang was an unusual ancient burial used to be practised by the Miao, Yi, Lisu and the Gelau people. This form of burial is like the cliff cave burial but with some differences. Evidence of this type of burial were seen in Sichuan, Yunnan, Guizhou, Fujian, Hunan, Hubei, Jiangxi and Taiwan. After a person had died, the corpse and belongings were placed in a coffin and taken to a high mountain cliff. If there was a precipice with a tree or branches in the mountain then the coffin would be placed on it. The higher the cliff the better as it was a form of respect and the deceased would be able to ascend to heaven early. If there were no steep cliffs with trees or branches, then wood had to be placed in an area to support the coffin. Coffins were also inserted in natural caves in the cliff. Usually, this form of burial was situated by a mountain cliff next to a river, both the river and the caves had to face the east. There were several reasons for this preference: facing the east had to do with worshipping the sun god; the river flowing towards the east was able to take the soul of the deceased to meet his or her ancestors. Coffins were usually made of a wood called nam wood, a hardwood that would not decay easily. Sometimes a coffin was just left on the precipice but sometimes after several years it was taken down for a ground burial. This ancient burial is still practised by some Gelau people in different areas.

According to history, the ancestors of the Gelau people used to live in natural caves in mountains. Although their descendants have moved out of the mountain caves long ago their lives are still very much linked to mountains. Not only do they like to live near hills and mountains but after their death they also like to be buried in stones and inside rocky mountains. The ancient Gelau people were buried in coffins made of slabs of stones more than an inch thick. These stone coffins were not buried under ground but were placed inside natural holes in rocky hills or mountains. Some holes had just one coffin, but some had two or even a few. Stone coffins can be found in nearly all of Guizhou's natural caves situated next to rivers. These coffins were just inserted into the holes in rocks and that was it, they were not covered with anything else. These kinds of natural caves were limited and when they ran out the Gelau people thought of another way to bury their dead. Stone tombs were erected on flat ground and

316

the stone coffins were placed inside them. Six slabs of stones were used to build each tomb, each about five to seven inches thick. One could say that it was a stone coffin within a stone coffin. Many of these stone tombs were carved with designs. The earliest designs were carved inside the tombs but in later periods the designs were on the outside. Usually more than one stone tomb was placed together. It could be as many as more than ten or just a couple. These stone tombs were called 'man zi fern', meaning, 'barbarian tombs' but in the Jin Sa district they were known as 'ming tombs'. Since the Manchu period, the Gelau people were into another kind of tomb building known as 'sen ji' which literally means 'live foundation'. This idea started in the north of Guizhou and the south of Sichuan. Similar to the Pharaohs of Egypt, the Gelau people started to build these tombs when they were still alive. In the past, a well off Gelau spent as much as a thousand dollars, eight to nine years building such a tomb for himself. To a Gelau stonemason this kind of tomb building was called 'siew shan', meaning, 'build mountain'. Sen ji was said to have developed from the stone tombs, the idea was Gelau burial culture influenced by Han-Chinese burial culture which led to them creating their own Gelau tomb form. Six slabs of stones were put together to form a tomb in the form of a building complete with a door and a window. In the middle of the bottom half of the tomb was the window with beams carved with lotuses, crabs, swords, Buddhist scripts and characters such as the Eight Fairies Crossing the Sea and the Mila Buddha. In the middle of the top half of the tomb was the headstone carved with characters such as the names of the deceased. At the top of the headstone were two small pillars each with a dragon coiled round it. The door of the tomb was wide and high was carved with meaningful characters. This form of tomb building has perpetuated till this day and is said to be as popular as ever among the Gelau people in the north of Guizhou.

Nuns and monks had their own burial called sitting burial. In Shaoxing, Zhejiang, nuns were buried in large pots called 'lily flower pots'. When a nun was dying, she would go into the pot and sit inside in a sitting position. After her death, the monks would finish the burial by placing the large pot inside something like a mini stone building, about two metres high and wide enough to place the large pot inside. Sometimes it would take a while for the nun to die and food and water would be fed to her until she died.

Pagoda burial was reserved for serfs' owners and living Buddhas. High quality spices were used to spread over the corpse. Afterwards the corpse was kept inside a gold or silver pagoda. These funerary pagodas can be seen in the Potala Palace in Lhasa where some of the Dalai Lamas were buried. The pagoda of the thirteenth Dalai Lama is over 30 feet high, is of gilded bronze, has three storeys and the body of the pagoda has carvings of figures and flowers and is inlaid with different precious stones. Silver and one gold funerary pagodas are also seen in the Ga Dan Monastery in Lhasa. In the town of Shigatse several funerary pagodas of Panchen Lamas are kept in the Za Shen Lun Bu Monastery.

Among some Menba people, after the death of a young child the corpse is cleaned with salt water. After that it is placed in a wooden box with sand inside. The box is then left in the attic room. (Most Menba people live in houses with three storeys). Usually, a year or several years later, an auspicious date is picked to bury the corpse in a water burial or a cliff cave burial. If a water burial is decided, then the box will be thrown into a river and left it to the current to wash it away. If a cliff cave burial is chosen, then the box will be taken to the top of the cliff of a mountain and will be inserted into a natural cave. The attic room burial is only part of the burial and it must be given a final burial either a cliff cave burial or a water burial, if not, there will be another death in the family.

Under the house burial is practised by some Menba people, only for dead babies. The corpse of the baby is wrapped with a cloth and is placed inside a gourd. Inside the house, the wooden floorboards are taken out and a deep hole is dug. After that the gourd is placed in the hole and is covered with earth and the floorboards. There will be no headstone and no worship. Outsiders are not informed about the burial and lamas are not hired to recite the sutras. It is a secret burial where only family members are present.

Bedroom burial was popular in Pingyang, Zhejiang. According to the practice, if a wife died before her husband, she would be given a ground burial. However, if a husband died first, he would not be buried straight away. The coffin would be placed in the couple's bedroom and would only be buried with the wife together after her death. Discrimination against women was the reason why this was being practised. Feudal law permitted a man to marry another wife or wives after the death of a spouse, but a woman had no such privilege. Even after death a husband continued to rule the life of a wife. Even if the woman was a young widow, she still had to accompany the bones of her husband all her life. Some people even placed the coffin next to the bed because it was believed, this way the deceased could control the wife. If a coffin were thin, foul water would leak out of it later and the smell would be unbearable for the wife. Some women suffered from infectious diseases and died as a result and some developed insanity due to fear of having a coffin in the bedroom.

Fu burial was known as fu zhang to the Chinese, 'Fu' means 'join' and 'zhang' means 'burial'. It was an unusual burial practice because the new coffin was buried on top of an old coffin. Before the deceased was to be placed in the coffin, a memorial service was held. During this service all the ancestors' tablets were worshipped. After this, the deceased was placed in a coffin and then placed on top of an old grave where a dead ancestor was buried years before.

BURIAL SITE TABOOS

Choosing the right site for the grave was very important to the Han-Chinese. According to the practice, the site of the grave could have an impact on the lives of the future generations, help them to acquire wealth or the opposite, and give them longevity or short life. This kind of concept made people carry out the rites of the funeral with care and respect for the dead. This also reflected people's religious concept of expecting and hoping that their dead ancestors would bestow prosperity on them. It can be argued that it was due to the idea that feng shui men played on people's fear of death and misfortune and their desire for prosperity, to extract money from them. This legacy is perpetuated to this day and it is a lucrative business in South-East Asia, especially in Hong Kong.

It was very important that the site of the grave was a lucky site. This idea originated in the early part of Chinese history. During the Jin Dynasty (265-316 AD), a text about funerals known as 'zhang jing', meaning, 'burial text', written by someone called Goi Pu, mentioned that burial sites could determine the fate of living descendants. Later the idea of choosing burial sites became more mysterious, hence, a new occupation was created for the man commonly called feng shui shen sen, who helped families to find burial sites. 'Feng shui' means 'wind and water' and 'shen sen' means 'mister'. These feng shui men who helped people to look for auspicious graves were no different from the feng shui men who looked for auspicious buildings. They were only exploiting people's ignorance, a superstitious occupation designed to cheat ignorant people of their money. Feng shui, with its endless taboos were complicated, invented by feng shui men to play on people's ignorance, saying that if a grave was built on the site where a dragon was lying then it would be an auspicious site and the living descendants would be prosperous.

Here is a folk song about the many taboo areas that were not suitable for burial which goes something like this:

'Do not bury on rough stoney ground.
Do not bury near running waterfalls.
Do not bury in a dead end area.
Do not bury on lonely hill.
Do not bury in front of deities and at the back of temples.
Do not bury in an area with difficult access.
Do not bury in a bleak and desolate wasteland.
Do not bury in an area lack of wind and water.
Do not bury on low lying land.
Do not bury on the head of a dragon or a tiger.'

For feng shui to work, it was said, it required good conduct from living descendants. There was a saying, 'If one wants a good land, one must have a good heart'. With a saying such as this any mistake made by the feng shui man was easily covered up, so if the living descendants were not prosperous, he could just blame it on their conduct. There was even such a poem which mocked the feng shui men. It goes something like this:

'Feng shui mister, you are used to telling lies.
Finger pointing at South, North, West and East.
If there is such a thing as an auspicious site in this world.
Why don't you find it to bury your own father?'

Other minorities like the Bai people also believed in choosing the right burial site and feng shui. Ideally, a burial site would be best situated with its back to a mountain with the green dragon on its left and the white tiger on its right. The green dragon and the white tiger were supposed to be the foot of the mountain. Among the minority known as the Lamor people, they buried their dead with the feet facing the mountain, if not, it was believed that the deceased's feet would be unsteady. This would have an impact on the longevity of the descendants.

In a place called Jilin, it was a taboo to erect a headstone for a person who died from a sudden death. In Honan, if two funerals were close to one another then the new grave was covered with a red paper first before burying the other one, if not, it would be unlucky. There was a saying which says, 'New grave see new grave, there will be more deaths'.

According to Bulang practice, every family will only bury their dead in their own graveyard where only Bulang people are buried. Even in the graveyard, the dead are buried according to their family name and are never mixed. If the dead people of different family names are buried together, it is said, they might not get on in the other world. Those who died from tragic deaths are not permitted to be buried in the graveyard, they are buried at the place where they died.

BURIAL RITES' TABOOS

Moving any funeral things was a taboo especially the coffin and the lid must not be opened at all otherwise it would be unlucky. Anybody, whether a relative or a friend with Eight Characters that were against the Eight Characters of the deceased would not be allowed to attend the funeral because it would be unlucky. For all those who suffered from certain diseases, pregnant women and those who had committed crime, it was a taboo for them to attend a funeral.

After the coffin was placed in the living room the floor must not be swept until before the funeral was due to start, a broom was used to sweep away the dust from the coffin. This was called 'sau chai', meaning, 'sweep fortune', signifying the fortune would not go out of the house.

In the past, after a person had died, a lamp was lit near the coffin until after the funeral. It must be lit all the time. It was said, the deceased in the other world would fall down each time the light went off because the lamp was believed to show the way for the departed.

In Fuyang, Zhejiang, the people there lit a lamp at the side of the deceased and a pair of candles were lit near the feet. Candles and joss sticks were also burned at the temple of the earth god so that the journey to the other world was well lit and the deceased would not have to walk in the dark. According to the people in Hainan, this lamp was the soul of the deceased.

The Ta Khan Er people also lit a lamp next to the coffin and different kinds of food were laid at the altar at night for the deceased. Until the funeral, the children of the deceased burned paper money every day and had to sit next to the coffin, sleeping on the floor at night as part of their filial duty. This practice was also observed by the Han-Chinese, with the male children on the right side of the coffin and female children on the left, all sat according to hierarchy.

Some minorities believed that if a person died a tragic death, to free the soul, an animal had to be slaughtered. Among the Buyi people, when someone died by a knife or a gun, an ox was slaughtered. This ox was used to die in the place of the deceased so that the soul would be freed.

According to Qiang practice, a goat was slaughtered after someone had died. This goat was called 'lead road goat' and was used as a guide for the deceased on the road. If the deceased was a male, a he-goat was slaughtered and if it was a female, then a she-goat was used. It was believed that the cause of death could be found in the goat's body. Before slaughtering the goat, someone would say, 'The goat will lead you. What illnesses did you die from? Please reveal it in the goat's body.' After this, the goat was slaughtered. A bowl was used to contain the blood.

Some barley straw soaked with blood was used to spread on the body of the deceased to let him or her know that the goat was leading the way. After this the goat was cut open to look for the cause of death. When the cause of death was found the whole family would cry together regretting that they did not know about the illness of the deceased. Perhaps if the illness had been treated, he or she would not have died. If a Qiang man fell over a cliff and died, a priest would be hired to 'call his soul' and a goat was pushed over the cliff the spot where he fell. If afterwards the goat was found to be alive, it was thought to be a bad sign, either the soul of the deceased was not yet free or that later there would be another person falling over this cliff.

Similar practice was seen among the Miao people, a pig was slaughtered to lead the way for the deceased. After this rite, the deceased was placed in the coffin. Before the funeral, another rite was performed; this time an ox was slaughtered. The head of the ox was held down and a big knife or an axe was used to strike at the head to cause it to be unconscious and then kill it. There was a history about this practice. According to one legend: in ancient times, the leader of the Miao people was killed by a rival, his general led the people from the North down to the South, on the way the general was killed by an arrow. The Miao people then buried their leader and his general, blowing the horns and beating the drums to scare away the tigers and other wild animals to allow the souls of the two deceased to have peace. When the horse of the general heard the sound of horns and drums, thinking it was going to war, it broke free from a rope, ran and stopped in front of the grave. When it saw that its master had died, tears flowed from its eyes and it refused food and water, dying several days later. Since then, the Miao people slaughtered an ox after someone's death, in memory of the general's horse, to represent it. This means that the ox would lead the soul of the deceased to the place of the dead ancestors. It also means that an ox was given to the deceased.

According to the practice of the Qing Yao, if the deceased is young, the ritual of slaughtering an ox is not performed but if the deceased is old and if financially well off an ox is slaughtered to feed the relatives and the guests. This ceremony is held before the funeral. Before slaughtering the ox, a dance is held known as the hunting dance, usually performed by about ten people each one holding a wooden pole about five to six feet long, dancing to the music of the drums. When slaughtering the ox, an important ritual is performed where firecrackers are set off; some will play the flutes, some will hold colourful flags, some will hold flowery umbrellas and walk round the village. During this time, the son-in-law enter the village gate with two men who will do the slaughtering. They bring with them white wine, rice, and glutinous rice cakes. Beef is distributed to every household in the village. The leftover beef is used to feed those who are attending the funeral. During this ceremony, a wooden ox horn and a wooden fish are nailed onto the coffin of the deceased. Agriculture is very important to the Qing Yao because it is their main source of income and oxen are important agricultural tools. Slaughtering an ox for an elderly deceased means that the living descendants are providing a working tool for the deceased in the other world. As for the hunting dance, it reflects the importance of the economy of hunting from the Qing Yao.

The Bai people carried out an unusual rite after someone had died. After putting new clothes on the corpse, it was wrapped with a rug and placed on a piece of wood with four ropes tying to the four corners. The piece of wood with the corpse on it was then raised up high, hanging on the beam in the middle of the room more than two metres from the floor. On the day of the death, a cockerel was strangled and placed on the chest of the deceased for a couple of hours. Afterwards the cockerel would be roasted and put into a sack bag, a bowl of cooked rice was also put inside. The bag was then hung on the beam near the head of the deceased as a sacrificial offering. A member of the family would say to the deceased 'These foods are for you and your dead mother and father to eat. Now you are not able to eat with us anymore, we are very sad. We hope that you will protect us in the other world. Now, you go to the place for dead people.' On that night, five or six women, each holding a stick, danced and sang underneath the deceased all night. The next day a pig or an ox was slaughtered as a sacrifice for the deceased. A hole was made in the left ear of the animal and a rope was used to tie the ear and the other end was tied to one of the wrists of the deceased. This means that the pig or ox would lead the soul of the deceased to the dead ancestors. When slaughtering the animal, people had to be careful not to let any blood splash on their bodies because it would be unlucky. The pig or ox was placed in front of the deceased as a sacrificial offering straight away and when it was cooked it was placed in front of the deceased again. Some wine was poured into the mouth of the deceased.

According to the practice of the Menba people, if a ground burial is decided the corpse is tied into a position like a foetus and a hada is hung over the head covering the whole face. The corpse is placed either in a large pot or on a few pieces of wood on top of some stones. In front of the corpse seven small bowls are placed, each filled with water, milk, wine, meat, tobacco, rice porridge and Tibetan money. Apart from these, bananas and peaches are also offered. Earrings, bracelets and rings and other daily used items and working tools are also placed near the deceased as a sacrificial offering. On the next afternoon after the death, the lama will perform a rite. On a piece of paper, names of the different demons and ghosts are written down and the lama will say some curses to it and then burn it. The ash is then mixed with some rice and is buried at the bottom of the stairs underneath. A piece of stone is placed on top of it and it is covered with soil. At the entrance of the village road, some demon figures, (made with rice flour) and little stones are scattered along the road to scare away the ghosts.

As stated by the Bulang people, when someone had died, the practice was to slaughter a chicken 'to call the soul of the deceased'. In Fuyang, after the death of someone, two pairs of straw sandals were burned on the roadside. These were for the messengers of the other world.

At the start of the funeral, the son had to break a salt bowl which belonged to the father. Since the father had died it was sad to look at it and so it was smashed to pieces. It was a taboo if the salt bowl did not break. Some people took it to the grave and broke it after the coffin was placed in the ground. In Thai An, Shandong, a small mud pot, used for burning the paper money, was placed near the coffin. When the coffin was about to be lifted to begin the funeral, the eldest son-in-law picked up the mud pot and placed it on the head of the deceased's eldest son and then threw it on the ground to break it. Breaking the mud bowl had the same meaning as breaking the salt bowl.

During the funeral of the Tartar people, the people who were carrying the stretcher had to make sure that the feet of the deceased came out of the front door first and then the stretcher was turned round with the head-first all the way towards the cemetery. Among the Buyi people, if the deceased was an unmarried girl her body was not allowed to be carried out of the front door but was carried out of the house by a side door. According to the She people, it was a taboo if the coffin hit the sides of the front door during the funeral. It was believed to be unlucky.

Among the Manchurians, Ewenke, Herjer and Ke-er-ke-zi people, the corpse was taken out of the house by the window not the front door. According to the people, the door was for living people to use so it was a taboo for the dead to use the door. For someone with a different family name and a dead infant they too had to be carried out of the house by the window, if not, it was unlucky. Similar practice was seen among the Dulong people where the corpse was not allowed to pass through the front door but through the floorboards. The Dulong people probably lived in houses similar to a long house which made it possible to do it this way. According to the people, if the corpse were carried out of the house by the front door then there would be another death in the family or even worse the whole family would die.

During the funeral, the Benglong people were very particular about how the coffin was being carried usually the feet first. This way, it was said, the deceased could not look back but had to carry on walking forward, if not, it would be unlucky. In the past, in Kaifeng, the graveyard was situated in the East or South of the city outside the walled city. When there was a funeral, only the North gate and two other gates in the North-East known as Sung Men and Chow Men were used but not the South gate or West gate. Although the graveyards were in the South and West people were only allowed to use the gates in the North-East and then went round to the South or West because it was a taboo to use the South and West gates for funerals.

During the funeral, the coffin bearers had to be careful not to say 'zong', meaning, 'heavy', it was a taboo. It was afraid that something might happen such as the coffin might tip over to the ground. In Honan, it was bad luck if the coffin fell to the ground during the funeral. The Muslim people used a stretcher provided by the mosque to transport their dead, carried by eight people. From the mosque to the cemetery the journey was by foot and the stretcher must not touch the ground all the way. In Jiangsu, during a funeral the neighbours placed their old brooms upside down outside their front doors otherwise they might get bad luck. In North and central China, neighbours did not like any wreaths, paper houses and anything associated with the funeral placed outside their front doors. It was believed to be unlucky.

328

In Hobei, during the burial, a small hole was made in the head of the coffin, and a small container with food was placed inside. It was to make sure that the deceased would not go hungry with rice to eat in the other world. In Fuyang, when the coffin was in the site, the people there placed one man tou, (a steamed bun), in each corner of the coffin and a vase with rice and vegetables was placed at the foot of the coffin. Lucky phrases were uttered by the feng shui man and he scattered some five grains, copper coins and nails for the deceased's children for them to bury at home. In the North, if the deceased was a female her natal family had to bring some puddings made in the shapes of different kinds of fruit especially peach, flowers, birds, and fish. During the burial, a bit of each pudding was thrown into the site or it was thrown into the fire when burning the paper money. This means that the deceased had already had some of the pudding and the rest were given to children.

In Thai An village, Shandong, the funeral was usually held in the afternoon. The coffin was carried out of the house and either it was placed outside the front door or on the street. A red cockerel was then placed on top of the coffin, it was to lead the soul of the deceased. At this moment, the family would kneel in front of the coffin and cry loudly. A temporary altar with food offerings was laid in front of the coffin and family and friends bowed to the deceased. At the grave, a temporary altar was set up here where food and joss sticks were offered. After the coffin was placed in the ground it was covered with soil into a rounded mound. The eldest son placed his funeral staff or stick, made with a willow stick with bits of white papers stuck on it, in the middle of the grave. This means that the deceased had sons and grandsons. Each family member then grabbed a handful of soil and took it home. After entering the house, each one of them had to sit on a sackcloth which was used for storing the five grains.

In Sichuan, at the start of the funeral, the eldest son of the deceased carried the tablet or a portrait and slightly bent his waist to take the funeral stick. This funeral stick was made with a bamboo stick about two feet long with flowers made of white papers. During the funeral someone carried a lamp, and someone carried a basket filled with paper money which was scattered along the way. This paper money was called 'mai lu qian', meaning, 'buy road money'. At the burial site, some cypress leaves and some copper coins were placed in the grave before the coffin was placed in it. The family prostrated themselves next to the site while the coffin was being lowered into it. Once the coffin was in the site the eldest son threw a handful of soil in it and followed by others. In Mianyang, when burning the paper house, the family's young people ran round the grave three times and each picked a cypress branch and a joss stick and ran home and stuck them into the urn on the altar. The one who reached the house first would have prosperity.

In Taiwan, some people practised a practice called 'jump over the coffin'. After the death of a wife, during the funeral, the husband would hold an umbrella in one hand and a bundle of clothes, shoes and hats that belonged to his wife in the other hand. When he was jumping over the coffin at the same time he would say, 'We want to return to Tang Shan'. This means that they wanted to return to China one day. In Malaysia, some Chinese there still called themselves 'Tang ren', meaning, 'Tang people' and China is known as Tang shan. 'Shan' means 'mountain'. By jumping over the coffin, it was said, the soul of the wife would be able to return to the ancestral village in mainland China. This practice revealed the feelings of some of the people in Taiwan. Although physically they were in Taiwan their hearts were in China.

In Shenlongjia, in Hubei, there was a practice called 'sit on the coffin'. At the start of the funeral, a son or a daughter of the deceased would sit in front of the coffin all the way till the funeral procession reached the burial site. The son or the daughter would hold a mirror with the back against his or her face. This means that two dead people were carried to the grave and so would be able to avoid another death in the family. Using the mirror to cover the face was to confuse the ghosts so that they would not be able to see clearly whether the one who sat in front of the coffin was alive or not.

Among the fishermen in the East coast, if a fisherman was lost at sea his family would carry out a rite called 'chao hoon', literally meaning 'tide soul'. A straw dummy was made, dressed with the clothes of the deceased. An altar was set up in the house. At the same time a Taoist priest was hired to attract the soul of the deceased by the sea. Usually, this was carried out at night when it was high tide. The family of the deceased had to be present by the sea during this rite. A temporary stand with a roof was erected by the sea and an altar was set up and the straw dummy was placed on it. The Eight Characters of the deceased was pinned on the dummy. When it was high tide the Taoist priest would start to chant some Taoist scripts. At this time, torches of fire were set up in front and at the back of the stand. Someone would carry a bamboo with roots and a basket with a chicken inside was hung at the end of it. While the priest was chanting the person had to keep shaking the bamboo. Some people carried out this rite in a different way. The family wore mourning clothes and carried lanterns painted with characters and cried out the name of the deceased, 'So-and-so come, so-and-so, come!' Then a young boy or a relative would answer, 'Coming, coming'. This would go on until the high tide was over then the priest would 'lead' the soul home. The next day the straw dummy was placed in the coffin and buried in the hill. There was even a folk song about this practice which goes like this, 'Ten coffins, there are nine bundles of straws', which means that straws were buried in nine coffins out of ten.

Usually, the Qing Yao people do not leave their dead at home too long. If someone died during the day the corpse will be buried that same night with the help of torches during the funeral. So unique is their funeral in that the funeral procession is required to walk through thorn bushes instead of roads. The worst thing is that people are not allowed to use big knives to hack their way forward but must suffer all the way through. According to the people, if they used knives to hack out a route there will be more funeral processions passing through this route.

According to the practice of the Yi people, the coffin is not carried by the family to the graveyard, but all the elders of the village walk beside the coffin all the way to the burial site. As they walk along whenever there is a table laid with a plate of rice puddings and sweets they will stop in front of that table and will place the coffin on top of two benches. Everyone including the caretakers, the elders, the family of the deceased, people of the village or from outside the village will help themselves to the food. Usually, there are quite a few tables laid with food along the street and the people will help themselves from one table to another. This custom is known as 'chuan jie' which literally means, 'string street'. This means that the deceased is having a last good time in his or her street, to have the last meal with the villagers. This 'last meal' custom is observed out of respect, out of love and out of memory for the elderly because most elderly people help to look after the children of the village.

Usually, the Miao people hold a funeral on the third day after death. During the funeral, the person who is carrying bow and arrows on his back will be in front, he is supposed to direct the way for the deceased. The children of the deceased will follow behind kneeling and walking all the way to the graveyard. In the past, the burial site was dug horizontally with one end facing the East and the other end facing the West. Since the Republic of China, the Miao people have abandoned this practice and are burying their dead in the usual way.

Before the funeral, the Ta Khan Er people will worship the deceased and all the offerings brought by the relatives and friends are laid out in front of the deceased. Someone will give a speech about the life of the deceased. Either a horse cart or an ox cart is tied to the coffin. This means that the deceased will ride in the horse cart or ox cart to heaven. After the worship, the animal will be slaughtered. When the coffin is in the grave the eldest son will start to bury the coffin and then everyone will help to erect a mound. All the belongings of the deceased and paper money are burned in front of the grave.

Usually, the site of a Menba ground burial is decided by the lama. Instead of the usual oblong shape, the site is unconventional because it is round with a depth about the height of a man. Pieces of wood are placed at the bottom of the site and three stones are placed on top of it in a triangular shape and on top of it a large basket is placed. The corpse is placed in the large basket (the corpse is tied into a foetus position) with the face facing the West. Belongings such as clothes, jewellery and working tools are placed all over the sides of the basket. Pieces of wood are placed against the walls of the site and wild banana leaves are used to cover the site. When this is done the site is covered with soil and a mound is erected about half a man's height. A bamboo and wooden fence is built round the mound to protect it from animals. Before leaving for home, everyone will say to the deceased, 'You are dead please do not be angry. You go to the place of the dead, do not come back to the village to harm human and animals. Protect your family and the villagers.' When people are leaving the site, they must not turn back and look. This means that they are breaking off the relationship between them and the deceased. If someone were to turn back and look, the dead soul will follow that person and later they will become ill or even die.

333

On the day of the funeral, the Hani people will slaughter a pig and distribute the pork among the villagers. Those who receive the pork will come to help to carry the coffin to the cemetery. All belongings including working tools of the deceased are buried with the coffin. Some Hani people slaughter a chicken, burying it with the coffin. Unlike other races, a headstone is not erected. According to the Hani, once a corpse is buried, the soul is sent out of the village and so it is not worshipped anymore.

When the coffin is lowered into the burial site, according to Bulang practice, a cup of wine and a cup of tea are buried near the head of the coffin and one candle is buried at each corner of the coffin. This means that the deceased has worked hard all his or her life and so should enjoy the fruit of his or her labour like the people who are alive. When the family are about to leave, they will ask the deceased to help himself or herself with the drinks. The candles are provided for the lighting to show the appreciation and love of the family. Like the Hani people, a mound is not erected over the grave and there is no headstone either. In fact, there is no trace of a grave.

Among the Benglong people, colourful papers are hung all over the coffin and a small bamboo house is placed on top of the coffin. At the start of the funeral, the people who are carrying the coffin must make sure that the legs of the deceased are carried out of the house first all the way to the grave. This means that the people are sending the dead soul forward and do not want it to come back. During the whole journey, shots are fired, it is to wake the earth god to receive the dead soul. Unlike other people, the site is not dug beforehand but during the funeral. The grave is dug horizontally instead of the usual way. Someone will go inside the site and walk round it three times. When the coffin is in the grave, the children of the deceased will each throw a handful of soil in it. After this everyone will help to cover the grave with soil, but a mound is not erected nor a headstone. When this is done, everyone will stand beside the grave and one of the elders will say some curses, 'The yang world and the yin world are two separate roads, the ones who are dead go to the place where you belong, those who are alive go home. Do not be entangled. Rest in peace.' After this everyone will pick a branch of leaves and brush their bodies with it once. There will not be any crying, and everyone will leave for the village and must not look back.

During a Uighurs funeral, the corpse is taken in a stretcher to the mosque. Women are excluded from the burial rite in the mosque. Everyone who attends the rite must wear a white cloth on the waist. The imam will start the rite by reciting some passages from the Koran, mention good deeds of the deceased and ask Allah for protection and wish the deceased rest in peace. When this is over the corpse will be taken to the burial site. The grave is about two metres in length, one metre in width and two metres in depth. At the side of this site, a hole is dug, and the corpse is buried in it with the head facing the West, the legs facing the East and the face facing the sky. The hole and the whole site are then covered with soil. Usually, the shape of the grave is a long square, but some are round. Some tombs are elaborate that look like palaces with a crescent moon on top. A wall is built round the tomb with design on the top of the wall.

During a Tadjik funeral, the corpse is wrapped with a rug and is placed on a stretcher. Every Tadjik clan have their own ancestral graveyard. Women are not allowed to attend the funeral procession. When lowering the corpse in the site it is important that the head of the deceased is facing the North, the legs facing the South and the face facing the West. According to the Elunchun people, it is a taboo for the deceased's face to face the direction where the sun is rising, it is believed to be unlucky.

In Honan, it was a taboo for pregnant women to go to the grave during a funeral. Usually, pregnant women were not allowed to have anything to do with funerals.

When the coffin was about to be lowered into the burial site the living descendants had to stand far away from the grave to make sure that their shadows were not in the grave. It was believed that if a person's shadow was in the grave, this person consequently would suffer bad health. Even the caretakers had to be careful that their shadows were not in the grave with the deceased. Among the Chinese in Malaysia, when the coffin is about to be lowered into the burial site all the living descendants and other mourners turn their heads away. It is a taboo to look as it might bring bad luck to the beholder.

After the coffin was being buried, the Han-Chinese believed that the dead soul of the deceased could get out of the grave and follow the people home, hence, the practice of walking round the grave three times so that the soul could not follow. During the journey home, the living descendants were forbidden to look back just in case they saw the shadow of the deceased as it would be bad luck for both sides. In Qinghai, the Mongolians who practised sky burial had a similar practice, after sending the corpse to the burial ground they had to jump over a fire and leave immediately without turning back. The oxen and horses which were used to transport the corpses to the burial site were not given any workload for a whole year as it was a taboo to let them work during this time.

In Qinghai, among the Tu people, when the coffin was buried in the ground everybody knelt and bowed to the grave. Funeral tools such as spades were not carried but were dragged all the way home. Before entering the house, people had to wash their hands and set up a fire outside the house first. Some people washed their hands with spirit. One reason was to do with luck so that there would not be any more funerals and the other reason was to wash away 'bad air.'

Things that were borrowed from people for the funeral were returned with some money in a red pouch. It did not matter how much but it had to be an odd number, double numbers were taboo and unlucky. This money is called 'lucky money'. Today, the legacy of lucky money is still perpetuated among the Han-Chinese in Malaysia, those who attend a funeral are still given some lucky money in a red pouch. As funerals are still seen as unlucky events and so people are given some 'lucky money' to take home with them.

MOURNING CLOTHING

Since ancient times, the Han-Chinese already had the wu fu, the five grades of mourning clothing. The first grade was made from raw linen with the hems unsewn, these were worn over white clothes. This type of raw linen was worn by sons and unmarried daughters, the oldest grandson and the wife of the deceased for three years. The second grade was made from not so rough raw linen and the hems were sewn, also worn over white clothes. This was worn by grandchildren for a year, great grandchildren for five months and great great grandchildren for three months. The third grade was made from treated linen not as rough as the second type. This was worn for one's paternal uncles and aunts, cousins, (sons of paternal uncles) and unmarried sisters for the duration of nine months. The fourth grade was made from softer linen, worn for the paternal cousin and wife of one's father, unmarried great aunt, (sister of grandfather), unmarried paternal aunt, maternal grandparents, wife of maternal uncle, maternal aunt, (mother's sister), for five months. The fifth grade was made from the softest type of linen, worn for uncles and aunts of the same clan, brothers and sisters of the same clan, maternal cousins, and parents-in-law, (only for men), for three months. These five grades of clothing were used to define degrees of relationship within and outside the family unit, therefore, from the mourning clothes an outsider could tell what relationship he or she was to the deceased.

According to the author, Baker, in his book 'Chinese Family and Kinship', he said, what was laid down by the Confucian orthodoxy was not what really went on in Chinese society. In fact, mourning did not necessarily follow the wu fu system and often the official prescriptions as how to dress and who should be mourned were modified by people in different areas.

Here is an example of one kind of diversity in contemporary Taiwan:

'Seen from a distance, from the top of a building or on one of the hills on which most graves are sited, the procession following a Chinese coffin is a colourful sight. The mourners wear long robe like gowns, some of rough dirty brown sackcloth, others of grey flax or grass cloths, and still others of unbleached white linen or muslin, scattered among these are blue gowns, red gowns, and, on the rare occasion. a yellow gown. Female mourners cover their heads with a hood that almost hides the face and hangs down the back to the waist; men wear a hempen 'helmet' over a short hood or one of two kinds of bag-like hats of unbleached or dyed muslin. A mourner's hood is sometimes of the same material as his gown, sometimes of a different material. The hood itself may be plain, or it may display a stripe or one or more patches of another material. A common combination is a tall spreading hat with a red stripe to which is sewn a smaller patch of grass cloth or blue muslin. I have never tried to count the number of mourning costumes in the Chinese repertoire but there must be at least a hundred immediately recognisable variants. A funeral procession of fifty mourners usually includes twenty or more different combinations of textiles and colours, (see Chinese Family and Kinship).

In Hong Kong, sackcloth is worn over white clothes. Women wear hoods that hang down their waists and men wear hempen helmets. In Malaysia, sack cloths are worn over black clothes. One difference is the colour of their clothes. The other difference between these two areas is that in Malaysia, maternal grandchildren wear only blue colour. The sack cloths are only worn before and during the funeral. Once the funeral is over, only black clothes are worn for a little while and after that people could wear grey, blue and green.

From looking at the mourning clothes of the Han-Chinese, the closer the blood tie, the coarser the material would be and as far as the workmanship was concerned, it was roughly made. This shows that mourning clothes were part of a self-punishment for the deceased's family, it was used to show their 'xiao xin', meaning, 'filial heart' or perhaps the family felt that they did not do enough filial duty to the deceased during his or her lifetime and this self-punishment was a way to express their filial hearts. In the past, during the period of mourning, it was a taboo for someone in state office to have anything to do with the business of the court. Even at the ceremony of the third anniversary of death, it was a taboo for a man to wear court ceremonial robes and hat and a taboo for the women to wear red clothes or clothes of bright colours.

White was the colour of mourning, therefore during the mourning period it was a taboo for the Han-Chinese to wear red and coloured clothes apart from white. However, other colours were worn in mourning according to people's relationship with the deceased. In Shandong, during the mourning period, sons and daughters were not allowed to wear bright colours such as red, yellow, or green, could only wear white, blue, grey, or black. In Rujong, it was a taboo for a pregnant woman to wear 'xiao tie', meaning, 'filial belt' or sash. It was afraid that the foetus might be hurt. Usually, a wife wore mourning clothes for her husband for three years. In the first year she wore white, the second and third year she wore green. During the mourning period, she was not allowed to remarry. For grandparents, parents, paternal uncles, and aunts the Ta Khan Er people wore mourning clothes for three months. If a maternal uncle and aunt died without children to mourn for them then nephews had to mourn and wore mourning clothes as though they were mourning their own parents.

Among the Ewenke people, when a maternal uncle had died, they wore mourning clothes for a month which was a mixture of white and other colours. When a husband died a wife had to wear mourning clothes but if a wife died a husband did not have to wear mourning clothes. When a paternal uncle 'shu shu', meaning, 'younger uncle', (younger brother of one's father), had died, a white sash was worn over the body and a sash round the waist. When parents died white mourning clothes were worn.

Among the Elunchun people, after a parent had died, not all the sons wore mourning clothes, only one of them. It was believed that the person who wore mourning clothes had less luck than others and would be less successful in hunting. This way, the other brothers who were not wearing mourning clothes could carry on hunting for food. The Yi people do not wear mourning clothes.

After the death of an elderly Hani, the whole village, men, and women, old and young were required to wear a piece of ginger on their clothes or hats. It was said, this was to prevent the dead soul coming near to bother them. Before the funeral, the deceased's family, old and young, did not wear shoes nor hats and hair was not combed, generally looking untidy in their appearances. Husbands and wives did not sleep in the same room during this period. It was to show their grief for the deceased.

 Among the Tadjiks, after the death of a husband, the wife and children were not allowed to wear bright red floral print clothes, they had to wear white sashes round their waists and wrap their heads with white scarves. When a Tibetan had died, Tibetan men would not wear nice clothes nor comb their hair within a hundred days. As a mark of respect and mourning, Tibetan women took off their earrings and religious beads.

According to a text of the Manchu period, it was said, in Kunshan, women wore red trousers as mourning clothes for their mothers for three years. The custom was said to have come from the belief that when a woman was giving birth there was blood everywhere and it was thought to be dirty and when she died, she would be cast in the hell of blood. It was believed, wearing red trousers would prevent the mother from this torment. Some men also followed this practice. This custom was unusual, but it was to show one's filial duty to one's mother.

In Honan, not everybody wore full mourning clothes only the deceased's sons, daughters-in-laws, daughters, sons-in-law, grandsons and grand- daughters in-law could wear mourning clothes in full, including hoods as long as seven feet. Wearing full mourning clothes was called 'ta xiao', meaning, 'big filial'. For the nephews, wives of nephews, nieces, and the not so close relatives, they only had to wear mourning trousers with hoods five feet long. For a daughter who was just engaged, it was a taboo to wear white, both her and her fiancé could wear blue.

Mourning hats were divided into three types, large, medium, and small and worn according to the relationship with the deceased. Great grandsons and great nephews wore hats with red threads on both the pointed ends. The meaning was similar to the present-day practice of a grandson wearing a black arm band with a little red material attached to it. This way of separating the different generations, it was said, to prevent the dead soul from harming the younger generation.

Sewing the mourning clothes in other people's houses was a taboo that was said to be unlucky. During the mourning period, those in mourning had to cover their shoes with white cloths. These white cloths must not be taken off by hand they must be left to wear themselves off. According to the practice, if it was torn off by hand, it was like tearing off the deceased's skin. Usually, the white cloth would have worn out after the 'wu qi', meaning, 'five seven' which was the thirty fifth day after the death. After this time, sons, daughters, and daughters-in law had to wear homemade shoes made with white cloth, one pair a year. Usually, a pair was worn for a father's death but for a mother two or sometimes three pairs were worn. Nowadays of course, no one will make these white shoes anymore, they are replaced by factory made white shoes. This legacy of wearing white shoes is still practised among the Han-Chinese today.

During the mourning period, it was a taboo to cut hair, comb hair and shave. The practice was said to have something to do with the younger generation wanting to thank the deceased for nurturing them and wiping their bottoms when they were babies! Another reason was, after the death of elderly parents the eldest son should grow a beard. It was believed children would die if there was no one with a beard in the family. In fact, not shaving the face, and not having the haircut was to show that people were still mourning.

TABOOS TO BE OBSERVED AFTER THE FUNERAL

Funerals usually brought the productivity of a whole village to a halt, for example, the Wa people had to stop all agricultural activities on the day of the burial. Especially the deceased's family, they had to stop work for six to seven days, then ten days later they stopped work again for three days, another ten days later, stopped work two more days, and another ten days later stopped work for a day. After this, agricultural activities went on as normal. If the deceased died from a tragic death the whole village had to stop productivity for a few days.

Among the Nu people, whenever an adult died, as a sign of mourning, the whole clan or people of the same village would stop all productivity for three days. When someone had died in the village the Hani people stopped work for a couple of days. For the Miao people, when a parent had died the son stopped work in the field for a whole month. In Tibet, among the Teng people, after the death of a man, everyone with the same family name, according to the custom, had to stop work for eleven days. If the deceased was a woman, work was stopped for ten days. A similar custom was practised by the Loba, Bai, Lahu, Dai and the Dulong people.

As funerals were seen as 'bad business', even the family of the deceased were people to be avoided during this time. People in mourning believed that if they engaged in agricultural work, they would harm the crops, for example, crops like wheat would have less yield or the crops would fail altogether. Another reason was because of respect and reverence for the deceased. In order to worship the deceased properly, it was necessary to stop productivity, so that people were able to use the time to mourn. People believed that if they did not worship the deceased properly something bad might happen, a rock might fall from the mountain or another person might die.

Certain days were considered as taboo to work in the fields and this was observed by the Han-Chinese and the Li people of Hainan island. Among the Li people, if someone had died in the family, the relatives were refrained from working in the fields on certain days for the next three years. Every twelve days there was a taboo day and so on this day all productivity must stop. This practice of course does not make economic sense and is now abolished. After the funeral, the Han-Chinese stopped work on one taboo day once a year for the next three years, five years or ten years. On this day, all work was put aside and the whole family went to the grave to offer food and to tend the weeds. Today, it is done on Ching Ming day, where all Han-Chinese who practised ancestors' worship sacrifice food and joss sticks to their ancestors.

After the funeral, the family of the deceased had to stop all social contact with other people outside the family, as people actually believed that at this time their luck was lower than usual, so it was best not to socialise with anybody just in case other people caught their bad luck as well. This taboo was observed by the Han-Chinese, Miao, Ewenke, Tibetan, Mongolian, Kazak and the Ta Khan Er people. During this period, the deceased's family refrained from all amusement activities, avoided quarrels with others, and did not pay any social visits especially not to visit sick people.

If it was Chinese New Year, the family could not stick red posters on their front doors, but blue and green colours were all right. The family could not visit friends nor attend any social gatherings. If relatives came to visit them, the family could accept the New Year gifts but could not return gifts to them.

If the deceased's family did not refrain themselves from social activities, then outsiders could intervene to keep them in line with the practice. Among the Ta Khan Er people, no one could take a person in mourning to the fisheries. Widows were not allowed to remarry during this period. After the death of a person, the Kazak people cut off the tail of his horse and no-one could ride on it again. According to the practice of the Ke-er-ke-zi people, a widow was required to cover her face with a head scarf.

In the past, after the death of a parent, a person in state office had to retire and mourn for a period of three years as his filial duty. According to a text, during the Jin period, a person in state office not only had to retire to his ancestral village to mourn his parents but also his grandparents, paternal uncles and aunts, brothers, sisters, and spouse. If not, the person would be criticised as not doing his xiao duty. 'Xiao' forms the subject of the Classic of Filial Piety known as Xiao Jing in Chinese, a work by Meng Zi, (known as Mencius to Westerners, a follower of Confucius).

FOOD TABOOS

There were food taboos to be observed during the mourning period. Among the Han-Chinese in many areas, wine and meat were forbidden on the funeral day as it was written in the Li Chi: 'on the day of the funeral, wine and meat should not be eaten'. Those who attended the funeral were also given vegetarian meals. In Anhui, when a child died from a tragic death the parents would stop eating pork for a month. As children were 'gu rou', meaning, 'bone and flesh' of parents, after their deaths, parents would not eat meat for a month as a mark of mourning.

Similar practice was observed by the Yao, Shui and Pumi people. Before the burial, the Yao people refrained from eating meat products, only chillies and green vegetables were eaten with rice. Before the burial, the Shui people only ate vegetarian meals but after the burial they were allowed to eat meat. Children of the deceased were forbidden to drink wine or slaughter animals during the mourning period, this was observed by the Pumi people.

However, although there were such taboos among the Han-Chinese they were not strictly practised by all the people. According to a text: 'the people of the Six Dynasties ate meat and drank wine during funerals even among the official class, there was no respect for the ancient practice'. This shows that this taboo was losing its grip on the people. Nowadays, banquets are still held after funerals in China and outside China. This wasteful practice is a legacy of the old days.

After the death of parents, the Miao people refrained from eating dog's meat for three years, if not, it was unlucky. If one child died after another in the family, the Lisu people refrained from eating mutton, garlic, and spring onions. If this were not observed, it was thought that it would upset the deities and ghosts resulting in greater disasters that would befall the family. In Taiwan, among the Gaoshan people, it was a taboo to eat fish during a burial.

In Yunnan, Guangxi and Guizhou, it was a practice of the Buyi people to offer beef to the guests who attended the funeral but sons, daughters-in-law and grandchildren of the deceased were only allowed to have vegetarian meals. According to an old rule, animal and animal fat were taboo food but it was all right to eat seafood. After the elder was buried, the family could eat meat again. An ox was slaughtered as a sacrifice, it was to show honour and respect for the deceased from the living descendants. Anybody who shared the same ancestor, same family name was forbidden to eat because the ox was slaughtered in the place of the deceased. It was believed that this way, the deceased would suffer less in the other world and because of this the family would not bear to eat the flesh of the ox which was slaughtered as a sacrifice.

According to the custom of the Hani people, pigs and chickens are slaughtered to worship the ghosts. If the family is wealthy as much as ten pigs are slaughtered and even a poor family will slaughter a couple to entertain the villagers. It is necessary to sacrifice a mother pig for the deceased to carry on producing piglets for the deceased in the other world.

Among the Yi people, when the funeral was over a simple meal was given to everybody who attended the funeral. Pork was cut into the size of a fist known as 'tour tour' and everyone was given a piece to eat with a puff ball snack called 'ku chiao ba ba' and washed down with white spirit.

Not only wine and meat were taboo food for the mourning family, but some other food was also taboo during mourning.

In Taiwan, if the mourning period happened to be in the Chinese New Year it was a taboo for the family to make nian gao, (New Year pudding), but they could only make 'lor paw gao', meaning 'turnip pudding', a kind of savoury pudding made from Chinese turnips and rice flour. If the mourning period happened to fall on the Duan Wu Festival, it was a taboo to eat zong zi, (triangular cakes). The family could only accept other food given by their relatives and friends. Making 'hong gui', meaning 'red tortoise', a kind of red dumpling in the shape of a tortoise, was especially a taboo. Everything was returned to normal once the mourning was over.

In the north and central China, it was a taboo for the deceased's family to eat noodles for seven days. It was thought that the deceased would suffer hardships in the other world because the noodles resembled iron chains. When a parent or someone in the village had died the Lisu and Miao people stopped eating chillies for a month. According to the custom, if someone did not follow this practice the person would be the enemy of the deceased.

In Hainan. among the Li people, those who attended the funeral were invited for a meal by the deceased's family. An ox or a pig was slaughtered to feed the guests. For the family however, it was a taboo for them to eat rice and they could only eat meat with wine and other snacks when they were hungry.

In Yunnan, before a burial, the Wa people could only eat rice and meat, it was a taboo to eat vegetables and other food such as noodles otherwise it would upset the deceased. If the deceased was upset, it would ruin the agricultural crops of the living descendants so that they would have nothing to eat except wild vegetables and other food. According to a text of the Tang period, it said, 'in the south, among a group of people called Wu Si Man, ('Man' means 'Barbarian'), after the death of parents, salt was eliminated from their diets for three years.'

Among the Han-Chinese and the Yi people, it was a taboo for the family of the deceased to eat with the guests after the funeral. Usually, the family ate separately from the other guests. As for the Yi people, before the funeral they had their meals on the straw mat next to the coffin to show that they were the family of the deceased.

SWEEP THE TOMBS

Certain taboos were observed during 'sau mu', meaning, 'sweep the tombs'. As mentioned before, pregnant women were forbidden to attend the burial, go near the burial site and in some areas, sweep the ancestor's tombs because people were afraid that the dead soul would jump at the foetus causing a miscarriage. According to the practice, if women swept the tombs of ancestors it was as if there were no men in the family, no male descendants.

In ancient times, criminals and those who were crippled because of punishment were not allowed to attend the funeral of their parents nor to sweep the tombs of ancestors. This had something to do with the teachings of Confucius: 'body and hair are given by parents, do not do anything to harm them'. According to the sage, one must do everything to protect one's body from harm. Those who had been in prison before were ashamed to see their dead ancestors. It was feared that the sorry state of the living descendants would upset the ancestors therefore anyone in this situation was forbidden to go to the tombs of his ancestors.

Any weeding and cleaning of the tombs must not be done by other people otherwise it would be a lack of respect for the ancestors and bad luck might befall the family. Sweeping the tombs must not be left to others because even Confucius himself had said: 'If one does not worship the ancestors himself might as well not worship at all'.

When burning the paper money at the tomb, it was a taboo to use a stick to stir at the paper money, if it all went to bits the ancestors would not be able to use it. If only half of the paper money were burned, it was a taboo to burn the rest. According to the practice, this leftover unburned paper money would turn into money, not in the real sense, but that the living descendants could expect some kind of fortune awaiting them. This unburned paper money was a sign that the ancestors did not want to take all the money but leave some for the descendants to use. It was believed that this unburnt paper money should not be burned again otherwise there would be no future generation. When going to the tombs, it was a taboo to visit relatives on the way or to do other things, the day must be devoted to the ancestors only.

Different areas had different times for going to the tombs. In Honan, after the burial, people paid a visit to the new tomb on the next day. After a sacrificial worship, the descendants had to return home via a different route as it was a taboo to return by the same route. This practice was called 'mi lu', meaning, 'lost way'. The idea was to confuse the deceased so that the dead soul would not follow the descendants all the way home.

In Heilongjiang, during the first three days after the burial, every night relatives went to the new tomb and placed a lamp on the tomb. If not, it was said, the deceased would be afraid of the dark in the night. The family had to bring their own fire and firewood for lighting the lamp as it was a taboo to borrow from other people. If the fuel and firewood were borrowed from other people, it was believed the deceased would not be able to see the light. In Sichuan, some people even built a small straw hut next to the new tomb and lived there as part of filial piety throughout the mourning period of three years.

After the death and burial of an ancestor, an ancestor tablet was installed in the home. In Malaysia, it is normally placed on a little wooden stand in a high position nailed on to a wall. The most common form of ancestor tablet is a narrow wooden block about one foot in height with a wooden base support. On it, the name, generation number and attainments of the ancestor are written and the inscription saying this is the 'ling wei', meaning, 'spirit place' of So and So. The wife or wives are usually written on a man's ancestor tablet, but sometimes separate tablets are made for each of the spouses. For those who could afford it, the ancestor tablet can be placed on a specially made Chinese design votive table where other deities such as the goddess Kuan Yin and the male deity Guan Di are worshipped alongside the ancestor or ancestors. Through the ancestor tablet, the ancestor is worshipped everyday with tea and joss sticks. An eternal light is kept burning before the altar, usually a small saucer of oil with a wick floating in it though a red-painted electric light has been popular in recent years in some modern homes.

During the early days of the burial, the family usually paid a visit to the new tomb to offer sacrifices every seven days, for example, on the seventh day, fourteenth day, twenty first day and so on. This 'seven' number was commonly used to divide each stage which would end on the 'qi qi', meaning, 'seven seven', the forty ninth day after death. This practice originated from ancient times, a text mentioned that after a person had died, on the seventh day, his relatives tried to call his spirit back to the yang world again. If after the forty ninth day, there was still no sign of the spirit coming back to life then the family knew there was nothing more to do. From this it shows that by hiring Taoist priests to chant Taoist scripts, offering sacrifices on every 'seventh' day, was to hope that the deceased would come back to life.

However, not everyone followed the practice, in Honan, Shandong and Zhejiang, it was a taboo to go to the new tomb to offer sacrifices on the 'fourth seventh', the twenty eighth day after death. This might be because 'four' sounds like 'death'. In some areas in Honan, if the deceased had only one son then there would be no sacrifices at the new tomb on the 'first seven'. If the deceased had two sons, then there would be no sacrifices on the 'second seventh'. Most people considered the 'fifth seventh' as very important. On this day, sons and daughters made 'shui jiao', meaning, 'water dumplings' as sacrificial food. One dumpling was made for each year according to the deceased's age. It was all right to make more but not less. After the sacrifices, the dumplings were eaten at the tomb but there must not be any leftovers as it was a taboo to bring it home. The sacrificial food for the 'sixth seventh' had to be cooked by the deceased's daughter.

In Honan and Shandong, it was believed that if one of these 'seventh' days happened to fall on the seventh day of the lunar New Year, seventeenth day and twenty seventh day or on the fourteenth day, twenty first day or twenty eighth day, the so-called 'shadow seventh' days, it was considered as unlucky. During the sacrifices, a small white flag was placed on the new tomb to chase away the evil spirits. In Jiangsu and Honan, it was a taboo to offer noodles as a sacrificial food to the new ancestor on the day of the seventh seventh because noodles resembled ropes, and this would frighten the dead spirit.

Within the first three days after the burial, according to the Miao people, the son must carry water in one hand and rice in the other to the new tomb on the first day. When he has arrived at the grave, he will say, 'Please wash your face and eat rice'. This practice was called 'sung shui fan', meaning, 'send water rice'. On the second day, he will carry the rice and water and leave it on the ground half-way to the grave. On the third day, the rice and water are left outside the front door. From the fourth day onwards, a bowl of rice and a pair of chopsticks are placed in front of the altar for the deceased. On the fourteenth day, the son will carry bamboo bow and arrows on his back to the grave and will 'fetch' the soul home to stay for two or three years, (not sure how this is done). After the duration, the soul will be sent back to the mountain.

On the third day after the funeral, the Menba people will go to the new tomb with the lama to stick a long narrow flag in the tomb. This was to invite the soul of the deceased to come home. During the service at home, the lama will draw the image of the deceased and his or her name on a piece of paper and tied it to an arrow. The arrow is then stuck into a dipper filled with uncooked rice. A hada is hung on the arrow. This is to be the spirit place of the deceased. Offerings are sacrificed in front of this spirit place. The lama will say to the deceased, 'You have died a few days, today your soul is invited back to your spirit place from the grave, do not be angry anymore. There are two roads, one is heaven, and one is hell, you have to choose carefully'. On the seventh day, another small rite is held at home. On the 'third seventh', another rite is held with two main activities. The lama will recite the sutras in front of the picture he drew earlier and will say to the deceased, 'You must have gone to heaven now, this is only a paper, a piece of paper without a spirit.' After he said this, he will burn the picture. At the entrance of the village, the family will stick a long narrow flag on the ground. Wealthy people often stick a hundred flags, three large ones and ninety seven small ones. Most people only stick one or two flags. On the 'seventh seventh', another big rite is held, which will last three days with many sacrificial offerings. Within one year, the family is not allowed to sing nor dance, not to slaughter chickens and ducks, not to marry and not to hunt. On the first anniversary of the death, a final rite is held, and lamas are hired to recite sutras for the deceased that he or she will ascend to heaven soon.

According to the custom of the Uighurs, worship services are held on the third, seventh and forty first day after burial, plus the first anniversary, in memory of the deceased. If the deceased was a young person, the services are simpler. Those who attend the service must bring gifts such as tea leaves, white fabrics and three Turkish biscuits, the last gift is a must. The gifts are sent to the deceased's family by women and are also received by women of the family. Usually, both husband and wife are invited together and if the wife is out or unwell, she has to pay a special visit on another day bringing some gifts along. Usually, the service is held in the afternoon. Men and women are segregated, men in one room and women in another. Food is laid out on a long table with white tablecloth. Different kinds of snacks and fruit candies are served to the guests. Music is not played, and people are not allowed to talk loudly. After serving tea, rice and meat are served. Elderly guests are expected to recite the Koran. Non-Muslims could also attend the service to express their sympathy to the family.

Pigs were seen as unclean animals by Islamic believers and because of this it was a taboo to raise pigs or to build a pigsty near the tombs. This was considered an offence to the ancestors and disasters would befall on those who committed the offence. Another group of people, the Kazaks, also treated their ancestors' tombs with great respect. When they were riding past the tombs they had to slow down, and women had to get down from their horses and walk with the horses until after they passed the tombs. Whenever there was a drought, people went to the tombs to offer sacrifices. If the goats were suffering from any form of diseases, they too were taken to the tombs and then stayed the night. The soil of the tombs were regarded as holy medicine by some people and were actually used to treat illnesses or mixed with water for pregnant women and women about to give birth to drink, it was hoped that they would have a smooth delivery. This was a belief in ancestors' spirits in the extreme and it shows clearly that people were sincere in their worship and they treated their ancestors' tombs with respect.

Planting cypress on tombs was an ancient practice. According to a text of the Zhou period, during the burial of a man named Fang Shiang, the family of the deceased saw a creature in the dug-out grave. This creature was fond of devouring the brains of corpses. It was said to be afraid of tigers and cypresses, hence, that was why cypress trees were planted and statues of tigers were erected in front of the graves. There was another reference at the times of Qin Xiao Gong, the King of the kingdom of Qin (ancestor of Qin Shi Huang Di), a man by the name of Chen Sher Ren dug something out of the ground that looked like a goat, wanted to give it away, met two boys on the way who told him that this thing was called 'wuen', and that it liked to feed on the brains of corpses in the ground! If he wanted to kill it, they said, just plant two cypress seedlings at the head of the grave. This legacy of planting cypresses in graves has perpetuated among some Chinese in Malaysia and the legacy of erecting statues of tigers has continued among the Chinese in Taiwan.

Besides cypress trees, willow trees were also planted in graves but there was no reference why they were planted. According to people, willows were planted because they were resilient and easy to grow. However, in Yubei, the people of this area did not want the willows to grow too quickly. When a willow seedling was first planted on the grave it was given a few shakes so that it would not root too quickly. Every time when someone was visiting the grave, the poor little plant was given a few shakes, this way, it was guaranteed that during the shaking period it would not grow at all. If the willow was growing too quickly it was as if the grave was not looked after, that the family had no filial sons and grandsons to tend the grave.

In fact, in high antiquity, the practice of sweeping the tombs did not exist. At that time, when a person had died the body was then buried, and that was it. There was no headstone, trees were not planted, there was no weeding and certainly no worshipping. According to the Li Chi, 'buried' means 'to hide'.

'To hide' is to put the corpse in a place where no one could see. The ancient text also mentioned that a person looked horrible when dead therefore it was placed in a coffin and buried away out of the sight of people.

Only in later times perhaps since the Shang period did people start to place importance in tombs and the practice of sweeping the tombs of ancestors became a very important part of people's lives. There was even a reference about Meng-zi, that he begged to be given some sacrificial food to eat. This reference shows that sweeping the tombs already existed in the Warring States period. By the times of the Tang and the Five Dynasties, sweeping the tombs was already very popular during the Han Shih Festival, (see Ching Ming Festival).

According to a text, the rituals of sweeping the tombs of ancestors have gone through many changes since ancient times:

1. In ancient times, a living descendant received sacrificial worship on behalf of his dead ancestor. In later periods, the ancestor's tablet and portrait represented the dead ancestor instead of the living descendant.

2. In ancient times, mugwort was burned and a kind of wine, (made with black jujubes), was poured on the ground. In later periods, joss sticks were burned in the place of the mugwort and spirit was poured on the ground.

3. In ancient times, during the Qin period, a type of cloth was buried with the deceased. During the Han dynasty, special underworld coins were buried with the deceased. In later periods, in the Tang dynasty, underworld paper money was burned.

4. In ancient times, the sacrificial rite was attended by male and female guests. In later periods, there were no guests and only men performed the rites but no women.

5. In ancient times, the sacrificial food 'jiao' was eaten according to hierarchical order. This jiao was made from rice flour and sugar. In ancient times, the elderly, the young and the sick lived on it. The modern jiao zi, kinds of round balls made from glutinous rice flour stuffed with vegetables and meat, originated from the ancient jiao. In later periods, all sacrificial food was eaten by the whole family at the same time.

6. In ancient times, after receiving the blessings from the dead ancestors, the living descendants had to give a kind of thank you speech to the dead ancestors. In later periods, after receiving the blessings, no thank you speech was given, however, the meaning still stands.

7. In ancient times, worship was carried out in hierarchical order. In later times, this practice has perpetuated till this day.

From this one could see that there were many changes in sacrificial rites since ancient times, however, the respect for ancestors and the hope for prosperity have remained unchanged.

Nowadays, great importance is still placed on the seventh seventh, the hundredth day, one year, three years, five years, and ten years anniversaries of death. During these times, families will get together in their ancestral tombs to offer sacrifices and will do the same in front of the ancestors' tablets in their homes and hope that their ancestors will bestow prosperity upon them.

These burial practices and customs of the Han-Chinese are more or less a thing of the past now. Burial practices have gone through reform and the people of China are looking at the concept of burial in a different view. In cities, a cremation service is now the norm. As cremation is now the only form of burial in cities, old burial practices and customs are nowhere to be seen now except in rural villages where some of the old practices still have a market. The minorities, however, are permitted to carry on with their own forms of burial outside the big cities.

356

Bibliography

English List

1 Baker, H.D.R. (1979) Chinese Families and Kinship, Macmillan Press

2 Bell, J.D. (1982) Things Chinese, Oxford University Press

3 Cotterrell, A. & Morgan, D. (1975) China – An Integrated Study, Harrap, London

4 Destenay, A.L. (1973) Nagel's Encyclopedia Guide – China, Nagel Publishers, Switzerland

5 Eberhard, W. (1958) Chinese Festivals, Abelard – Shuman

6 Ebrey P. (1981) Chinese Civilization and Society, The Free Press

7 Gernet, J. (1962) Daily Life in China, George Allen & Unwin Ltd

8 Han, S. (1968) Birdless Summer, Jonathan Cape

9 Han, S. (1965) The Crippled Tree, Jonathan Cape

10 Hook, B. (1982) The Cambridge Encyclopedia of China, Cambridge University Press

11 Kong, D. & Ke, L. (1988) The House of Confucius, Hodder & Stoughton

12 Pan, L. (1985) China's Sorrow, Century Publishing

13 Van Gulik, R.H. (1974) Sexual Life in Ancient China, Brill, E.J., Netherlands

Chinese List

1 Chang, R.C. (1993) Hong Bai Xi Shi, Beijing Yan Shan Press, Beijing

2 Chen, D.Y. (1937) Zhongguo Funu Shenghuo Shi (A History of the Life of Chinese Women) Shang Wu Yin Shu Guan, Shanghai

3 Cheng, R. (1993) Zhong Guo Min Jian Jin Ji, Han Xin Wenhua Shiye Youxian Gungsi, Taiwan

4 The Editorial Department of Jiang Men Wen Wu Chuban Youxian Gungsi, Taiwan

5 Wang, Y.L. (1994) Zhong Guo Wen Hua Yu Funu, Hong Kong Educational Publishing Company

6 Xiao, G. (1992) Min Su Feng Qing, Shang Wu Yin Shu Guan, Hong Kong

7 Yang, Z.D. & Chang, Z. (1993) Zhong Guo Min Su Feng Qing Ta Guan, Shanxi Teachers' Training University Press

Index

317, 346
Guo (fief) 5, 7, 14, 35, 42, 46, 87, 135, 141, 150, 151, 159, 175, 191, 205, 211, 212, 213, 234, 262, 281
Gu-zhoong 28, 128
Gwor Ta Li 54, 56, 57, 58, 357
Hakka 4, 57, 175, 176
Hainan 138, 323, 343, 347
Han Dynasty 6, 20, 42, 136, 141, 355
Hani 22, 24, 34, 54, 80 88, 89, 102, 127, 149, 216, 218, 219, 228, 229, 230, 234, 235, 238, 242, 272, 288, 291, 298, 334, 340, 343, 346
Han Suyin 60
Han Wu Di 136
Happy sweets 141
Heilongjiang 116, 209, 221, 233, 234, 349
Herjer 214, 290, 305, 308, 327
High antiquity 5, 10, 11, 26, 42, 50, 79, 111, 113, 120, 133, 162, 165, 181, 193, 300, 301, 354
Hobei 306, 329
Honan 38, 71, 73, 74, 106, 114, 115, 123, 156, 157, 158, 159, 184, 198, 199, 202, 208, 209, 210, 213, 226, 229, 233, 236, 237, 241, 242, 250, 252, 254, 259, 270, 274, 275, 277, 279, 281, 283, 284, 291, 293, 296, 298, 301, 302, 322, 328, 335,

341, 349, 350, 351
Hoon (time of wedding) 6, 76, 331
Hong Kong 57, 69, 86, 97, 115, 138, 147, 153, 154, 173, 320, 338
Hou (Queen) 8
Huang Di 354
Hubei 55, 61, 101, 104, 195, 204, 237, 242, 315, 330
Hui Chinese 48, 72, 116, 139, 154, 156
Hui Niang Jia 156, 157, 159, 161
Hunan 51, 65, 106, 107, 199, 258, 263, 264, 268, 315
Islamic 72, 94, 95, 103, 139, 169, 170, 304, 353
Imperial examination 74, 75
Introduction agency 191
Jade Emperor 53
Jiangbei 215
Jiangsu 114, 141, 176, 181, 182, 215, 258, 306, 328, 351
Jin Dynasty 320
Jilin 322
Jino 9, 12, 218, 253, 254, 311
Jin Ping 33, 78, 128
Jing 22, 26, 27, 49, 56
Jingpo 12, 16, 17, 22, 24, 37, 168, 178, 308
Jin Sa 317
Jin-siu 166
Kank 105, 114, 135, 136, 137,

Dien Wen 227

Dong 16, 70, 116, 118, 239, 263

Dong Xiang 21, 27, 147

Double Bliss 33, 46, 51, 74, 75

Dowry 24, 55, 58, 59, 60, 61, 62, 70, 78, 147, 164, 167, 170, 188, 299

Dulong 9, 35, 214, 215, 328, 343

Eight characters 27, 31, 35, 39, 40, 41, 42, 43, 45, 50, 130, 144, 225, 226, 274, 331, 322, 331

Elunchun 9, 14, 15, 123, 196, 202, 203, 209, 214, 220, 242, 254, 290, 308, 311, 312, 335, 340

Emperor Sung Hui Zong 43

Emperor Qian Long 59

Empress Ci Xi 44

Engagement 26, 27, 28, 29, 30, 31, 185

Enuchs 59

Ewenke 9, 12, 27, 48, 87, 88, 122, 149, 150, 199, 209, 214, 222, 304, 305, 311, 327, 340, 344

Fang Shiang 354

Fan-yu 112, 174

Feng Shui 106, 320, 321, 329

Filial piety 6, 344, 349

Fire crackers 54, 73, 74, 76, 90, 97, 102, 111, 166, 145, 218, 325

Foetus education 211, 213

Fujian 48, 57, 62, 63, 97, 315

Full month feast 261, 262, 264, 266, 267

Funeral 71, 73, 108, 110, 123, 126, 189, 203, 204, 239, 254, 256, 279, 282, 285, 286, 293, 295, 297, 299, 300, 301, 302, 304, 309, 311, 320, 322, 323, 324, 325, 327, 328, 329, 330, 331, 332, 333, 334, 335, 336, 337, 338, 339, 340, 342, 343, 344, 345, 346, 347, 348, 353

Fu-ren (consorts) 8

Fu-Xi (mythical emperor 5, 32, 39, 193

Fu-yang 100, 131

Ga Dan Monastery 318

Gansu 21, 81, 91

Gaoshan 34, 84, 164, 167, 232, 346

Ge lao 64

Genghis Khan 18

Goi Pu 320

Golden Orchid Society 173

Gou Zan 36

Guan Di 271, 274, 350

Guangdong 26, 49, 56, 64, 69, 71, 112, 145, 150, 153, 155, 172, 173, 175, 187, 243, 246, 249, 263, 266

Guangxi 13, 22, 26, 34, 77, 89, 115, 127, 128, 166, 174, 263, 292, 346

Guishan 86

Guizhou 25, 26, 49, 233, 229, 245, 268, 289, 292, 315, 316,

Printed in Great Britain
by Amazon

21430743R00210